Peter's Kingdom

Peter's Kingdom

Inside the Papal City

Jerrold M. Packard

CHARLES SCRIBNER'S SONS • NEW YORK

Copyright © 1985 Jerrold M. Packard

Library of Congress Cataloging-in-Publication Data

Packard, Jerrold M.
  Peter's kingdom.

  Bibliography: p.
  Includes index.
  1. Papacy.   2. Vatican City.   3. Catholic Church—
Government.   I. Title.
BX955.2.P33   1985   262′.13   85-22086
ISBN 0-684-18430-3

Published simultaneously in Canada by Collier Macmillan Canada, Inc.
Copyright under the Berne Convention.

1 3 5 7 9 11 13 15 17 19   F/C   20 18 16 14 12 10 8 6 4 2

Printed in the United States of America.

Contents

St. Peter's Basilica

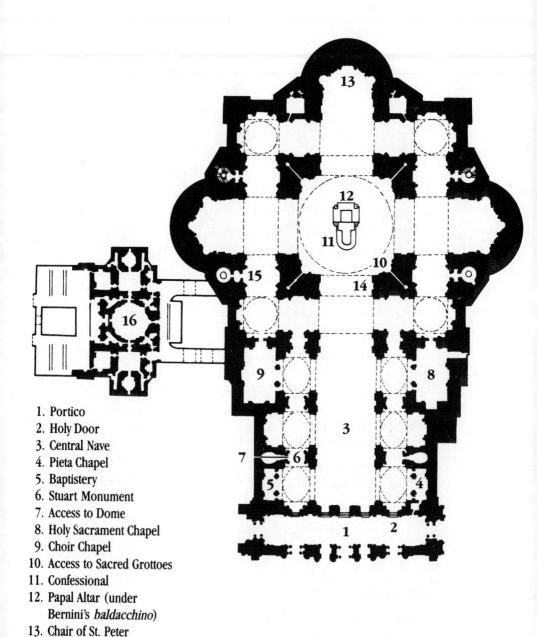

1. Portico
2. Holy Door
3. Central Nave
4. Pieta Chapel
5. Baptistery
6. Stuart Monument
7. Access to Dome
8. Holy Sacrament Chapel
9. Choir Chapel
10. Access to Sacred Grottoes
11. Confessional
12. Papal Altar (under
    Bernini's *baldacchino*)
13. Chair of St. Peter
14. Statue of St. Peter
15. Entrance to Sacristy
    and Treasury
16. Sacristy

Introduction

At the heart of the Universal and Holy Roman Catholic Church is an enigmatic and vexatious doctrine, one that both inspires and infuriates millions of its members. It is the principle that the basic beliefs of the Church—its dogma—have remained unchanged throughout the history of the faith, that its fundamental substantive issues are not and never have been negotiable. Perhaps *interpretation* changes, but interpretation is only the human attempt to uncover unalterable truths. On one side, this heritage of a single doctrinal thread two thousand years old comforts millions of Catholics who consider it the core of their faith, a link to the man-God who founded their Church, and a living conservation of his legacy. For others among the Church's claimed membership of nearly eight hundred million people, this same conservatism often represents at best an irrelevant, and at its worst, a mean-spirited and un-Christian, denial of the reality and consequences of an undernourished and overpopulated planet. These conflicts, conundrums, and militantly differing views meet head on in a small enclosure of historic and sovereign territory, a site long venerated as the burial place of the first successor to the Church's first head.

1

Il Stato della Città del Vaticano, the world's smallest independent state, is the legal framework guaranteeing sovereignty in international law to the world's largest and oldest organization and its most ancient authority. Described by many of its interpreters as hidden behind a curtain of secrecy and unfathomable mysteries, a less colorful but more realistic interpretation as well as a key to understanding the Vatican is the recognition that it is the headquarters of a colossal bureaucracy, not entirely dissimilar in its structure to other multinational organizations governing vast holdings. What seems mysterious is, to a great extent, the result of an inability to absorb the complexity of the Holy See. And like its fellow conglomerates, each of the Church's actions and its decision-making process in general are not for public consumption. If all church activity were held up to public scrutiny, the ability to direct its global domain effectively would be crippled.

At the pinnacle of both Vatican and Church structure is the papacy, the world's single supranational office wielding substantial power and influence. The power of the office to rule the Church is, in theory, uncontested; the degree of its influence to shape society and exert control over its membership is in large measure dependent upon the personality of the man occupying the papal throne. With the ascendance of Pope John Paul II, that influence is again on the rise after a generation transformed by the discarding of verities in the wake of the Second Vatican Council.

Both Catholic and non-Catholic are aware of the modern papacy's power to influence events. A precondition to better understanding of this phenomenon is an examination of the city-state that gives the popes their kingdom and the Roman Catholic Church its unique status as a sovereign international entity. This is meant to serve as a guide to the little monarchy in the shadow of St. Peter's Basilica.

1

God's Kingdom on Earth:
The Vatican City-State

"La Santa Sede non è uno stato;
La Santa Sede a uno stato"
(The Holy See is not a state;
the Holy See has a state)

Monsignor Ritter of Berne

In a well-intentioned but wholly symbolic act, the United Nations in 1960 solemnly declared the Vatican city-state to be in its entirety a "war-free zone," an enclave off-limits to all belligerents in future military conflicts, presumably including nuclear threats. Since the Vatican city-state is totally surrounded by Rome, the capital of one of the Western military alliance's leading guarantors, it is highly doubtful that such well-meant concern would do much toward saving the world's densest concentration of living history in the event that the planet's enmities explode in another world war. Regardless of the unenforceable nature of the United Nations decree, no other country has been deemed worth cosseting under such an aegis.

But labeling the Vatican city-state a "country," though technically accurate, is highly misleading. This minuscule enclave is more easily understood as a kind of headquarters compound for, say, a multinational organization doing worldwide business on the level of a greatly magnified IBM or a Boeing Company. Think of it as a legalistic formula designed to ensure that the Catholic Church—which until just over a century ago really did have its very own country—would assume parity with all other sovereign nations, and you begin to understand the nature of this highly idiosyncratic entity. (For a plan of the Vatican City-State, see Illustrations.)

3

Today, the papal state is one of the world's few remaining absolute monarchies, albeit the only one in which the monarch can come from any country or any class of society, including the poorest in either category. It is a state free of violent crime, welfare, decaying streets, and graffiti-defaced walls. It is a state unique in that it does not exist to serve the usual purposes of national sovereignty, but rather to function as the material support division—including diplomatic—of a far larger and infinitely more consequential entity. Its reestablishment in 1929 as an independent state, following a half century of official limbo, was a specific act on the part of the Italian kingdom to guarantee independence and sovereignty to the governing bodies of the Roman Catholic Church. Entirely independent of Italy and thus free from Italian law, the Vatican is nonetheless an integral part of the Italian economy, the wellspring of billions of lira earned each year in foreign exchange. The Vatican is not only the spiritual focus of Roman Catholics worldwide, but it is also the focus of the world itself at those chapter openings in Christendom's history marking the ascension of fresh pontificates, the periodic passing of the old and known, the periodic emergence of some new direction for the Church. Beneath its age-old palaces and venerated basilica lies the earth of pagan Rome, uniting with the material splendors of the Church both classical antiquity and the Christian faith, two of the three sources of Western civilization.

To the visitor's unfamiliar eye, the face that the Vatican presents to Rome isn't immediately discernible from the larger jumble that makes up the Eternal City—a clutter of domed churches and palazzi and monument-topped columns, and streets many of which are charm itself but almost all of which are traffic-clogged speedways. For most of Christian history, it wasn't necessary to separate the Church's chief shrine and future headquarters in the Vatican from the larger entity of Rome itself—until 1870 the entire city served as the capital of the secular Papal States. What is now the State of Vatican City was until 1929 simply a complex of palaces and museums clustered around the Mother Church of Christendom and the locus of Europe's Christian pilgrims, St. Peter's Basilica.

St. Peter's still rises out of the low, dome-dotted profile of modern Rome just as the jeweled cross crowns the pontifical tiara. From almost any vantage point in the city, the enormous baroque temple appears to float above a forest of lesser temples. Divided unevenly by the River Tiber, as the Thames cuts London and the Seine separates Paris into disproportionate halves, Rome's larger and more historic left bank was the primary setting for the city's ancient imperial splendor, as it is still today its commercial heart. Across the river, on the less elegant, less mercantile right bank, the ecclesiastical quarter has, since Constantine built the first St. Peter's, crowded around the front of the Vatican hill, forming its own little city. Today the sight of cassocks and Roman collars and a sea of distinctive habits is as much a part of the district's coloration as are the ubiquitous peddlers' carts filled with tangled rosaries and cheap medallions bearing the fuzzy image of the reigning pope.

Most of the Vatican state's international boundary is clearly defined by the sloping gray Renaissance wall—quoined with marble at its corners—that nearly surrounds the complex. Pointing arrow-straight into St. Peter's Square, the only part of the state not enclosed by the wall, is the modern Mussolini-inspired Via della Conciliazione, a sterile and wholly artificial-looking thoroughfare built to commemorate the treaty between the Vatican and the Italian state, ending a fifty-year political face-off. For this token of conciliation the ancient clerical quarter, known as the Borgo, was nearly decimated. The Conciliazione is joined to St. Peter's Square by the smaller connecting Pius XII Square, once called the Piazza Rusticucci after the town palace of Cardinal Rusticucci; the space is framed by the pair of twin Fascist-style buildings erected as part of the Conciliazione set piece and that today house nine of the Holy See's congregations, or ministries. The St. Peter's end of the Conciliazione has been visually narrowed with protruding arcades, an architectural device intended to recapture some of the lost visual "surprise" strangers experienced when leaving the cramped streets of the Borgo to find themselves suddenly facing the immense open space framing Europe's most majestic architectural mass.

Arguably the finest public space in the world, St. Peter's Square is a keyhole-shaped piazza enclosed by the pillared arms of Bernini's double colonnade; the boundary between Italy and the Vatican state, a white strip set in the cobbled pavement, continues the curving line that would connect the two ends of the colonnade. This immense forum is a brilliant composition of three conjoined spaces. Linked to the basilica by cascading steps that make up about half its space is the trapezoid-shaped Piazza Retta, named after its rectilinear plan. Emerging from it is the key to Bernini's design, the Piazza Obliqua, in translation meaning not "oblique" in the modern sense but simply nonrectilinear, the primary seventeenth-century connotation of the word. Outside the Vatican's modern boundaries but nonetheless part of Bernini's overall plan, the Piazza Pio XII is now a kind of forecourt to the larger masterpiece.

The square has evolved into the world's most heavily utilized outdoor theater. During all but the winter months it is the scene of Rome's most colorful happenings. These include the weekly general papal audiences, dozens of other ecclesiastical ceremonies and gatherings that draw throngs of people, and celebrations ranging from the solemn pomp of papal enthronements and funerals and the world-famous Christmas and Easter blessings to the enormous and carnivallike Italian Catholic youth rallies.

Except for the piazza and the colonnades, the 2.53-mile boundary between the two political entities follows city streets (in a few places, territory that is legally part of Italy makes minor incursions into the area ordinarily treated as part of the Vatican), the precise limit of the papal state defined by the point where the sidewalk touches the foot of the wall. To the north of the square (on the right when facing the basilica), the border follows the outer edge of the front half of the colonnade, cutting deeply into the narrow courtyard between the colonnade and the Swiss Guards' barracks, an area inaccessible to the public. It then turns north at the Via di Porta Angelica and continues along the edge of the Piazza del Risorgimento and the Via Leone IV, busy torrents of traffic separating constantly tumultuous Roman middle-class neighborhoods from the far quieter business and maintenance quarter of the Vatican. The sidewalks along these thoroughfares serve as the chief open-air emporium of the slightly seedy souvenir merchants doing a brisk commerce with the unending stream of tourists, Gypsy beggars imploring pilgrims for a few coins, and freshly emptied moving vans doubling for their drayers as temporary cardrooms on wheels.

The remaining circumference of the Vatican's walled boundary is bordered by the suburban-feeling Viale Vaticano, a relatively unimportant and altogether ordinary residential street, not particularly meriting its designation as a *viale,* an avenue. The Roman neighborhood on the Vatican's little-known back side, mostly developed since World War II, is a monotonous, low-rise working-class apartment sprawl which grew to displace the farm fields that until a couple of generations ago covered most of this northwestern part of Rome. The atmosphere is still one of pallid newness in contrast to the time-worn, polychromatic districts on the city side of the papal enclave.

After nearly encircling the city-state, the Viale Vaticano changes briefly to the Via Stazione Vaticana before turning into the Largo di Porta Cavalleggeri, which itself turns the corner and becomes the Piazza del Sant'Uffizio—the Holy Office Square—before reaching the south colonnade and St. Peter's Square again. In this jumble of piazza and palazzo, the actual boundary between republic and monarchy zigs into the closed Vatican grounds, legally splitting the Nervi Audience Hall into Italian seats and a Vatican stage, leaving the Palace of the Holy Office—once called the Palace of the Inquisition—and the German College next door entirely in Italy. For all practical purposes, however, this southeast corner is wholly treated as a part of Vatican territory and is off-limits to the public behind its tall wrought-iron fence.

The 108.7 acres (an area considerably smaller than the U.S. Capitol grounds, which cover 131 acres) within the boundary, shaped like a rough triangle with the "front"—St. Peter's Square—as its base, is composed of four main areas: St. Peter's Basilica and St. Peter's Square; the palaces and administrative buildings to the south of the square; the papal residential palace, museums, and business quarter to the north; and, behind these three, the private complex of gardens, villas, and fountains. For most purposes, the only parts of the Vatican open to the public are the square, the basilica, and the museums; the latter are accessible only through their own special entrance in the Viale Vaticano. Saving the Vatican's primary attraction—the basilica—for the next chapter, we'll take a tour of the rest of the little state now, starting with its "downtown."

The Porta Sant'Anna—the St. Anne Gate—is the busiest and least ceremonial of the entrances into the nonpublic areas of the Vatican; it can, for most purposes, be considered the tradesmen's entrance. The St. Anne district of the Vatican is the only one that could pass for an ordinary Roman neighborhood, although the relative lack of Rome's murderous traffic dulls the comparison. Priests and nuns make up the better part of a steady stream of pedestrians jostling along the narrow stone sidewalks bordering the cobbled streets, with the balance composed of Romans employed by the Holy See as civil servants, and customers for the various Vatican services.

At the ornate steel-reinforced gate, fitted with a smaller pass door to allow entrance to pedestrians after the main section itself is closed an hour before midnight, a contingent of blue-uniformed Swiss Guards, the popes' private army, mans the fort. Small knots of tourists gather at this break in the Porta Angelica sidewalk to stare at and past the guardsmen and further into the tantalizing mysteries of the little city, a place where tourists may not casually enter. Every few minutes one of the camera-clad travelers will politely ask to be admitted and, in the absence of a reason acceptable to the Swiss guardian, is as equally politely turned down.

Just inside and to the right of the barrier is the small church of St. Anne of the Palafrenieri, the parish church serving the thousand or so people who actually make their home in the Vatican. Erected in 1573 as a chapel for the pope's grooms (palafrenieri), it was then merely one of a galaxy of churches that dotted the precincts of St. Peter's. In theory, the pope is the parish priest of St. Anne's. Today the Augustinian order is in charge of the little church, and in the crypt below its stone floor Vatican citizens have the right to be buried.

A large tile-roofed barracks housing the hundred or so halberdiers of the Swiss Guards faces the church on the other side of the gateway. Around the corner from its main entrance in the ancient Colonnade Courtyard, one of the most secluded corners of the Vatican, and nearly lost in shadow against the clifflike bulk of the papal palace rising above is the tiny classical Chapel of the Swiss Guards, the smallest church in the state. I remember especially its quality of timelessness, embodied in a pair of nuns in their crisp habits quietly lost in prayer in the chapel's dusty half light, enjoying a privacy completely unknown to the throngs of tourists in the immense square a few dozen feet away on the other side of the colonnade wall.

Once a visitor has passed the relatively cursory perusal of the Swiss Guardsmen directly inside the gate, another, more formidable obstacle has to be faced: the dark-uniformed officers of the Corpo di Vigilanza, successor to the Papal Gendarmerie, the primary Vatican police force and the real protector of the state's peace and security. A small Vigilance office, staffed by all-too-typical Roman bureaucrats, is responsible for deciding on requests for passes. If a visitor's entreaties sound reasonable, he is allowed to go to the second step in the process and complete a questionnaire that, after being examined by the attendant, may or may not be approved. For the non-Italian-speaking visitor, this little ritual has all the charm of an IRS audit.

Bearing off to the right in front of the Vigilance office, the Street of the Pilgrims—the major thoroughfare of the St. Anne district and once the last stretch of the old pilgrims' road that led south to St. Peter's from the heights of Monte Mario—is lined with a dun-colored mix of offices and shops providing many of the routine services that stoke the machinery of the Holy See's headquarters. A small placard identifies the famous Vatican newspaper, *L'Osservatore Romano*—"The Roman Observer"—next door to the church of San Pellegrino. Named for St. Peregrinus, whose name meant "pilgrim" in Latin, the church is the second oldest in the Vatican, built at the end of the eighth century, and now the official chapel for the Vigilanza.

The farther one penetrates the St. Anne business quarter, the more it resembles an American military installation, roughly of the dreary kind peppering West Germany. At the north end, close to the wall that cuts it off from Rome, the buildings are fairly tatty low stucco affairs, serving as garages, machine shops, and mechanical plants; this seldom-seen part of the Vatican shares very little of the glory that graces the rest of the pontifical state. The occasional patrolling Vigilance officer will ask to see the pass of any suspicious-looking visitor, but otherwise there's little excitement. A glimpse of the shiny tanklike papal Mercedes heading for its garage makes an unusual memory for those with the good fortune to encounter it.

A large triangular complex in the center of the St. Anne area shelters a brace of activities: the Vatican's own printing press and publishing house and its famous grocery store. Called the Annona, a corruption of the Latin for "provisionary," the A&P-sized market is usually the scene of small, well-controlled mobs and what passes for traffic jams in the Vatican. The Annona is a much-coveted perk for those who live and work in the little state, and occasionally even for those who only *know* someone in that privileged category, although a recent austerity drive has cut down on such abuse. Most of the foreign goods are appreciably cheaper than they would be in Italy, which is usually the result of their exemption from Italian import duties imposed on merchandise sold on the other side of the wall. Across the little street fronting the grocery store, called the Via di Tipografia—"Printer's Street"—is a well-stocked pharmacy, like the Annona open only to those with Vatican identification cards. The pharmacy shares its quarters, the unpalatial Belvedere Palace (not to be confused with what is often called the Belvedere Palace, the far larger building housing part of the Vatican museums), with a number of administrative offices.

At the junction where the Belvedere Palace and the publishing house meet is the stately post office, where the surest thing in the world is that the nun directly ahead of you in line is there to take care of her convent's complete annual postage stamp purchase. (The other two windows will, of course, be closed at the time.) A large, new-looking oak writing table dominates the center of the post office's public space, but it is the same table seen in decades-old photographs of the building's interior, an observation that attests to the orderliness and lack of anything resembling vandalism in this very law-abiding state.

The enterprising tourist/stamp collector can wangle his way in for an educational walk through this part of the Vatican if he can convince the Vigilanza that he plans to make a particularly large or complicated purchase, but most of the post office's customers are, as might be expected, priests, nuns, and Vatican residents. For small purchases, a post-office van that looks like a house trailer has been set up in St. Peter's Square; its Italian counterpart is parked a few yards away on the other side of the border in Pius XII Square.

Framing the St. Anne district to the south and west is the enormous architectural mass appended to St. Peter's, the complex of buildings that together make up the Apostolic Palace and the Vatican museums. More than ten thousand rooms connected by nearly a thousand flights of stairs make it the largest such structure in the world.

The Apostolic—or Papal—Palace juts off the northeast corner of the basilica in an unbalanced jumble of loggias and courtyards that mirror the haphazard course of its construction over a dozen centuries. Although primarily the residence of the pope, it also serves the Holy See in many other capacities. The buildings, with the Sistine Chapel at the junction where they join St. Peter's Basilica, are pierced by a series of historically named courtyards—St. Damase and Sixtus V, the Sentinel, the Borgia, the Parrot, the Marshal. The portion of the palace where the pope actually resides (and the last major element to be built) is a four-story building surrounding the courtyard of Sixtus V, with entry to the pope's own fourth-floor suite through the courtyard of St. Damase.

Nearly every wing and floor of this maze at the heart of the papal kingdom was added onto earlier portions built by individual popes, the primary reason for the uncoordinated external appearance the palace presents. The "Noble Apartments," equivalent to the state rooms at the White House or Buckingham Palace, are a series of interconnecting, marble-floored salons surrounding the Sixtus V Courtyard on the third floor of the residential palace and are used mainly for private and semiprivate papal audiences. (For a plan of the Pontifical Audience Apartments in the Apostolic Palace, see Illustrations.)

Also overlooking this same courtyard are the historic and once open-air loggias off which are located the Secretariat of State, the senior administrative arm of the Church's hierarchy. Ranged primarily along the third-floor loggia bordering two sides of the courtyard, their deliberate nearness to the pontifical private quarters allows the cardinal secretary of state to be instantly available to the pope. The cardinal also enjoys, as a benefice of his position, his own substantial private apartment suite in the residential palace.

Tucked into this confusing architectural hodgepodge is the incomparable Sistine Chapel, plain to the point of severity on the outside, backdrop for one of the world's most sublime art treasures within. A veritable cataract of tourists constantly flows through the chapel built by, and commemorating, Pope Sixtus IV. Recently this flow of visitors has been forced to make an end run around a team of technicians restoring the chapel's frescoes, work funded by a Japanese television company in a quid pro quo exchange for exclusive rights to make a television documentary chronicling their efforts.

Many of the spectacular chambers in the vicinity of the chapel, including the Pauline Chapel, the Sala Ducale, and the Sala Regia, are not shown to the public. The Pauline Chapel, with its two opposing walls displaying murals by Michelangelo—the Crucifixion of St. Peter and the Conversion of Saul—is sometimes opened for an occasional pontifical mass and even a rare—a very rare—wedding performed by the pope. Shortly after his accession to the papacy,

John Paul II performed a unique private marriage ceremony in the chapel in response to a request from a young Roman woman named Vittoria Ianni, who must have been staggered by the pope's assent and her own good fortune. The Sala Regia—the "Royal Salon"—is under the constant vigil of a Swiss Guardsman in token of its past significance as the principal site of papal receptions for crowned visitors. Doors from the Sistine Chapel are open to tourists for a brief look into the lavishly decorated chamber, but a barrier across the doorway prevents them from entering; usually so many bodies are jammed in the opening that it's difficult to see much of this masterpiece of Renaissance interior architecture.

The grandest element of the Vatican's northern group of buildings is the massive Vatican Museums building, essentially an enormously long quadrangular structure with three courtyards formed by two wings crossing its open center. Besides its status as the world's largest museum open to the public, this series of galleries, chapels, former papal apartments, and pleasure resorts looking out on magnificent vistas is also home to the Vatican's Secret Archives and Library, two independent institutions that attract both lay and clerical scholars from all over the world.

Serving as the public entrance and exit for the museums is a "new" (built in 1932—yesterday, by Vatican standards) portal from the Viale Vaticano; crossing its threshold, one steps into Vatican territory. The arched entry was built into the seventeenth-century bastion at the order of Pius XI, whose purpose was to stem what had become an unmanageable flow of visitors who, through lack of an alternative, were forced to enter the museums through a palace entrance off St. Peter's Square.

For five thousand lire—about three dollars—an art lover can spend an entire day wandering through Roman Catholicism's artistic heritage: paintings that range from the majesty of Raphael and drama of Caravaggio to the angst of forgotten Victorians; tapestries so finely woven and mosaics so minutely constructed that they seem to be composed of delicate brushstrokes; exquisite souvenirs and knickknacks presented to dozens of popes, remembrances extending from the altarpieces commissioned by papal vassals for the pope-king Julius II to the moon rocks given to the ecumenical pope Paul VI by Richard Nixon; and galleries neatly lined with thousands of Greek and Roman busts.

The least art-conscious place in the museum complex is the Posto Ristoro—the Vatican's single restaurant open to the public. A modern chrome and plastic cafeteria built into a partially buried site at the north end of the museums, it is one of the rare places in Italy where overcooked pasta can consistently be found.

Continuing on our counterclockwise circumnavigation of the papal state, the next major element—and the one that takes up half the total acreage—is the garden, a partly formal, partly rusticated private park sprinkled. with a handful of widely spaced villas, today serving mostly as office buildings. The Casino of Pius IV, the jewel of the gardens and one of Europe's treasures of Renaissance architecture and landscaping, is a composition of four complementary structures facing each other across a marbled courtyard: a small villa—the "little house" itself—on the west (to which Pius XI added a wing), an elegant loggia enclosing a grotto framed by cascading fountains opposing it, and miniature twin kiosks to either side.

The gardens of the Vatican are like an arboretum designed for humans, a gently hilled refuge light-years away from the maelstrom of modern Rome. This very private park was never meant as a public pleasure ground but only as a sylvan retreat for the sole enjoyment of the pope, with his court alone permitted to share its isolated beauty. Today, only the twenty gardeners wander freely through the paths of the partly manicured, partly semiwild papal grounds, where Pius XII daily covered the same few feet of garden path, which John XXIII and Paul VI essentially ignored and which John Paul II rarely visits because of security considerations. Populated mostly by small lizards, seen darting across hidden paths under the shadows of pine and palm trees, as well as the ubiquitous stray cats that are a permanent component of Rome, the gardens are strewn with all manner of fountains and statuary art, the latter mostly of middling quality— fragments of ancient marbles, or an odd bust of some forgotten pope.

Tourists are able to see a large part of the gardens from the Vatican's tour buses, which pass along the main roads. But the fortunate few who can receive official permission to explore the gardens on their own may find themselves musing on the popes who have walked these same shaded lanes, worrying over problems and bedevilments that have passed out of both time and history. Some of the nearly hidden paths in the wilder parts of the gardens near the northern wall appear not to have been trod for decades, so overgrown are they with weeds and vines. Every few yards, you discover a little stone fountain or piece of statuary that looks as though it hasn't been touched since the days Michelangelo was wrangling with Julius II. But the illusion is carefully wrought—many of these decorations are new, at least as the word is understood in the context of Vatican history, and the look of timelessness is a proudly crafted product of the gardeners' skill.

Adjoining this rustic wildwood are the more formal esplanades and court-type gardens to the south, typical of those found adjacent to nearly every palace in Europe and looking, in the phrase of Aubrey Menen, like a "spa out of season." Most are elegantly precise, a few cooled with bright flower beds set in patterns, many enlivened with the felicitous sound of splashing fountains.

The largest building in the gardens is the Palazzo del Governatorato*, the administrative headquarters in which the temporal affairs of the Vatican city-state are handled. The structure was built in 1930 in a ponderous and even then antiquated wedding-cake style to serve as a seminary; a more pressing need for administrative offices brought about by the Lateran Accords, establishing the Vatican state, quickly outweighed this original purpose. The architect, Giuseppe Momo, a close friend of the reigning pope, Pius XI, designed the building that today houses not only the main offices of the state's bureaucracy but also the clothing and dry-goods store that stocks the black clothing worn by many of the Vatican's clerics. Perched somewhat pompously on top of the building is its chief identifying mark, a sort of bourgeois classical temple crowned with a statue of the Virgin.

Between the Government Palace's sloping front yard and the back of St. Peter's is the famous flower bed carefully arranged after each papal election in the coat of arms of the new pope, and so maintained throughout the remainder of his pontificate. Just to the south is the Vatican Railway Station, a gift to Pius XI from Mussolini in commemoration of the signing of the Lateran Treaty. Precisely why the Fascist leader thought the Holy See's new little state needed an ornate and oversized train station has never been adequately ex-

*In Italian, the word *palazzo* carries no regal connotation—it simply means a large urban dwelling.

plained (important visitors even then came by car, through St. Peter's Square), and the decaying depot can probably be fairly described as Europe's most underutilized facility of its sort. Grandly and solidly built in marble and large enough to serve a population many times larger than the Vatican's, the passenger facilities of the station have been used infrequently, their only real spurt of activity—a minor spurt—coming during the Second Vatican Council. Today the station is undergoing preservation work to keep a leaky roof from caving in and the marble walls from crumbling. The track behind the platform is technically a spur of the Italian state railway system, and the small loading dock serves as the primary receiving area for the Vatican's supplies.

In the farthest reaches of the grounds, at the apex of the Vatican triangle, a landing pad for the pope's helicopter was built over tennis courts that once bordered this sharply angled bastion in the wall. Between the pad and the Governatorato are buildings housing Radio Vaticana, the official broadcasting station of the Holy See. Nearby is the Ethiopian College, an ecclesiastical academy under pontifical control. The college, depot, and government palace were all designed by Momo. Maintenance shops are hidden along the inside perimeter of the boundary wall.

The final area of the Vatican is the smaller clerical business section on the south side of the basilica, entrance to which is through the Arch of the Bells at the foot of the basilica's steps. Like the St. Anne Gate, this entrance is continuously manned by a pair of halbardiers of the Swiss Guard, constantly beseeched by tourists, pilgrims, and the simply curious eager for permission to enter the off-limits area of which a small and tempting part is visible beyond the barrier. The Guards, like the Beefeaters at the Tower of London, are perfectly amenable to being photographed standing next to any manner of tourists, an amenability that occasionally leads to some memorable juxtapositions.

The elegantly designed square immediately through the arch is called the Piazza dei Protomarteri Romani, named for Rome's first Christian martyrs, who died on this ground when it was the site of Nero's enormous and often bloody imperial circus. Straight ahead, through a series of arches connecting the basilica with its sacristy, is the Canonical Palace, housing not only a small museum displaying the greatest of the Church's sacramental treasures but also the apartments of St. Peter's canons, the priests who regularly say mass in the basilica.

Through the sacristy is another, much larger square, named for St. Martha, with two major office buildings on its perimeter, the Palace of St. Charles and the Palace of Justice, both containing administrative offices. The major tenant of the former is the Pontifical Commission for Social Communications, the Holy See's public-relations office. There are also a number of apartments in the building for permanent staff clerics; clotheslines with their laundry flapping above the roofline are a visible mark of their residence.

The southeastern corner of the state is almost literally filled with two of the largest buildings of the Vatican, the Paul VI Aula and the Palace of the Holy Office. The Aula (or auditorium), the last major building erected in the Vatican, covers a site on which once stood a number of smaller structures demolished in the 1970s to accommodate it. The international boundary courses directly through the enormous but relatively inconspicuous Nervi-designed hall on an approximate line with its proscenium arch. The depressing-looking palace housing the Holy Office (formally the Sacred Congregation for the Doctrine of the Faith, famed as the agency of the Church responsible for the Inquisition), is completely outside the Vatican limits, but, like the Aula, is an extraterritorial possession of the Holy See. Finally, between the Holy Office and the left arm of the Bernini arcade is a large open space where the Petrine Museum stood until it was torn down to provide a more spacious entrance area for the Aula.

History of the Vatican

As Rome itself is the source of so much of the fabric of Christian civilization, the Mons Vaticanus—the Vatican Hill—is the source of the greatest riches, both spiritual and temporal, of the Roman Catholic Church. In the time before man made this place the capital and point of convergence of the Western world, the region where the Tiber begins to leave the hills and breaks into the coastal flatland was as sharply divided socially as it was physically by its muddy river. The mighty entrepôt, from which armies conquered lands beyond numberless horizons, itself remained through the early Christian centuries almost exclusively on the stream's left bank, a layer of commerce, marble, and power covering the many hills that corrugated the land. The forgotten bank—the marshy, fever-plagued Vaticanum, as the Romans called the ill-defined area along the other side of the Tiber—stretched from the Janiculum Hill on the south, northward to where the Milvian Bridge would be built and eventually play a legendary role in the establishment of Christianity as the dominant force in the West. In the time of Christ it was home only to a few small farmers, and, because of clay-rich soil, a scattering of potters and makers of brick and tile.

Even the origin of the word "Vatican" has still not been settled on with any unanimity. One eighteenth-century source has the presumed original Latin—*vaticinii* or *vaticinium*—meaning "prediction," or "prophecy," named for the oracular god Vatican, who was purported to have resided on that fetid side of the river. Others attribute it to some long-vanished Etruscan town that once may have stood on the unrewarding ground. Whatever the meaning, the Vatican remained outside the city proper's development until Nero's midfirst-century reign. Only the making of a reputedly bad red wine was added to the few enterprises up to then established.

But as the newly imperial Rome inevitably outgrew its confines, even this forlorn area began to attract speculators who could see its potential as the source of a few quick talents of gold. Agrippina, Emperor Caligula's much-unloved mother, had the marshy lower parts drained and garden terraces built on the hills, one of which—in the gardens of today's Vatican state, behind St. Peter's—rose to 264 feet above the level of the Tiber. Because it was outside the city proper, Roman law permitted the area to be used as a burial ground, a portentous factor in its future fame. The charioteers from the nearby racetrack had a particular penchant for building elaborate mausoleums among the tombs of their more sedentary fellow citizens, some of whom were converting to a treasonous new religion named for an itinerant Jewish evangelist put to a state execution in one of the most underdeveloped colonies of the empire. These Christians, as they called themselves, were often interred in the Vatican area cemeteries right alongside the charioteers and their pagan compatriots. This last development is, in short, what caused this unlikely speck on the face of the earth to become a shrine to that itinerant evangelist and his first apostle, and the seat of the faith he founded.

In the fifteenth year of Emperor Nero's reign, sixty-four years after the crucifixion of Jesus in Jerusalem, a seminal event occurred that would change forever the obscurity of the Vatican hill. Simon, called Peter, chief among Jesus's disciples, was condemned for treason and, at his own request, nailed upside down, so tradition claims, to his execution cross so as not to imitate directly the manner in which his master was put to death. In a story based more on tradition than verified history, it is said that Peter was then buried in a nearby cemetery, a place that came to be honored with a small memorial raised over the gravesite by the growing community of Christians. For the three centuries after Peter died, these Christians of Rome would be persecuted with varying degrees of fiendishness for their "treasonous" faith, and some of the persecutions would be carried out in the circus near Peter's grave. All would have the quite unintended and unforeseen effect of strengthening the young and rapidly growing faith.

In the meantime, the Christians picked leaders from among themselves to act in the role of Peter's successors as vicars of the faith Christ left. These chief priests—or bishops—of Rome's Christians, later reckoned as the first popes, managed heroically to keep the Church alive but were themselves martyred to a man in the process. The emperors banished several of them to the worst hellhole in the empire, the dreaded lead mines of Sardinia. There, to ensure the docility of new arrivals, each had the nerve at the back of his right knee severed, his right eye gouged out and the socket cauterized with molten iron, and, if under thirty, was castrated. Arriving "popes," considered eminently expendable enemies of the state for defying the official emperor-centered pantheistic religion, were not excepted from these brutalities.

In the Christian year 312, all the officially sanctioned abuse of Christians suddenly and momentously came to an end. A signal event in both religious and world history took place at Saxa Rubra, about nine miles from Rome, an event that would shape the complexion of much of the world for many centuries to come and that helped define the basic configurations of modern Western society. On October 28, 312, General Constantine of the Romans won a decisive victory over his rival warlord, Emperor Maxentius, who after his defeat tried to escape back to Rome over the Milvian Bridge, then at the outskirts of the city. Maxentius was drowned when the frightened and stampeding populace crowding the bridge caused it to collapse. Constantine looked for an explanation of his good fortune in the stars and found it in the divine intervention of the God of the Christians. The new emperor, Constantine, not only ordered the immediate end to the long-standing persecutions of Christians suffered under almost every emperor since the founding of the sect but also declared with all solemnity that Christianity would henceforth be the official religion of the empire.

Constantine then set out to perform a spectacular act of piety to honor the Christian God, one that switched the center of authority in Rome from its ancient seat on the Capitoline Hill to the formerly undesirable circus and cemetery area across the river. The emperor reckoned that the deed that would best serve the one deity was to honor his first earthly vicar, Peter, with a splendid basilica rising over his grave. This would eternally mark Peter's burial place and signify the fullest honor it was in his ability to bestow.

The new church was named, of course, for Peter. How this basilica was built is the subject of the next chapter, but it should be stated here that from its very beginnings it was the primary temple of Christianity, outstripping in religious significance if not in veneration even those sites on the eastern Mediterranean littoral associated with the birth, life, and death of Jesus. Constantine soon forever forswore the Rome he had never particulary liked in order to establish a new capital, at Byzantium, for the eastern half of his empire. Accordingly, the bishop of Rome he left behind as his suzerain would within a few decades become, in effect, the chief civil authority in the old western half of the empire. The first papal residence was built on the Vatican hill shortly after the final collapse of the western empire. Here, Bishop (Pope) Symmachus constructed a dwelling for himself near the forecourt of the Constantinian basilica. (The later western emperors had their court in Ravenna, to the north, until their half of the empire finally collapsed in 476.)

After the western empire fell in 476, the popes remained nominally loyal to the rulers in Constantinople, as Constantine renamed his capital at Byzantium, at least until 692, when Emperor Justinian tried to order the arrest of Pope Sergius II for an infraction of imperial authority. In response, the pope's soldiers sent the emperor's representatives fleeing back to the Bosphorus. For better or for worse, the popes had by now become the de facto temporal rulers in addition to serving as their Church's chief priests. This duality would grow to such proportions in later centuries so as to present a grave, almost fatal danger to the existence of the papacy and to Roman Catholicism itself.

Because the new basilica built over the alleged site of Peter's grave attracted pilgrims from all over Europe, its precincts naturally turned into a small village of shops, lodgings, and bathhouses. This new commercial quarter, which came to be known as the Borgo, rapidly grew to fill the space between St. Peter's and the Tiber, eclipsing in importance the nearly separate city on the other bank of the river. (The Borgo wouldn't become officially integrated into Rome's administrative system until the end of the sixteenth century.) The first major elements that constitute what is today Vatican City were two *episcopia*—hostels for the bishops who came to say mass at the church of St. Peter.

As Rome increasingly fell prey to marauding armies of invaders, it lost its importance as a commercial center, and Church activities became the primary reason for the city's existence. Other basilicas were built in the city; one, dedicated to Christ, had been built by Constantine at the eastern edge of the city on property once owned by the late-empire Laterani family, and was dedicated to the pope at that time, Melchiades, and later renamed St. John Lateran. A palace was built alongside that became home to popes for a thousand years, as well as the administrative headquarters of the Church. (It—not St. Peter's—still serves today as the cathedral church of the diocese of Rome.)

From time to time, though, popes went to live at the new palace being built in the Vatican, usually to escape the political riots and turmoil that were a constant danger to life in the center of the old city. The new Apostolic Palace was started by Pope Eugenius III in the midtwelfth century to replace a rickety structure that Charlemagne, the first Holy Roman emperor, had built in the eighth century to serve as his residence when he visited Rome; Innocent III modernized the palace a few decades later.

Rome continued to be an irresistible target for repeated waves of invaders. Most of these enemies of Rome in the earlier postempire years were fellow Christians and thus to a great extent respected the sanctity of Peter's tomb, still unprotected in contrast to the city proper, whose ramparts were built centuries earlier by Emperor

Aurelian. This situation changed abruptly after the zealous Islamic hordes came in search of plunder and the furtherance of their religious cause in 846. They completely stripped the basilica and burned most of the Borgo quarter that had grown up in its lee. Pope Leo IV, outraged by this sacrilege, immediately ordered the building of a protective wall around the entire ecclesiastical area. The forty-foot-high "Leonine" wall, completed in 852 and containing four gates and forty-eight towers, began at the Tiber, rounded the crest of the Vatican hill, and went down again to the river, forming an enclosed town of the Vatican and Borgo that came to be called the Leonine City. It was, in essence, a fortress of the faith.

The chief defensive point of this religious village was the enormous cylindrical tomb built by Emperor Hadrian as his own monument on the right riverbank of the Tiber, midway along the Leonine City's river frontage. During a plague in 590, Pope Gregory had "seen"—probably after too much mulled wine—the image of an angel atop the structure, a sign he interpreted as an end to the pestilence. He reverently renamed it Castel Sant' Angelo—the Castle of the Holy Angel—and had apartments built for himself and his court in its bastions. A covered walkway, constructed on top of an aqueductlike structure between the apartments and the new pontifical palace being built north of St. Peter's, became an escape route from the Vatican to the fortress; almost a thousand years later, in 1527, this passage—called the Passetto—saved the life of Pope Clement VII under hot pursuit by a blood-crazed mob of imperial mercenaries.

The actual beginning of the Papal States—that part of the Italian peninsula ruled directly by the pope as a temporal kingdom—came about as a result of the so-called Donation of Pepin, a "gift" from the French king to Pope Stephen II in 754. After Pepin and his army came to the pope's rescue by kicking out the Lombards, one in a long line of invaders of central Italy, the French monarch placed the provinces under papal rule, guaranteeing them Frankish protection. All future popes through Pius XI considered this act both a precedent and a theoretical basis for their ensuing civil rule over much of the area. This region would become part of a unified and temporal Italian state in 1870.

Eugene III's Vatican Palace, the nucleus of today's Papal Residence, was enlarged many times. The portion around the Courtyard of the Parrot, the oldest part of the present structure, was finally finished after Innocent III, Nicholas III, and Boniface VIII added new wings and floors. Boniface's last additions probably were constructed toward the end of the thirteenth century. These popes still generally stayed at the Vatican palace for only short periods of time, although the more lavish Lateran Palace continued to serve as their primary residence.

Both Rome and the Vatican suffered a nearly fatal calamity in 1309 when Clement V moved the papacy to the infinitely more agreeable city of Avignon in his native France, a largely politically inspired maneuver related later in the book. This might have been the papacy's permanent site were it not for Catherine (later St. Catherine) of Siena. Clement's six immediate successors remained in Avignon, all maintaining that they planned to return the see of Peter to Rome. However, the pressures from the French court and the comforts of this "Babylonian captivity" outweighed any desire to return to Rome's discomforts and political maelstrom. In 1377, according to popular tradition, the nun Catherine convinced Gregory XI that he was driving the final nails in the coffin of the Church. When the papal see was finally and with little good grace brought back to its original home, Gregory found the derelict and unprotected Lateran vandalized and in ruins. He was forced to take up residence in the Vatican "palace," finally making it the permanent site of the papacy and its court.

Today's Vatican is largely the result of the plans commissioned by Nicholas V, the pope who in the middle of the fifteenth century took the first steps toward realizing a new St. Peter's, continuing the extension of the still crude palaces, and ordering the restoration of the by then decayed Leonine walls. Perhaps most significantly, Nicholas moved the remainder of the church government from the Lateran (whose adjacent church, even though the diocesan cathedral, the Christians of Rome had never embraced as they had St. Peter's), thus making the Vatican the undisputed hub of papal administration. The magnificent monument he left as his personal legacy, the famous Chapel of Nicholas V, was so beautifully decorated that it helped its artistic creator, Fra Giovanni da Fiesole, earn the more appropriate name "Angelico." This extraordinary period of construction lasted for more than a century, the Vatican's rebirth coinciding with the birth of the greater Renaissance then beginning to transform a medieval continent into modern Europe.

The Vatican's most famous architectural feature (other than the basilica itself) was the chapel built by one of Nicholas's successors, Sixtus IV, between 1473 and 1481, and at 44 feet wide by 130 feet long, the same dimensions as the biblical temple of Solomon. Named the Sistine Chapel after the pope, it was to serve as both a chapel proper and as a chamber of state (it was, in fact, intended primarily as a grand setting for the conclaves that elected new popes), but it soon became more famous for Michelangelo's interior decoration than for its remarkably clean architecture.

Julius II, a successor of Sixtus, hired the Florentine sculptor/painter to transform the blue-painted ceiling, then set with golden stars, into a great allegorical fresco mural depicting the creation in the Book of Genesis. The chapel was then thirty-three years old, about the same age as Michelangelo when he started the work. Twenty-two years after finishing the ceiling and window lunettes, Michelangelo continued the chapel's interior embellishment with the Last Judgment on the altar wall. Together the two works are considered one of the world's most enduring artistic achievements. Shortly after Michelangelo finished the latter work, a knot of pious and unfortunately influential papal advisers led by the pope's chamberlain labeled them pornography. The chamberlain called the frontal nudity "more fit for a house of ill repute than a house of God." The advisors persuaded a successor to Julius to order Daniele da Volterra, the master's pupil, to cover strategic areas of the figures in the Last Judgment with wisps of painted-in fabric. Providentially, original studies of the frescoes still exist, and it is thus possible to see the work the way Michelangelo meant it to be seen.

What is today the Vatican museum complex was started by Innocent VIII at the end of the fifteenth century. Originally built as a summer residence, the first element of the palace—named the Belvedere Palace for its splendid panoramic view across the city—was situated at the northern extreme of the Vatican area, nearly fronting on what is today the Viale Vaticano. Later Alexander VI added the Borgia (the Italianized version of his Spanish family name) Tower to the corner of the new palace, enabling its northwestern side to be more readily defended against armed attacks. Julius II,

Michelangelo's first patron, joined the older Apostolic Palace with the newer Belvedere in a gigantic complex, with Bramante serving as his chief architect.

The splendid new palace originally encompassed an enormous open quadrangle, a courtyard terraced in steps to accommodate the grade of the hill on which it was built, and the first great Roman pleasure garden laid out since the end of the empire. Spectacular— and utterly nonreligious—entertainments, ranging from jousts to theatrical musicales, were staged for the papal court's entertainment. Later popes put an end to this vast open arena by building two arms across the center, the first to house the Vatican library, the second a museum wing. There are now, as a result, three courtyards, named from south to north the Courts of the Belvedere, the Library, and, because of its giant bronze ornamental pine cone at one end, the Pine. The library wing, built at the end of the 1580s by Sixtus V, still houses the Vatican collection of books and manuscripts in addition to the administratively distinct Vatican Secret Archives. Its Sistine Salon, originally the library's reading gallery and today seen by visitors on the museum tours, is as a result of its opulent golden walls and intricately vaulted ceiling one of the most strikingly beautiful rooms in the entire papal state.

Since Gregory XI had returned from Avignon to find the living quarters in the Lateran uninhabitable, expansion of the Vatican palace became a priority for his next several successors. Their apartments grew in artistic splendor in direct proportion to the increasing secularity of the Church. Nearly every pope was responsible for the addition of some new tower, floor, or wing, and generally the less spiritual the incumbent, the better the artistic additions he commissioned. Very little was done in a coordinated manner, with a new wing simply being tacked on to the last one. This lack of any kind of overall plan resulted in the unbalanced, yet nonetheless impressive appearance the complex presents today.

At the end of the sixteenth century, Sixtus V built the last major addition to what had become a layer-cake palace, the structure in which today's actual private papal suite is located. A large, square building surrounding a courtyard, named the Court of Sixtus V, for its patron builder, was designed and erected by Domenico Fontana and situated east of the loggias that Bramante had created earlier that century for Julius II. The palace's main entrance is in the

Courtyard of St. Damase, once the *hortus secretus*—the private garden—of the medieval popes. The building's four stories overlook the open campus before the basilica, and it is from a window high up on the southern side of this wing that popes still bestow their apostolic blessings to the crowds that gather below. With a few more small additions in the decades after Sixtus V's reign, by the midsixteenth century the palace existed essentially as it is today.

After the new basilica of St. Peter's was completed in 1614, it was obvious that the unsightly public forum facing it was a completely inadequate frontispiece for Christendom's grandest cathedral. Fortunately, considerable thought was devoted to solving the problem of space, and the result, a sort of "amphitheater of the Christian universe," as it has been called, forever enshrined the architect/sculptor responsible for it. Alexander VII chose Gian Lorenzo Bernini to design an ensemble to present both a suitably magnificent setting for the basilica itself and to frame the Egyptian obelisk that Sixtus V had earlier placed in the center of the square, unfortunately just off line with the basilica's central axis. The designer had to meet two crucial requirements imposed upon him by the pope: Everyone in the square must be able to see the benediction loggia on the facade of the church used by the pope for appearances on particularly solemn occasions, *and* the window of the pope's apartment in the Vatican palace, used for similar but less formal blessings, must be equally visible.

Bernini's solution—one upon which the imagination cannot conceive improvement—was the two semicircular colonnades, joined to the atrium of the basilica by straight and slightly converging wings, the whole made up of 284 marble columns, each nearly 50 feet high, and a pediment topped with 140 travertine statues of martyr and confessor saints. The degree of importance of each particular saint is greater the closer his statue is to the basilica. Bernini added a second fountain to match an older one in a corresponding position between the obelisk and the north arm of the colonnade. The completed ensemble—then able to hold twice the population of baroque Rome—became in its majesty a metaphor for the arms of the Church embracing all those who enter the square, and, in a larger sense, for all who enter the faith.

By the time St. Peter's Square was finished, the basic outlines of the Vatican we see today were in place. Many of the subsequent additions came in the form of the walls, museums, and business quarters that fill out the modern city-state. A major reason that so many of the enclave's most prominent features were not superseded by later replacements was Gregory XIII's removal of the primary papal residence back across the river to the center of old Rome in the 1570s, this time not to the Lateran but to a new palace built on the ancient Quirinal Hill. Beginning with Gregory, the major Vatican buildings were left relatively undisturbed, as each of his successors preferred as he did the comforts and healthier air of the Quirinal to those of the comparatively low-lying and thus still malarial Leonine City. It is, however, important to point out that this action didn't imply an "abandonment" of the Vatican. The entire city, it should be remembered, served as the capital of a papal kingdom. The Vatican itself did not yet represent an entity politically distinct from the greater city.

The crumbling first-millennium walls of Leo IV had been restored by Nicholas V in the fifteenth century, but in the century between 1540 and 1640 much-needed new walls, enclosing a considerably larger territory, were built around the Vatican by Pius IV, Pius V, and Urban VIII. These walls became what is, for the most part, the modern boundary of the city-state when it was established in 1929. At the time the walls were built, they served a defensive as well as a decorative purpose. Embattlements were built along the top, with sections of the perimeter extended to allow protected firing fields.

About fifty feet high and a bit over 2 miles in circumference from one end to the other, the slightly sloping wall is broken by only two entrances in ordinary use from the St. Anne Gate counterclockwise to the Holy Office: that into the Vatican museums, and the Porta Fabbrica, leading into the railway station, the latter portal used only by trains supplying the Vatican's provisions. At the top of the Vatican hill, where the walls form a sharp angle at their westernmost point, a papal helicopter pad has been tucked into the battlement. It is used both by John Paul II for the frequent flights to and from his summer residence at Castel Gandolfo, and by his state visitors who are sometimes airlifted to the city-state from Rome's international airport at Fiumicino.

The Vatican's final massive building spree changed the Belvedere Palace into the public museum complex it is today, a transformation that has continued into the last quarter of the twentieth century.

From the time Julius II placed the statue of the Apollo Belvedere in the Belvedere's courtyard in 1503, usually reckoned as the beginning of what eventually became the modern Vatican museums, to the 1973 opening of the new Missionary-Ethnological Museum and the underground Historical Museum, the growth of the Holy See's galleries into the world's largest public collection of art represents both the triumph of the Roman Catholic Church and one of its greatest gifts to posterity.

The gardens of the Vatican as they now exist are, for the most part, a creation of the twentieth century, although they were first planted four hundred years ago. The forty-two acre modern park—nearly half of the city-state's total land area—was laid out at the turn of the century by Leo XIII, but many of the buildings were erected in the area long before the formal patterns designed for Leo were drafted. The oldest structures, such as the ancient towers of the remaining fragments of the Leonine walls, have been adapted for practical use. The tower at the highest point of the Vatican hill houses administrative offices of Radio Vaticana, while another less importantly conceals the only public toilet facilities on the grounds. The most interesting structure, called St. John's Tower, was converted by Pope John XXIII late in his papacy to serve as a summer residence and hermitage in which he sought solitude from the considerable pressures of the Second Vatican Council. He was, sadly, able to use it for only a few days before his death. Still immaculately cared for and with John's arms emblazoned over the entrance, the modern living quarters built into the ancient stone tower serve today as a guest apartment for John Paul II's most important visitors.

The greatest treasure in the Vatican gardens is the Casino of Pius IV, named for the sixteenth-century Milanese Medici who built additions onto the small retreat started by his immediate predecessor, Paul IV. Beginning with Innocent VIII in the late fifteenth century, most popes built personal or summer villas in the vicinity of Rome, although the Belvedere Palace was the only one within the Vatican enclave. Paul started his villa higher up the steep Vatican hill to remove himself from the enervating heat that blankets Roman summers. Pius finished the relatively simple loggia and fountain that Paul had begun, induced partly, according to legend, by his desire to get away from the noise of the construction then being carried out on St. Peter's dome. He turned it into an elaborate four-building complex. The villa and the loggia are small masterpieces of the mannerist style in architecture, and the most delicate of the major Vatican architectural settings.

Since 1922, this site has served as the headquarters of the Pontifical Academy of Sciences (originally called the Academy of Lynxes—after animals considered to be symbols of intellectual farsightedness—when it was founded in 1603), a group of seventy scientists of international repute—mostly university teachers and including twenty Nobel laureates—all chosen personally by the pope without regard to religious belief. Their main charge is to advise him on scientific issues, including providing documentation for his increasingly frequent speeches on scientific matters. One of the Academy's earliest, and probably most illustrious, members was Galileo Galilei, condemned by Urban VIII for astronomic views that ran counter to church dogma. Today, discussion of the radiation effects of a nuclear holocaust or a complex study of leprosy are apt to engage the members during their biennial meetings. The Academy, whose annual budget stands at $400,000, is permanently staffed by a single Jesuit administrator assisted by two secretaries.

After the Vatican became an independent state in 1929, the government palace and railway station were built. Basically they are symbols, and fairly pompous ones, of the territorial independence of the new state. Incidentally, the station suffered the only damage in the Vatican from air attack during World War II. Four German bombs fell behind St. Peter's, missing the basilica itself by a frighteningly small margin; instead, only the windowpanes in the station were blown out. The bombing has remained officially unexplained by German military historians, but some writers attribute it to German furor over the Vatican granting asylum to refugees.

Much of the St. Anne business district has been developed since the establishment of the independent Vatican state: the maintenance facilities, the fire station, the waterworks, electrical and heating plants, the post office, the Annona, and a barracks for the Vigilanza have all been constructed since 1929.

Chances are that twenty-first-century pilgrims—and maybe even twenty-first-century art critics—will regard the Paul VI Audience Hall, the Vatican's newest major building, if not a masterpiece, as at least a first-rate example of late-twentieth-century architecture. Paul ordered the auditorium built to provide a large indoor setting for winter general audiences, something the huge structure handsomely provides. Its creator, the internationally acclaimed Italian architect Pier Luigi Nervi, was severely circumscribed by the site restrictions, limitations that could not be overcome because of the inflexible nature of the Vatican's setting and the artistic and historic value of many of the structures on and near the proposed site. A location behind the Holy Office was decided on, to the left of the basilica as it is seen from St. Peter's Square. Nervi was able to provide a hall seating sixty-three hundred people, twice as many standing when some of the rows of seats are removed. Because the architect realized that planning a building in the lee of the world's greatest cathedral was an act of considerable audacity, he designed it so that it is all but invisible from most of the traditional public sight lines in the Vatican. The best—probably the only—way to see it in its entirety is from the cupola at the top of St. Peter's.

Even within its acutely constricted limits, this city of God has continued to grow, no longer at the pace of the builder popes of the Renaissance, but enough to meet the needs of a largely desecularized but still infinitely important see of Peter. Given the lack of areas in which to expand, future occupants of Peter's throne will probably have to content themselves with a Vatican much as it is today: a tight little kingdom filled to bursting with corridors of ecclesiastical power and serving as a testimonial to the enduring power of the craft, beauty, and majesty with which Providence has imbued the creative capability of man.

2

The Church of the Fisherman from Galilee: *St. Peter's Basilica*

*"You feel something lies behind it
you are not meant to see.
Something does.
It is the Vatican."*

Aubrey Menen

Most people seem never to notice it at all; the few who do have probably made many visits before it caught their attention. Framed against the golden fantasy of Bernini's *cathedra* in the Basilica of St. Peter's stands a severely plain unpainted wooden cross, perhaps eight feet high, planted in an equally severe white marble plinth. In another setting, an object of such size might impose on its surroundings, but it is so overpowered by the glories of Christendom's chief temple that it seems almost nonexistent there.

St. Peter's Basilica is, of course, the reason for the Vatican's existence, and it is both the primary reason for the hosts of pilgrims, visitors, and tourists who have come to this site for nearly eighteen centuries, and the reason for the continuing presence of the popes on this tiny sliver of earth. The floods of the faithful and the curious continue, even in our overbearingly cynical age, to be drawn to St. Peter's permanence and sense of connection to the spiritual force that made and guides this world. That plain, unpainted cross may not be what people come to St. Peter's to see, but it is the essence of the basilica's power to command their veneration.

The church the apostle Simon Peter founded in Rome was not one of mortar and brick, but simply of small groups of Christians who met in one another's homes to practice their proscribed religion quietly. The presence of Jesus's closest collaborator, the man he chose as his first vicar to continue his stewardship of the new faith, was deemed a profound honor by these earliest Christians, who were often among the least prosperous and most disenfranchised elements of the population. Scores went to their deaths in persecutions designed as a diversionary spectacle for Rome's massive underclass; a hoped-for side effect was the quashing of this undesirable fledgling sect. When Peter followed his fellow Christians to martyrdom, his body became an icon to those who remained. The enduring myth from those essentially protohistoric times—but a story now officially endorsed by the Church—is that Peter's remains were given to his friends and buried in a tomb built at the foot of Vatican hill near the site of his crucifixion, where he was covertly venerated for some three hundred years. Their religion remained proscribed, their community in continual danger because of their "treason," and their faith challenged by an increasingly hostile state that had stopped regarding the growing sect as inconsequential.

It was over Peter's grave-shrine that Constantine, Rome's first emperor to convert to Christianity, decided to erect his temple to the memory of the first pope. As emperor, amassing the considerable financial resources needed to achieve this task was not an insuperable barrier, but another, more delicate concern gave pause even to imperial wishes. The area surrounding Peter's gravesite was, in effect, a cemetery city, with streets of tombs housing the earthly remains of Christian and non-Christian alike. Roman law had its blind spots, but the violation of cemeteries was a deeply held taboo, and the emperor was treading on sensitive and even dangerous ground with his plan to build a temple—Christian or otherwise—over *any* graves. But the wily Constantine harbored another, more subtle consideration when he chose the relatively remote Vatican site. By removing his new church from the center of the then existing city, as he had done with the church he dedicated to St. John, he was hoping to avoid antagonizing both the strongly pagan Senate, for whom the emperor's religious beliefs remained very much his own private affair, and Rome's formidable first families.

Constantine's monumental temple of homage was to be in the form of a five-aisled "basilica." The word, from the Greek *basilike,* originally was the feminine form of "royal" and probably derived from Athens' *Stoa Basilike,* where magistrates had once carried out juridical duties inherited from kings of earlier times. The Romans applied the term to the buildings they copied from the general form of the original Athenian *stoa* (or covered colonnade), and it thus came to signify rectangular structures lighted by windows high up the walls of the central hall, with low-colonnaded aisles to either side. Constantine's earlier shrine dedicated to the new religion, built near the palace of the Lateran family, was the first basilica in the city.

It was this form, greatly magnified, that Constantine chose for his churches. From the outset, the second church was deliberately designed to be the world's largest such temple. This was part of an effort to convince his Roman subjects that if Christianity was worthy of such opulence and such commitment from the emperor, then it was a worthy replacement for paganism as the new state religion. In this he succeeded magnificently. Christianity spread over the empire with astonishing speed, and the form chosen for these earliest churches—purposely different from the classical temple associated with the old paganism—became the model for the most important Christian places of worship.

The church Constantine built on the site of Peter's entombment stood for over one thousand years, more than twice as long as its stone and brick replacement existed. Begun in about the year 320, most of the huge structure was completed before Constantine's death in 337. (Ironically, Constantine remained unbaptized for nearly his entire reign, apparently in the belief that he would be a more effective peacemaker among all factions; he agreed to receive the sacrament only on his deathbed.) Considering the many factors involved, especially the terrain upon which it was built, we can have little other than profound admiration for a feat accomplished in such a relatively primitive era.

Not only did the emperor want the monument-*cum*-temple to be the largest in the world, but he also insisted that it be placed squarely over the site that had been the center of Christian worship in Rome since Peter was martyred. (For some time, Peter's bones had been hidden in one of Rome's catacombs; Pope Silvester returned them to the Vatican site at the emperor's request.) However, the Vatican hill's slope rises fairly steeply to the immediate north and west of the site where the remains were believed to have been entombed. To accommodate the imperial wishes, the basilica's

builders first had to create a flat foundation by digging an escarp-
ment (a set-back niche) into the side of the hill for one end of the
church, and, second, build an extended platform—in some places
30 feet high—out over the side of the hill on which to construct the
other end. In a time when motive power was very closely related to
muscle power, and keeping in mind that from its front door to its
apse the church was over 350 feet long, the significance of this
fourth-century engineering achievement can better be appreciated.
Constantine himself is said to have ceremonially participated in the
construction by carrying a token twelve baskets of earth, the number
in commemoration of the Twelve Apostles.

This first St. Peter's in the basilica form was to serve primarily as
a monument marking the tomb of Peter. It was thus positioned so
that the actual tombsite was the church's focal point, with a col-
umned shrine over the apostle's grave at the far end of the center
nave, backed by a semicircular apse serving as a visual frame and
ambulatory, or walkway, around its rear. Three centuries after it was
completed, the church was further embellished with an atrium
added onto its front wall and nearly doubling the total length. The
new courtyard created by the atrium, popularly called the Garden of
Paradise after the palm trees painted on its walls, acted as a kind of
forum/marketplace for the thousands of pilgrims who were attracted
to the spectacular church as well as for the merchants who were ever
eager to serve these early tourists. Perhaps a decoration from an ancient Roman bath, a huge Roman bronze pine cone (the same ornament that today decorates one of the museum courtyards named for
it, and one of the few relics remaining from the first basilica) loomed
over the center of the open court, and to the north the first crude
elements of what would later become the papal palace were built.

For a tumultuous twelve centuries, Constantine's brick and wood
church endured heavy daily use, raucous commerce, nearly fatal
pillagings, and architectural dabbling. Chapels, courtyards, and
belfries were added, with palaces to the side and structural tinkering
with the arrangements of the shrine over the apostle's grave. It
witnessed uncounted papal coronations, funerals, and ceremonies,
and—most memorably—the almost accidental crowning by Pope
Leo III of the Holy Roman emperor, Charlemagne, in the year 800.
The core that the first Christian emperor built survived hordes of
attacking outland bandits of one vague ideological stripe or another,

the fires endemic to the times, and endlessly changing fashions in ecclesiastical architecture. But one assault it couldn't withstand was old age, and by the time Julius II started construction of a new basilica with which to replace it in the early sixteenth century, old St. Peter's had fallen into an advanced and—with the skills then available—irreparable state of decay. This condition, incidentally, little bothered Julius, who felt a new church would be a far more appropriate setting for his eventual tomb anyway. Sadly for history, the only remaining parts of old St. Peter's Church likely to be noticed by tourists are the large bronze doors shielding the new basilica's central entrance, commissioned in the early fifteenth century by Eugenius IV from the sculptor Filarete.

The first basilica had been built as a monument to mark Peter's gravesite, so it stood to reason that its replacement would have to be sited precisely as had its predecessor. But to accomplish this, the builder popes couldn't simply pull down the old and erect the new. For one thing, cathedrals aren't built quickly—neither today, nor, far less so, in the sixteenth century. Peter's shrine needed to convey a sense of continuance and permanence, and the only possible way to accomplish this was bit by bit, to tear down some of the old and build some of the new, and so on to completion. The engineering and architectural complications inherent in this sort of thing were and are staggering, and without the genius of four of the supreme artists in history—Donato Bramante, Michelangelo Buonarotti, Carlo Maderno, and Gian Lorenzo Bernini—there is little question that the St. Peter's that slowly evolved would be far less than the masterpiece it is.

The earliest serious plans to remodel St. Peter's substantially were put forward by Pope Nicholas V in the midfifteenth century. His grand plan was to reconstruct the entire city of Rome, with St. Peter's as its chief ornament. Nicholas envisioned leaving the church's main nave standing and adding three more arms of equal length, the crossing topped by a dome. With his death, these papal dreams came to an abrupt halt, his successors having their own, quite different priorities. But at the beginning of the sixteenth century, one of history's most forceful and self-assured popes came to the papal throne and set the stage for remaking the basilica and the Vatican into what they are today. Julius II, more warrior and all-around Renaissance man than spiritual leader, had the great good fortune to live in the same age as a superbly capable architect who shared his vision of a Rome restored to its long-lost imperial grandeur. Although Donato Bramante's design for St. Peter's was never realized, it was nonetheless the inspiration and model for what eventually rose from the venerable but rotting hulk of the old and bound subsequent architects to the general foundations he laid.

The first thing to be noted about Bramante's design is that it represented a plan for an entirely new church, not merely further additions, upgrading, or remodeling of the Constantinian basilica. The vision Bramante had for his once-in-a-lifetime commission was nothing less than monumentally audacious. Four colossal piers had to be built to support the colossal dome he planned over his Greek-cruciform (a cross with four equal arms) church. The exact point where the arms would cross was to be precisely over Peter's tomb, emphasizing the basilica's special nature. When construction started, a temporary yet elaborate templelike structure was built over the tomb to protect it, both from any material workmen might drop from above and from the elements to which it would be exposed when the old basilica's superstructure itself was razed. Construction of the first pier was hurriedly begun in 1506, even before the architect's final plans had been worked out. On April 18, 1506, a white marble cornerstone was laid in Julius's presence. On it, the pope inscribed his pithy testament for posterity: "Pope Julius II of Liguria in the year 1506 restored this basilica, which had fallen into decay." To help meet its costs, income from the sale of indulgences was applied toward financing this most massive and expensive of papal whims and was to portend a major cause for the coming cataclysm in Western Christianity.

In the past, the death of a pope had almost always brought building projects to a virtual halt, and it did so once again. Julius died in 1513, and Bramante's death the following year began two decades of inactivity on construction of the new basilica. A major part of the reason was the serious preoccupation on the part of Julius's successors Adrian VI and Clement VII with the foreign military forces then creating havoc in the papal capital. The most brutal rape of Rome since the Islamic attacks of the eighth century occurred in 1527, the famous Sack of Rome by the mostly mercenary forces of the Catholic Hapsburg Holy Roman emperor, Charles V. Clement had the utmost misfortune to be pontiff at this perigee of the papacy. He escaped with his life only because of the willingness of many of his Swiss Guards to give up theirs. Paintings and drawings of the Vatican from the period show St. Peter's construction site, with its forlorn, half-completed piers, looking very much like any of the authentic ancient ruins dotting the other side of Rome.

After the tides of invasion receded, Clement's successor, Paul III, appointed a new chief architect in 1534. Antonio da Sangallo came up with a plan based on a modified Greek cross with four equal arms and a short nave attached to one arm, giving it the appearance of a Latin cross (a cross with a longer fourth arm). His plan was properly grandiose, yet the floor arrangements of the interior space below the central dome were extremely complex and potentially dangerous. It was feared that ne'er-do-wells might lie in wait in the dark passages among the piers to relieve pilgrims of their purses. In reality, the chief drawback was a lack of an unimpeded central space in which to conduct to best advantage the grand ceremonials so central to the basilica's purpose.

Most of the rest of Sangallo's life was spent building a wooden model of his plan rather than pursuing work on the real thing. (This model is on display in a Vatican museum.) When Sangallo died in 1546, Paul appointed Michelangelo, seventy-one years old, with the bulk of his work on the Sistine Chapel long since completed, to take over the project. In spite of this towering genius's usual protestations of "lack of ability," he nonetheless immediately condemned Sangallo's work as "overly busy" and came up with his own, much-simplified design, tearing down most of what little of Sangallo's plan had actually been built. And it was back to the plain Greek cross form again.

But even Michelangelo was bound by the essentials of Bramante's design, primarily the great piers whose vaults had been built much too sturdily, massively, and expensively to alter them significantly. Michelangelo's plan really amounted to the inner perambulatory— the circular area surrounding the altar—of Sangallo, minus Sangallo's outer wall; in effect, Michelangelo stripped one layer off his predecessor's composition. Michelangelo's most significant contribution, however, was the design for a new dome, one with major differences from those envisioned by both Bramante and Sangallo.

The first part of the job was the southern apse, the rounded wall at the end of the church's left cross arm. One of the most beautiful architectural features on this outside wall was Michelangelo's treatment of the attic floor, that part of the structure sitting above the formally pilastered and friezed main section: The dramatic and deeply recessed arches on the plain attic surface were among his singular design glories. Although construction had started on the opposite apse (that on the north side) when Michelangelo died in 1564, much of his design died with him, as most of his plans were ignored by his successors. The drum to support the dome (which together were to be supported by Bramante's original four piers built on the floor of the church) was nearly finished during Michelangelo's stewardship of the basilica's construction, but it would wait for twenty-four years after his death until the dome was to close and crown the gaping hole of the drum.

The basilica's design remained confused, with elements of both the old and the new churches, and stood without any kind of façade other than the remaining broken eastern end of old St. Peter's. The exact progression of the basilica's construction and even the identity of minor architects to whom credit is due for various elements are in doubt for the next portion of its history. What is certain is that the major deviation from Michelangelo's plan was a mistake, especially the transformation of his strong vertical openings in the attic floor into prettily embellished horizontal portals, the form in which they are preserved in the present church. The major building pope during this period, Sixtus V, oversaw the transformation of much of Rome during his five-year papacy, and had he lived another five years he might well have been able to get final construction of St. Peter's irreversibly under way. As it was, the one element of the basilica he saw to near-completion was the dome, which to the world today is *the* supreme symbol of the Vatican, the papacy, and—to many—of Roman Catholicism itself.

The design for Michelangelo's dome was hemispherical—half of a perfect sphere. This was how it was completed on its underside, the part seen by those inside the basilica looking up. But the spherical outside surface of the double-walled dome was changed to an elongated form, the typical baroque profile. Giacomo della Porta, Sixtus's architect, was the author of this major new element, although Michelangelo was for centuries credited not only with the drum but with the dome as well. Sixtus lived to see this main element of the cupola finished, but the lantern with its orb and cross weren't completed until three years after his death, during which time three popes came and went in what were even then unusually short reigns.

Early in the seventeenth century, Paul V finally gave the order to demolish the last standing section of old St. Peter's, the entrance area at the eastern end of the new structure. The last element barring completion of the church's exterior was a portico and façade. However, before a new front could be built, it was necessary to decide the burning question of whether to finish it in the Greek cross plan of Michelangelo, or add a long nave to transform the plan into a Latin cross. Paul chose the latter course, for not doing so would have left barren a large part of the ground covered by the old church. Additionally, a longer nave facilitated better (that is, bigger) ceremonies. Finally, Latin cross-style churches were by Paul's day simply the more fashionable design mode.

There now came on the scene the third of the church's primary architectural quadrivirate, the man responsible for what is by far the greatest controversy over the basilica's final form. Carlo Maderno's major contribution to the exterior of the basilica, the façade looming up over the piazza, has been for centuries severely criticized for its proportions: too wide for its height, the dome invisible from most of the square, and the two end bays projecting out from either side of the church both unnecessary and unattractive. There is truth in all these charges, but there is also considerable justification for each.

As for the first point, the great height of the façade was judged by Maderno to be necessary primarily to hide the pitched roof over the nave; had the façade been lower, the dome would have been visible from more of the square, but so would the markedly unattractive and unbaroque triangular end of the nave roof. When the decision was made to extend the church into the form of a Latin cross, it may have been determined that the damage this would do to the perspective of the dome from the square was less important than *not* having the longer nave. The extension of the nave was considered the more important issue.

Finally, the extensions of the façade into an extra bay on either side were originally done so a bell tower could be built on each, a design that would have made ample sense had it been carried out. It is clear to anybody looking at the church today that the two end bays were an afterthought: after the façade was completed as

Maderno planned it, and before Paul ordered the extra bays built to support the belfries, an inscription—IN HONOREM PRINCIPIS APOST. PAULUS V BURGHESIUS ROMANUS PONT. MAX. AN. MDCXII PONT. VII ("In honor of the Prince of the Apostles, Paul V Borghese, Roman, Supreme Pontiff, in the year 1612, the seventh of his pontificate")—was incised along the top of the main frieze; the letters clearly *don't* extend to the two later end bays. By the way, it isn't clear whether the placement of these words was papal flattery on Maderno's part or whether the pope ordered it thus, but it was no accident that PAULUS V BURGHESIUS ROMANUS is nicely centered right over the church's main door.

One interesting and little-known detail about Maderno's design for the basilica is that the building's façade is—purposely—not quite at a right angle with its nave. To place it at a true right angle would have meant that the already implanted obelisk in the center of the square would have been off-axis with the church. A two-degree turning of the façade prevented an unaesthetic appearance and kept the obelisk in line with the center of the portico and the dome. This device would later greatly facilitate a symmetrical plan for the church's piazza.

The architectural design work Maderno drew up for the *inside* of St. Peter's is, happily, beyond criticism, and his two major contributions—the portico and the nave—are indisputable glories of the baroque. We'll examine the interior of the church shortly, but in fairness, it should be mentioned here that Maderno's place among the four great architects of St. Peter's is securely founded, irrespective of criticism about the façade. Maderno was responsible for the virtual completion of the actual church building, and on November 18, 1626, supposedly the thirteen-hundredth anniversary of the consecration of the original basilica, Pope Urban VIII was at last able to consecrate a new St. Peter's.

The next pontiff central to the story of the basilica is Urban VIII, born Maffeo Barberini, and to whom we owe credit for much of the interior of the church. His friendship of over twenty years with the sculptor Gian Lorenzo Bernini gave that consummate artist a position of unequaled creative eminence in the papal kingdom, but rarely in history has eminence thus achieved been so genuinely deserved. When we think of the glories of baroque art, the image that often comes to mind is a Bernini masterpiece, very often a masterpiece created for St. Peter's. After his election to the papal throne, Urban is said to have remarked to his already eminent friend, "It is your great fortune, O Cavalier, to see Cardinal Maffeo Barberini pope, but much greater is our own that the Cavalier Bernini lives during our pontificate." Some have criticized Bernini for his overeagerness to return such flattery—one biographer remarked that Bernini's greatest talent lay in "bringing out the picturesque"—but today's St. Peter's is unimaginable without the ornaments given it by this most flamboyantly talented artist.

Ironically, after his first great success on the basilica's interior— the fantasy baldacchino over the papal altar—Bernini's fortunes followed a rocky path. When Maderno died in 1629, the pope's friend was named architect of St. Peter's, and his first major task in that position of considerable authority was to build the towers on top of the two bases on either side of the façade that Maderno had provided for that purpose. Maderno had compensated by building the south base with considerably wider footings than its opposite number because of pesky underground springs, an annoyance considered too expensive to drain properly. Bernini evidently didn't give sufficient attention to the matter, and soon after two of the planned three stories of the south tower were built, the whole thing started to sink and otherwise show signs of imminent collapse. An alarmed pope, of course, ordered that work be immediately suspended. Plans for the north tower were abandoned, the sinking south tower was demolished, and Bernini had to suffer a storm of opprobrium for bungling St. Peter's. Fortunately, amends to the artist's reputation were soon made in a spectacular way.

Bernini lost his patron and protector in 1644, and under Innocent X, the new pope, the artist suffered a temporary loss of influence. This state of affairs lasted throughout Innocent's reign, but when that pope was succeeded by Alexander VII, Bernini again had a patron who appreciated his artistic talents. No sooner was Alexander crowned than he commissioned Bernini to enclose and beautify the haphazard piazza fronting the church, and his stunning success with the square enhanced immeasurably the total majesty of St. Peter's. So successful is Bernini's piazza that it has the quality of an indispensable frame for the basilica, almost an architectural element of the church itself.

During the century it took to build the basilica's walls, the design and decoration of the interior were proceeding at a less spectacular but nevertheless steady pace. One of the most fundamental differences between the interior of the old church and that of the new was the floor level. What is today called the Sacred Grottoes, a level varying between twelve and eighteen feet below that of the new basilica, was the original floor level of old St. Peter's. A ceremonial entrance from the new floor to the tomb of Peter on the preserved Constantinian floor was built in a horseshoe-shaped double stairway in front of the papal altar, a design that probably was Maderno's last contribution to the building. A major difference between the appearance of the new church as it looks today and how it looked in the years soon after its completion was its earlier relative simplicity. The "richness" we now think of as an integral part of St. Peter's interior is in large part attributable to the baroque ornamentation later applied to surfaces originally designed in a classical mold.

Among the final parts of the interior to be completed were Maderno's nave and portico, both of which awaited the destruction of the last bits of old St. Peter's before they could be built. Maderno was justifiably most proud of his design for the portico, the part of the church serving essentially as a grand "entry hall" and a transition space between interior and exterior—the five entrance doors from the portico into the nave correspond precisely to the five doors leading into the portico from the outside. At the north end of the portico is the entrance to the Scala Regia, the Royal Stairway leading up to the Royal Salon and Sistine Chapel and into the Apostolic Palace itself.

The supreme ornament in St. Peter's—unequaled in any other church in the world—is the *baldacchino,* or canopy, which Bernini built for his Barberini patron to cover the high altar, the church's central place of devotion reserved for papal masses alone. The story that the massive amounts of bronze that went into its construction—186,392 pounds, to be precise—came from a papal raid on the Pantheon portico and dome isn't really true, but it gave rise to the snide jest that "what the barbarians didn't destroy, the Barberini did." It is certain that Urban had the Pantheon bronze removed for use elsewhere, but it has never been proven that Bernini used it on his baldacchino. Bernini did, however, appropriate seven of the bronze ribs supporting St. Peter's dome, replacing them with lead.

Construction of the hundred-foot-high baldacchino—the equivalent of an eight-story building—required sinking massive founda-

tions to support its ninety tons, footings that extended far below the
level of the Constantinian floor, destroying an unknown number of
graves and relics dating from the first Christian centuries. This
caused such consternation among both the superstitious workers and
the general population that protest marches were organized to stop
the "sacrilege." The situation eventually quieted down, and Bernini
got his men back to work by offering them bonuses, but the affair
gave the baldacchino an unsavory reputation in its early years.

The great canopy, which is not precisely centered under the dome
but a bit to the west, is the focus of every eye from within the
church. (This canopy matches the location of the canopy over Peter's
tomb in the old basilica.) Deceptively fragile, what appears to be
fabric swagged into draperies decorated with daintily corded tassels
is, of course, solid gilt bronze (the gliding alone cost forty thousand
golden crowns), the whole so soundly and brilliantly engineered by
Bernini that it is as stable as the basilica itself. The artist added a
flattering fillip by festooning the immense and theatrical structure
with all the Barberini emblems, especially the famous bees from
which came the papal family name.

An additional Bernini ornament in the basilica straddles the line
between sculpture and architecture. The Cathedra Petri—the Chair
of Peter—is the name given the colossal golden composition over
the altar in the apse, hard against the far end of the basilica. With a
background of golden clouds, a brilliant sunburst, a chorus of
winged cherubs bearing the papal keys and crown, and four
fourteen-foot high bronze statues of the Fathers of the Church, the
stylized baroque throne at its center conceals, behind the grille under its cushion, what was for centuries one of Rome's most venerated
relics. It is now known to be both less sacred and less ancient than
its long-presumed heritage.

A chair thought to have been actually used by Peter had been a
prized relic in the old basilica's sacristy since late in the first millennium and had come to symbolize the divine authority of the
Church's first pope. In fact, this oak chair hidden in Bernini's
flamboyant case is now known to be no older than the Carolingian
age, a date confirmed by carbon testing during an examination allowed by Paul VI in 1968, and may even have been a throne chair
used by Charlemagne himself. But in Bernini's day its authenticity
as a genuine Petrine relic was still uncontested. During the Counter

Reformation the Church stressed the authority of the pontificate as descended in an unbroken line from Peter, and therefore Bernini was commissioned by Alexander VII to give the ivory-paneled chair new symbolic weight in its prominent location at the western end of the basilica. Unfortunately, soon after the monumental reliquary for the chair was finished, Church scholars came to doubt its authenticity and accorded it a more simple value as a metaphor for the "see of Peter"—the role of the Vatican as the center of the Church—and less as an actual relic.

In Bernini's first two designs for the *cathedra,* his plans for the monumental encasement for the throne were limited because of a window at the apse's second-story level. In his third design, he struck gold. *Using* the window on the apse wall rather than being *limited* by it, he enlarged the scale of the sunburst structure so it covered the opening, allowing natural sunlight to filter through the central oval of the sunburst and illuminate the golden rays surrounding the dove at its center. For sheer theatricality, few set pieces anywhere in the world can match the magnificent confection built to enshrine and glorify the little wooden throne.

It is this same golden light spilling through the twisted columns of the bronze canopy over the papal altar to which the visitor's eyes are irresistibly drawn on entering the basilica. The basilica's individual statistics, which blur into an overwhelming grandeur, are nonetheless impressive: 710 feet long, 500 feet across the transept, 335 feet from the level of the piazza to the tip of the lantern that caps the dome, 240 feet around each of the four clifflike piers supporting the cupola, 290 windows, 800 chandeliers, 27 chapels, 48 altars, 390 statues, 748 columns, the cornice above the nave wide enough for a two-person footrace. Brass letters set into the floor of the nave mark the length of the world's other great cathedrals—all, of course, falling far short of the full extent of St. Peter's. If not the cathedral church of the pope, this most majestic of temples is surely the cathedral of the papacy.

One of the verities of Rome is that St. Peter's and its piazza is the center around which the city's pilgrims and tourists turn. There is little doubt that modern Rome without the Vatican would be unimaginable, and the fact is that a great deal of the money spent to enjoy the papal kingdom enriches the republican capital. There isn't really a tourist "season" in Rome anymore; masses of foreigners, as well as non-Roman Italians, are attracted to the Eternal City year-round. And every one of them finds himself, usually sooner rather than later, on the Via della Conciliazione heading for St. Peter's and the riches in its orbit. (For a plan of St. Peter's Basilica, see p. viii.)

A large percentage of people arriving at the basilica do so in tight little groups under the aegis of one of a countless number of tour operators. Their sleek, usually German-built buses are parked in Pius XII Square by the dozen, tightly wedged together, like huge slugs. Each tour group has its own readily identifiable standard to rally round, something like a telescoping pointer, a garish parasol, or a jangling bracelet. I remember one husky German conductor waving a painted Spanish fan over her head as her symbol of touristic authority, looking like a Teutonic Carmen.

Inside the five monumental doors at the top of the cascade of steps fronting the basilica is Maderno's magnificent portico, itself larger than many cathedrals and a staging point for the visitors' entry into the main part of St. Peter's. Guards at the entrances check to see that everyone is dressed in at least the minimally acceptable clothing, which translates into no shorts or bare midriffs for women, no bare chests for men, and no bare feet for anyone. A surprising number of women still show traditional respect by covering their heads, a requirement long since abrogated in the wake of the Second Vatican Council. A long table against one wall is staffed with volunteers who offer assistance to bewildered pilgrims, for many of whom the visit represents a rare excursion from remote and still very unsophisticated rural areas. Banks of receivers are set in the wall to translate (for fifty lire) all this confusion into seven languages, Polish having recently been added to the traditional Italian, French, English, German, Spanish, and Portuguese. Additional guards man the entrances from the portico into the nave.

During the rare times it's open, most people head for the famous Holy Door, through which traffic flows in only one direction. Many visitors, especially nuns making their once-in-a-lifetime visit to their Church's chief shrine, kneel on the threshold for a few moments before passing into the church. This portal, the farthest right

of the five entrances from the portico into the church proper, is completely sealed with brick and masonry at all times except Holy
Years, special ecclesiastical celebrations decreed by the pope, usually
at twenty-five-year intervals. An unusual off-year Holy Year was declared by John Paul II in 1983 to mark the Year of Redemption.
This celebration highlighted the 1,950th anniversary of the death of
Jesus and vastly increased the Vatican's normal tourist traffic. Some
reports attribute the papal proclamation of this most recent Holy
Year, with its enormously beneficial impact on the Roman
economy, as a favor—an "olive branch," as financial writer Rupert
Cornwell put it—from John Paul to the Italian government to help
remedy the losses the latter suffered in the Vatican banking scandal
(see chapter 8).

The differences that separate peoples—the barriers of language,
disparity of wealth, differing ways of worshiping or not worshiping
God—all seem to fall away upon entering St. Peter's. The power of
this temple even cuts through the inharmonious thumping and
banging that always seems to fill the building: chairs being either
set out in neat rows or collected again, great wooden derricks rolled
around to change a light fixture hanging high above the marble
floors, the shuffle of the crowds that fill the aisles and eddy around
the dozens of altars, chapels, and intricately carved confessionals,
the rattle of hand-pulled flatcars loaded with equipment for television crews or with flowers to decorate the altars, or the pope's throne
on its way to being assembled for the pontifical masses said under
Bernini's canopy.

The nave of St. Peter's, the long arm of the Latin cross that runs
east toward the main doors from the papal altar, is lined with
wooden barriers to form a middle passage directly down the center.
This helps separate the traffic heading straight for the altar from that
stopped to inspect the side chapels. These barriers also serve to form
a protected passage for the elaborate papal processionals assembled
in the large off-limits staging area near the bottom of the Scala
Regia. Two side aisles run parallel to the nave, separated from it by
fifty-six pillars set in rows. Twelve of these columns, those nearest to
where the cardinals sit during ceremonials, are marble, the remaining forty-four stucco imitations, the result of a builder pope's
purse having run dry. The ceilings over these aisles are considerably

lower than that over the vaulted center aisle. Many of the church's chapels, including the two largest ones—those of the Choir and of the Blessed Sacrament—open onto the nave's side aisles.

Near the right entrance is the chapel of the Pietà, the artistic and historic magnet that attracts every visitor to the basilica yet is today sadly closed to public entry behind a massive and utterly disruptive sheet of plate glass. Viewers now see the statue from about twenty feet away. In 1972, Michelangelo's sculpture of the Virgin cradling her crucified son was hideously damaged, primarily around Mary's face, with a ball-peen hammer wielded by a vandal named Laszlo Toth. As a consequence, when the restored statue was returned to the chapel in which it had been displayed for centuries, the glass barrier was installed to prevent a future miscreant from again defacing Michelangelo's masterpiece. Probably as long as St. Peter's stands, this most glorious sculpture and its historic setting will be kept at a distance so people can no longer examine it or the chapel at close quarters, an unhappy reminder of the effects of vandalism on our heritage and our environment.

The church's central point is the convergence of the main nave and the papal altar. The part of the nave extending to the rear of the high altar is called the apse; the side arms, equal in length to the apse, are the transepts. The four piers supporting the dome, each 240 feet in circumference, are commemoratively named after four early saints—Longinus, Andrew, Veronica, and Helena—each of whom is represented on his or her pier with a sixteen-foot-high statue. A niche on St. Longinus's pier holds a spear, venerated as that thrust by the centurion into the side of Jesus as he hung on the cross. The artifact was a gift to Innocent VIII from the Ottoman emperor Bayazet III.

The breathtaking spectacle of Michelangelo's dome, the largest and most magnificent in the world, automatically draws every eye up, far above the *baldacchino*. The golden frieze, a seemingly narrow ribbon around the inside of the drum, is decorated in six-foot-high blue mosaic letters with the famous passage from the sixteenth chapter of Matthew, TU ES PETRUS, & SUPER HANC PETRAM OEDIFICABO ECCLESIAM MEAM, & TIBIDABO CLAVES REGNI COELORUM—"thou art Peter, and upon this rock I will build my Church . . . and I will give unto thee the keys of the kingdom of heaven." Above the frieze, sixteen tall windows allow the

Roman sunlight to illuminate the floor of the church's crossing hundreds of feet below. Sixteen gilded ribs converge over the windows at the inside of the lantern crowning the dome, from whose smaller windows more light is admitted. Near the very top, just where the lantern meets the ribbing, another Latin inscription around the opening proclaims that the dome was completed during the reign of Sixtus V.

Many rewarding and even adventurous side excursions can be made in St. Peter's in addition to exploring the vast interior of the basilica itself. The sacristy, a major appendage to the church completed in 1784, is today primarily a museum. A sacristy originally provided a place for priests to robe and store vestments and linens used in the liturgy, but St. Peter's enormous size and special purpose obviates this use. Today it houses chapels as well as the Treasury of St. Peter's, opened to the public as a gallery in 1975. Here visitors see an exact copy of Peter's throne chair, the original of which is encased in Bernini's cathedra. The exhibit is filled with reliquaries and altar candlesticks masterfully crafted in precious metals and studded with gems, as well as historic fragments of the old St. Peter's, including one of the twisted columns that stood over Peter's tomb, a motif borrowed by Bernini for his *baldacchino,* and the gilt weathercock that once topped the Constantinian church. One little-known facility in the sacristy is its cafe/bar, closed to the public but used by priests after they have celebrated mass in one of the basilica's chapels. It is a right and treasured privilege of any Catholic priest.

Two subterranean levels are open to the public, one visited routinely by the majority of tourists who come to the church, the other a semisecret hidden treasure seen by only a tiny fraction of the basilica's visitors. The Sacred Vatican Grottoes, at the first underground level, were built just above the original floor level of the earlier structure and extend from directly below the apse to about halfway down the length of the nave of the church above. Their floor plan still roughly corresponds to that of the church that the sixteenth-century structure replaced. The oldest parts of this undercroft, called the Grotte Vecchie, are the three long passages built in the late sixteenth century that extend under the nave. The Grotte Nuove is the semicircular ambulatory that runs under the corresponding semicircular apse above and was added a generation later. Ten rooms were later built onto this newer section by Pius XII, including a chapel for his own tomb situated in one of the most historically significant sites in the entire basilica.

Through the reign of Pius XI, the grottoes were simply a cramped, cellarlike place, damp in the extreme, little seen and then only by torch or candlelight. They were, to quote Baedeker, "no fit place" for the unwieldy skirts and hoops of pre–twentieth-century female visitors. Through the nineteenth century, in fact, women were allowed to visit this area only once a year, on Whitmonday, or otherwise only with special permission from the cardinal archpriest of St. Peter's, which required a petition addressed to the pope. The primary attractions then were the rows of sarcophagi, mostly holding the remains of popes and a few "civilians," most notably a handful of royal Stuarts, commemorated in a famous monument by Canova on the floor above. Beginning in 1935, the forlorn crypt was transformed at great cost into a finished and usable undercroft. The floors were lowered thirty inches, walls relined with marble, tightly packed rows of sarcophagi thinned out, ten extra rooms added to the ambulatory, electric lights installed, and the existing chapels rearranged and some reinaugurated to commemorate more up-to-date subjects.

Today, entry to the grottoes is a simple matter, freely allowed whenever the church is open. A low door opening under the *baldacchino* side of the St. Longinus pier leads to a narrow flight of spiral stone stairs. Visitors enter the crypt at this end of the ambulatory, follow the low-ceilinged passage around various chapels, and come out into the more open main area from which the all-important semicircular Confession is seen through a plate-glass wall.

Two of the grottoes' primary attractions face each other at the top of the ambulatory: the chapel-tomb of Pius XII and St. Peter's Chapel, the former previously called the Clementine Chapel, after Clement VIII, who enlarged and decorated it at the end of the sixteenth century. St. Peter's Chapel is not open except on the *scavi* tours (see below). Pius's tomb, placed in this central position of special honor closest to Peter's remains, and done so at his request, is, as might be expected of the quietly ascetic pope, subdued in mood and finished in an icy, marbled luxuriousness.

In strong contrast, St. Peter's Chapel behind its gilded gate is a palette of baroque colors, textures, and shapes. The rear of the funeral monument Constantine built over the grave of Peter is barely visible though an iron gate behind the small altar. This Petrine altar is directly below the papal altar on the basilica's main floor.

After coming out of the semicircular corridor, you enter the main part of the grottoes. It is divided by three rows of low columns interspersed with marble tombs, with those of the more recent popes most prominently positioned. The area's major interest is its nearness to the Confession behind the plate-glass screen, allowing pilgrims the best view of the Vatican's holiest shrine. The stairs down to the Confession, as well as the small open space directly in front of Peter's tomb, are never open to the public. The pope occasionally descends to this area for special sacramental rites. Until recently, photographs of the recessed Confesione, or reliquary, taken from the railing surrounding it on the main floor above showed Canova's twice-life-size marble statue of the eighteenth-century pope Pius VI facing Peter's tombsite in a kneeling position. The statue was removed several years ago to a less prominent site in the grottoes, and the solid wall behind it replaced with today's glass screen. This enables grotto visitors to see through to the sanctuary on its own level.

The least-known parts of St. Peter's open to the public are the Scavi, the twentieth-century excavations (whence the word *scavi*) exposing the pre-Constantinian necropolis below the level of the Sacred Grottoes and constituting, in effect, the Vatican's basement. A visit to the extremely cramped Scavi takes a bit of effort, however. A request for a specific date for a visit is made at the Uffizio Scavi, the Excavations Office in the sacristy, entered from St. Peter's Square through the Arch of the Bells. This is one of the few purposes for which the Swiss Guardsmen on duty will allow tourists to pass through the portal. The office will arrange small manageable group tours of about fifteen people, by language. The applicants will be telephoned at their hotels, generally within a week of their request, regarding the date and time they should arrive.

A palpable electricity charges the air outside the Uffizio Scavi as the groups are marshaled for entry into the Roman city of death, and people jockey for what they perceive to be the most advantageous positions. Leaving daylight and the splendors of the Vatican behind, the guide leads his little band into the first century of Christianity.

The providential 1939 discovery of the necropolis was made by a workman digging up the floor of the grottoes in preparation for the placement of a sarcophagus for the recently deceased Pius XI. While the work on his predecessor's tomb was in progress, the newly crowned Pius XII ordered the workers to extend their excavations in a treasure hunt for Peter's fabled tomb. A breakthrough in the grotto floor to the ceiling of one of the Roman burial chambers was immediately reported to the pope, who unhesitatingly gave orders to continue the search. The only restriction Pius placed on the excavations was that the other graves be treated respectfully in the search for the site of Peter's interment.

Ironically, while constructing his basilica, Constantine disregarded the pagan burial ground surrounding Peter's grave and thus preserved it for posterity far more effectively than any other course of action he might have followed. His orders for the construction of the church were simply to build over the tombs and if possible use them as foundations, foreseeing a considerable saving in costs. As a consequence, the streets of Roman tombs, both pagan and Christian, were filled with earth by the emperor's workers and became part of the foundation of the basilica, preserving the relatively intact chambers from the succeeding waves of destructive armies that later washed over Rome. During sixteenth-century foundation work on the new church, workers did, in fact, uncover a small part of the early tombs, but no exploration was carried out because of both papal reverence and popular superstition.

The unearthing of this archaelogical treasure continued throughout the 1940s, including the war years when the city above was in considerable danger from both withdrawing German and advancing Allied armies. When a tomb thought to be Peter's was located directly under the basilican altar of Constantine, the researchers knew that they might have hit paydirt. But the excitement truly peaked when they opened the tomb. There was a box holding the bones of a man, judged to be between sixty and seventy years old, strewn with bits of earth and shreds of purple and gold fabric, the burial or reburial clothing for those of exceptional importance. This fit the scriptural description of Peter as well as the logical manner in which he would have been interred and led to the understandably irresistible conclusion that the remains of Jesus's first vicar had been uncovered. In 1968, Pope Paul VI gingerly made the "happy announcement" that in the eyes of the Roman Catholic Church the bones were "satisfactorily identified" as those of Peter. It is neither disrespectful nor excessively skeptical to state, as many historians do, that there still is no evidence *beyond a doubt* that the bones are, in fact, those of Peter, nor to broach the more fundamental proposition that it hasn't yet been conclusively proven that Peter ever *visited* Rome. Religion is, by definition, a matter of faith, and the specifics of Peter's life and death must also be acknowledged on this basis until the unlikely time that they can be ascertained with absolute historical certainty. In any event, for both the dedicated history buff and the single-minded tourist who make the pilgrimage to St. Peter's basement, the effort will be thoroughly worthwhile, the rare glimpse afforded of the inner working areas of Vatican City alone worth the effort.

Although the necropolis was probably one of the largest in Rome, only slightly over two hundred feet of it have been excavated—an area extending from the papal altar to the position of the Chapel of the Blessed Sacrament in the basilica. The first part of the tour concentrates on the Roman tombs. There are spots where pieces of masonry from the second, third, and fourth centuries can be seen in close proximity, the quality clearly diminishing as the Roman empire declined. All, however, appear superior to the modern masonrywork on the stairs leading down to the tombs. The guide cheerfully attributed this to a "lack of unions" when the original work was carried out.

The high point of any visit to the Vatican, and one of the most awe-inspiring historical experiences in the world, comes when the group ascends from the Scavi back to the level of the grottoes and is led into St. Peter's Chapel. Behind the altar at the rear of the chapel, visible through a grille, is the back of the Constantinian shrine over Peter's grave, the nearest anyone can come to the actual tomb. On my visit an unexpected power failure caused the lights to go out, leaving us for a few seconds in inky blackness, the only sound the choristers' chanting seeping down through the floor grates from the basilica overhead. For that moment we had the rarest chance to feel the sleep of the man whose bones represent for so many the heart of Christendom.

From an adventure that touches on the mysteries of faith to one which belongs entirely to the magic of man as builder, the final exploration of St. Peter's takes the visitor to the otherworldly landscape of the basilica's roof and dome. Except when a papal ceremony is taking place in St. Peter's Square and security is a consideration, tourists are allowed free access to the church's upperworks. Free, that is, if you choose the lung-searing climb by foot up the spiral staircase. Otherwise, it is fifteen hundred lire for an elevator ride.

On the roof terrace, you are immediately in the realm of the serious tourist. Magical landscapes aside, most people head directly for the well-stocked souvenir emporium tucked neatly under the nave's overhanging roof. The dedicated nun-clerks handle the saleswork with amazing good grace in the face of a welter of animated queries in an endless number of languages. A post office next door to the souvenir shop allows visitors to mail home cards with the double cachet of a Vatican frank *and* an address from St. Peter's roof.

Besides the world's largest dome looming overpoweringly toward the rear of the roof, there are two other large cupolas, both designed solely to frame in miniature the central dome. The cupolas do not correspond to any architectural features inside the church. Additionally, there are six small oval cupolas with lanterns set in rows on either side of the main nave and illuminating it from within, and four somewhat larger cupolas lighting the chapels at the ends of the transept. Toward the east, across the strangely undulating surface of the roof terrace and past the little oval cupolas set in their fenced wells, is the front edge of the basilica, directly over the papal benediction loggia hanging on the façade of the church. Lined up on its front edge are the nineteen-foot-high carved figures of Jesus, John the Baptist, and eleven of the Apostles, excluding Peter because the whole Church is theoretically represented by him. In your excitement to look out at the panorama, take care not to bang your head on the bottom of the Baptist's staff, as I did.

The formidable climb up the dome is the final trek of this journey through St. Peter's and should *under no circumstances whatsoever* be missed unless your health dictates prudence. Access to the goatpathlike spiral ramp is up a graceful little double-flighted staircase and through a small door in the southeast side of the great cupola's drum. Two paths are arranged between the inner and outer shells of the dome so that the narrow ascending and descending spirals are separated, a highly functional idea on the designer's part. A stopping point where the simple curve of the drum reaches the bottom of the complex curve of the cupola leads through a doorway into the interior wall of the dome and a narrow, vertigo-inducing parapet around its perimeter. The view down onto the crossing of the naves and the top of Bernini's *baldacchino* is an almost indescribable spectacle, causing many who venture out around it to blanch visibly. From this unique vantage point, you are literally face to face with the mosaics that look as delicate as oil paintings from the floor far below but are seen here to be relatively crudely fashioned from large pieces of colored stone. According to the Vatican's public-relations office, the greatest danger posed by continued public access to this site is the almost inevitable time when a tourist's camera, poked through the railing's wide openings, will drop to the basilica's floor, a lethal missile if it hits one of the throng below.

From this point, the hardest part of the climb to the top begins along the rising curve of the dome to the lantern. Once on the ascent, the narrow path makes stops difficult because of those bringing up the rear, but an occasional pause to read some of the more creative graffiti gives you a chance to catch your rapidly disappearing breath. More culturally rewarding is the opportunity to see at close range the wonderfully intricate way the builders put this enormous dome together, the wooden beams and inner and outer shell platings a fascinating lesson in Renaissance building methods.

The final step and ultimate goal is the balustrade around the lantern, usually crowded with hearty pilgrims—some rewarding themselves with a quick, although officially illegal, smoke—their cameras snapping away at the ethereal views around the entire compass. Thousands of little vessels that once supported tallow candles in vellum holders and were used to illuminate the cupola on festive occasions are still in place along the glacis of the dome's surface. Each of the decorated eyelids over the windows lighting its interior is inscribed with the name and arms of the pope responsible for its placement there.

A few years ago, professional photographers found that this site was a good place to take candid photos of the pope on his strolls around the roof terrace atop the Apostolic Palace. Guards now bar access to the dome to anyone with photographic equipment that looks as though it might be used for this nefarious purpose. The view across Rome from this vantage point also clearly confirms the declining ecclesiastical character of the Eternal City: Toward the old imperial center, domes are clustered in a forest of Christian temples; toward the raw gracelessness of the endlessly sprawling suburbs behind the Vatican, they hardly exist.

In years past, the public was allowed access even farther up into the lantern, to the interior of the bronze ball that represents the world under the dominion of Christianity. The seven-and-a-half-foot-diameter orb, topped with the cross that marks the peak of the basilica, holds sixteen people on a bench fitted into its interior perimeter. It has been closed since World War II, officially for safety reasons.

On the eighteenth day of April in 1506, Pope Julius II laid the first stone for the new church of St. Peter's. Eighty-seven years later, on the morning of November 18, 1593, the gilded bronze orb and cross destined for the basilica were blessed in the Gregorian Chapel by Pope Clement VIII in preparation for their placement on the dome's lantern. That evening, workers hoisted them up with block and tackle and fixed them in place. A gallery of builder popes, architectural geniuses, mechanical innovators, and dedicated laborers gave the world, over the course of the sixteenth century, one of its greatest gifts and once more proved the power and magic of man's ability to create.

3

Vicar of Christ, Bishop of Rome: A *Profile of John Paul II*

> *"You are Peter.*
> *On you I will build my Church."*
>
> *Jesus, to Simon Peter*

Slowly growing over Poland's tumultuous and troubled centuries, gray and anonymous Wadowice has always been overshadowed by its prestigious neighbor to the northeast, the mellow old university and cathedral city of Cracow. But a few miles away on the other side of the little industrial city, a smaller town, named Oświęcim, and one that attracted history's notice only as a middling railway junction, would in the years when Karol Wojtyla of Wadowice was growing into manhood become better known to the outside world than either of its neighbors. Under its German name, Auschwitz, it became a synonym for hell. In the time when the Polish people were suffering the worst agonies in their pain-plagued history and young Wojtyla was preparing for his life's work, he may already have realized that his mission would be far more concerned with the flaws in humankind represented by what happened at Auschwitz than it would with man's virtues mirrored in the glories of Cracow.

Wojtyla's road to the Apostolic Palace was a notably short one— bishop at thirty-eight, archbishop at forty-three, cardinal at forty-seven, pope at fifty-eight, early recognitions of special ability by a Church that historically puts great emphasis on seeing that its prelates are tempered with suitable age. His experiences dealing with the dark side of human existence gave him unique preparation for his destiny, preparation his fellow cardinal-electors hoped he could bring to focus on a Church pressed hard up against a growing spectrum of troubles.

Born a year and half after World War I ended, Karol was in childhood known by the diminutive Lolek among his circle of lower-middle- and working-class friends. He was raised at home jointly by his father and older brother after his mother died when he was nine. His brother, Edmund, later became a doctor and succumbed in his early twenties to scarlet fever. The future prelate did not have the usual background, the artificial hothouse atmosphere of a seminary, of so many of the men who reach the church's highest ranks. Instead, the bright and athletic Lolek attended an ordinary high school, and when he reached college age, was admitted to Cracow's venerable Jagellonian University to study in philology. He was extroverted enough to be an amateur actor and talented enough to be a success at it, but the shattering intervention of war with Germany suddenly focused Wojtyla's life, and he decided to train for the priesthood, an illegal activity under the New Order of the Germans, who made Cracow the capital of their rump "Generalgouvernement." Providentially, he had the extraordinary fortune of coming under the personal patronage of Cracow's powerful and well-connected archbishop, Prince Adam Cardinal Sapieha, a leader treated even by the Nazi occupiers with something approaching caution.

Ordained a priest on November 1, 1946, when his devastated country was exchanging a Hitlerian tyranny for Stalin's marginally more subtle version, the new Father Wojtyla was immediately sent by Sapieha to Rome for two years of theological study at the Dominican-run Pontifical Angelicum University. This site was a training ground for future leaders of the Church and a sign that his superiors had already taken notice of the obviously special neophyte priest. Wojtyla wrote his doctoral dissertation in Latin on St. John of the Cross, the sixteenth-century Spanish poet and mystic. This experience imbued the young cleric with a deep mystical sense of his own spiritual life. He also spent time during these two years working in Western Europe with Polish refugees, a part of the tidal wave of displaced persons then sweeping over the Continent. A side benefit to this work, later to prove enormously useful to Wojtyla as pope, was his becoming conversant in several European languages.

After returning to Poland, he spent the next six years gaining firsthand pastoral experience in small parishes in and around Cracow, more study at Jagellonian University, and service as the university's student chaplain. In this latter capacity he developed a close rapport between charismatic priest and students. The university staff remembers him from those days as an "eternal teenager," but he was also busy in writing many of the five hundred essays, poems, articles, and plays that he would create during his priesthood. (One example and indication of his interests: "On the Possibility of Constructing Catholic Ethics on the Basis of the System of Max Scheler.") Although it was a time of great intellectual growth for Wojtyla, these were also the most brutal days of Stalinism in Poland, striking out with particular vengeance against the Church: Warsaw's Stefan Cardinal Wyszynski, the Polish primate, was jailed along with the nine bishops and some eight hundred priests.

The step that led directly to his promotion to the episcopate was taken in 1954, when he began teaching at the Catholic University in Lublin, the only Catholic center of higher education, as well as the only one not controlled by the state, in any Communist country. The popular Wojtyla advanced the next year to the highly visible post of head of the ethics department, delivering lectures that his audiences remember as "spellbinding" and drawing the close attention not only of the Church's hierarchy but also that of the state. His teaching reflected a quick mastery of the art of maintaining a balance between the moral requirements of his Church and the political realities of a Marxist state, a valuable talent the Polish Church doesn't overlook. He became auxiliary bishop of Cracow in 1958.

Bishop Wojtyla's initiation to international attention—and to that of his fellow prelates—came with the Second Vatican Council in 1962. He made a series of eight speeches before the assembled prelates, one on religious liberty and another on freedom of conscience—two matters on which he had become an authority in a country whose government saw one of its primary missions as the destruction of both—gaining him celebrity among the assembled bishops. He was promoted to archbishop of Cracow in 1964.

In his new and highly influential post, Wojtyla suddenly found himself in the position of having to deal with the state authorities on a routine basis. Although he let Wyszynski, by now freed from his imprisonment, take the major share of the limelight as primate of

Poland, the less autocratic Wojtyla won religious concessions by his
methodical efforts and through the strength of his forceful personality. The archbishop valued the benefits of dialogue, and though he
often and loudly denounced the oppression usual under totalitarian
regimes, he never let himself get carried away with rhetorical excess.
He knew that to do so would have only disastrously negative results
on his ability to reason with a hostile government.

Archbishop Wojtyla was highly regarded by Paul VI for both his
intellect and his pluck in standing up to the Communist authorities.
Although the two men had widely divergent views on the priorities
and directions that the Church should take, Paul's admiration for
the Polish prelate resulted in Wojtyla's being raised to the cardinalate in 1967 at the age of forty-seven, a youth in Vatican prelatial
terms. Soon after, the pope invited the cardinal to conduct a Lenten
retreat for himself and his household, a signal ecclesiastical honor.

Once back in Poland, the now Cardinal Wojtyla exacted a huge
propaganda victory over the government. As a result of his patient
but relentless pressure on the authorities, a Catholic church was constructed in the new industrial town of Nowa Huta, a showcase socialist city originally planned by Poland's political leaders to be free
of the "corruption" of religion. In spite of the fact that it is a Marxist
state, Poland is paradoxically one of the most intensely Catholic
countries in the world, and the victory turned the new prince of the
Church into a popular hero to millions of his fellow Poles.

This kind of quiet success, together with the attention he received
from his worldwide travels, including two visits to the United States
as a cardinal, made the Pole a dark-horse candidate for the papal
throne on the death of John Paul I. Probably nobody in the Sacred
College, including his strongest partisans, really expected a non-
Italian to succeed the Venetian cardinal-archbishop Luciani, who
had reigned for thirty-three days as Pope John Paul I. But a deadlock between two Italians, the more conservative Siri of Genoa and
the less conservative Benelli of Florence, produced the compromise
that elected Wojtyla. As Luciani had taken the name of John Paul to
honor his two immediate predecessors, so Wojtyla extended the
honor when he chose to be the second John Paul.

At the moment Wojtyla accepted the will of the cardinals, he
ceased being a Polish citizen, a private person, or a man who would

ever again experience even occasional anonymity. In an instant he became sovereign head of state of an independent national entity, the religious leader of a fifth of mankind, and an immediate new chapter in the history book of the world. And since the day of his enthronement he has also been—by a considerable margin—the most visible spiritual leader of our time.

If he can never again be anonymous, he can at least within the confines of the Vatican find a little privacy and even moments of relief from the overwhelming responsibilities of his office. Since he became pope, John Paul's private life has been centered in two palace suites: the historic but relatively modest range of rooms on the fourth floor of the Vatican's Apostolic Palace, and the marginally airier apartments in the Papal Palace at Castel Gandolfo, in the Alban hills outside Rome. There is no string of additional estates or holiday retreats in the manner of many of the world's major leaders; he briefly used the elegant John XXIII Tower in the farthest part of the Vatican gardens when his Apostolic Palace apartments were being redecorated, but it is not a usual thing for him. In a first in modern papal history, John Paul for a short while escaped his office and, even rarer, his pontifical vestments in a July 1984 skiing holiday in the Italian Alps. His partner, a highly unlikely one, was Italy's socialist president Sandro Pertini, the two men having built a close personal friendship since John Paul became pope. Exchanging white cassock for a blue ski suit and with an audience made up of Pertini and his own personal staff, the pope repeatedly schussed a twenty-three-hundred-foot-long slope, after each run hauled back to the top in a snowmobile. Commented his secretary, Father Stanislaw Dziwisz, "I've never seen him look so happy or relaxed."

Access to John Paul's Apostolic Palace suite is through an entrance in the historic and well-guarded (by elements of the Swiss Guard and the Vigilance) courtyard of St. Damase, hidden behind the Bernini colonnade at the foot of the three major palace wings. A private elevator, which starts in the palace's basement at a level with the Belvedere on the opposite (St. Anne) side, ascends to the fourth floor of the Sixtus V quadrangle section of the Apostolic Palace, one floor above the lavish suite of official Pontifical Apartments containing the formal reception and throne rooms. The nearest anyone, other than private persona guests, is allowed to the fourth-floor papal living quarters is the iron grille at the end of the loggia that continues the corridor occupied by officials of the Vatican's Secretariat of State and the Council for Public Affairs.

John Paul's private inner sanctum is a very small part of the sprawling palace, far removed from the grandiose luxury that was the natural state of popes for much of the papacy's history. The modernizing and deglorifying that Paul VI ordered for the palace generally was also extended to the private suite, with a sort of Milan-modern look filled out with teak furniture and the original palatial gilt and scarlet walls neatly hidden under baize coverings. The pope's own rooms consist of a small library, a dining room, a chapel decorated with an ultramodern look, and a combined study and bedroom that is, in effect, his living room. Staff quarters are nearby, which include an office for Father Dziwisz, longtime secretary and now holder of the title of second-grade minor official in the Secretariat of State. John Paul brought Dziwisz with him from Cracow, while the pope's second secretary, Monsignor Emery Kabongo, hails from Zaire and is the first black African in the household retinue of a modern pope. A bedroom for the papal valet, and a cloistered dormitory-type room for the corps of Polish nuns who serve as his personal servants make up the rest of the quarters. The women are members of the Polish Order of Maria Bambina who looked after John Paul when he lived in Cracow's Episcopal Palace; besides cooking and serving meals, they see to the Pope's laundry and other domestic chores around the private apartment.

For a head of state who is also head of the world's largest religion, the pope's daily morning routine is largely free of any kind of gratuitous pomp. Arising between 5 and 6 A.M., John Paul starts his day without any kind of assistance from a valet. Freed from having to make a choice of dress, he unvaryingly puts on the unique uniform of his office: a collarless white dress shirt with French cuffs, a Roman collar, trousers, white socks, burgundy slip-ons, and his signature garment—the thirty-two button (with a hidden zipper) white simar, a cassock worn only by the pope. The final item is his white leather-lined skullcap, which completes the outfit. Fifteen minutes of prayer at his bedside *prie-dieu,* a quick cup of coffee (milk, no sugar) with his secretaries, and he's ready for his first public appearance of the day.

It is the same duty shared by thousands of Roman Catholic priests everywhere in the world—the celebration of mass, the Church's central act of devotion, common to the pope and the most junior of his priests. John Paul often invites clerics studying in Rome to be his assistants, an honor beyond measure to these young men. Joining him in the ultra-modern little chapel with its white marble walls and a conspicuous icon hanging over the altar of Our Lady of Częstochowa, the Black Madonna and Poland's patroness, are other special invitees recommended to the pontiff: perhaps a group of nuns, or visiting officials from a Catholic lay fraternity such as America's Order of the Sons of Italy, in which case John Paul will say mass in his heavily accented but serviceable English. The mass, incidentally, gives the pope a welcome chance to try out different languages, especially those he will be using on upcoming pastoral journeys.

The ranking guests will often be invited to join the pope for breakfast, served by his nun-servants in the dining room. This custom is totally different from the habits of the aloof Pius XII, who often had visitors at the table to inform or amuse him but *never* actually to join in the meal. Breakfast usually follows the normal Italian menu: coffee, the peculiar pentagonal hollow buns few Romans start the day without, and marmalade; occasionally the smell of ham and pungent Polish-style sausage permeates the suite. Given a choice, the pope naturally prefers Polish food, something in which the sisters oblige him for at least one meal a day.

After breakfast, John Paul habitually returns to the desk in his spacious bedroom-study for the next two hours, set aside for his daily personal reading and writing. Even this activity, though, excludes any "pleasure" reading or writing of poetry, activities he could occasionally indulge when still only a cardinal; most of the time is spent on papal messages, written in Polish and sent out by his secretary for immediate translation into the languages of the recipients. The study of new languages is also sometimes squeezed into the two hours; he has added passable Portuguese, Dutch, and some pidgin English to his several other languages since coming to the pontificate. The pope is briefed, first on his daily schedule by Pontifical Household head Bishop Jacques Martin, and then on the Church's most important diplomatic developments by the secretary of state Cardinal Agostino Casaroli. This is also the time when John Paul, as the Church's arbiter of last resort, makes decisions on those matters, usually thorny by the time they reach his desk, that only he can adjudicate.

Many are judgments that will affect enormous numbers of people; some are more limited in scope. Occasionally he still has to order the Church's most severe punishment, a mandate of excommunication. Such an order was given in April 1983, when eighty-five-year-old Archbishop Pierre Martin Ngo Ding Thuc, former head of the Vietnamese archdiocese of Hue, was excommunicated for a deliberately improper ordination of three bishops. John Paul's personal touch often is evident, as when, for example, the death of the last Italian Savoyard king, Umberto II, left the Church heir to the deposed monarch's greatest possession, the famous Shroud of Turin. The pope was petitioned by thirty thousand Turinese to leave the treasure in the custody of Turin's cathedral rather than take it to the Vatican. In an act of typical John Pauline tact and diplomacy, the pontiff named the people of Turin the shroud's custodian, and left the revered artifact where it had been displayed since the sixteenth century.

The two or three hours before lunch constitute his "people's work" time—mostly private and semiprivate audiences and diplomatic formalities. For these daily obligations, John Paul leaves the secluded fourth floor and descends to his "official" and considerably larger office in the grander and more elegant third-floor Pontifical Apartments.

Its component parts flowing into one another in the manner of royal palaces all over Europe, L'Appartamento Pontificio della Udienze is a suite of audience chambers little known to all but the tiny fraction of the public with either sufficient rank or sufficient importance to be permitted attendance at one of the semiprivate papal audiences held in them. Many are now less baroquely formal since Paul VI had some of the rooms' brilliant scarlet and gold walls hidden under beige velvet in 1964, and they contain little furniture other than a papal throne. However, their walls are hung with a magnificent selection of the Vatican's bottomless reserve of paintings, a large number of which are museum-quality masterpieces.

The Clementine Room, largest of the seventeen chambers and centrally located at the head of the Sistine Palace stairs, is the most used and the most exotically decorated; through the reign of Pius XII, general audiences were held in this room. Named for Clement VIII, his six-starred Aldobrandini coat of arms is prominently reproduced in the center of the highly polished marble floor. Nearly equal to the Clementine Room in size and splendor is the Room of the Consistory, still used primarily by the College of Cardinals for that purpose.

I find the most graceful room in this polychromatic sea of splendor the Room of the Evangelists, primarily because of the impact of its memorable throne. Evocative of an ancient throne chair but ultramodern in its effect, this symbol of papal authority is simply a beige backboard, scalloped at the top and flush against the wall, with a simple block seat approached by three marble steps. The armrests are the sole "decoration"—two fourteenth-century brackets with sculpted figures of Sts. Peter and Paul, ornaments that for centuries were features of the middle door of old St. Peter's.

The formal Papal Library is the most private part of the apartments, reserved for the highest category of state audiences in which the head of the Church receives monarchs and heads of state and government. A desk, one not actually put to use for routine deskwork, is at the far end of the room, and grouped stiffly in the center are a throne chair for the pope and side chairs for his guests. A collection of Bibles fills a glass-fronted bookcase on the long wall. The windows on the opposite side of the room overlook the same view of St. Peter's Square that is seen from his private suite on the floor above.

After the audiences, each averaging perhaps fifteen minutes, John Paul heads back to his bedroom/study, sometimes slipping off the silk sash that decorates his cassock the moment he gets through the doorway. Lunch might be pasta or Polish borscht, but whatever it is, it will likely be taken with company, table guests in the middle of the day making the meal a social event for a very social pope. Lunch is followed by a short nap and a walk in his rooftop garden.

John Paul's twelve-hour working routines are not greatly different from those he spent as a bishop, and, as then, he still makes every effort to work in an hour of exercise. In a gesture of rare indulgence, the frugal Paul VI had the roof garden built over his private fourth-floor apartment; connected to the papal suite by an internal staircase, it is discreetly concealed from view by a false roof to all but the tourists who make the ascent to St. Peter's cupola. After the exercise and a change into a fresh white simar, the normal afternoon work schedule begins—perhaps visits to churches or religious orders, masses celebrated to commemorate special persons or events, meetings, endless paperwork, more meetings. On Wednesdays, the papal schedule almost always includes the lengthy and elaborate noontime general audiences, Hollywood-style extravaganzas that could stagger a well-trained athlete.

Dinner, usually at eight, may be in any one of the dozens of religious institutions and orders dotted around Rome, where the pope's attendance naturally becomes an historic evening for his hosts. If he is dining in the Vatican, guests—perhaps old friends from Poland—sometimes are included. John Paul sits at one side of an eight-foot-long table, with his two secretaries at either end and guests ranged along the opposite side; if extra guests need the end seats, the secretaries dine elsewhere. No one ever sits next to the pope at the dinner table, but mercifully for the occupant of Peter's throne, the old conventions are gone when to have sat at the papal table at all would have been an unthinkable breach of Vatican etiquette. Conversation can go until ten-thirty or eleven, when John Paul finds another hour's worth of paperwork to be done before the light goes out in his bedroom window above St. Peter's Square.

Even on Sundays a busy schedule faces the pope, one including the famous papal blessing from his bedroom window, for which he ascends a little raised platform in front of the shuttered opening, making him clearly visible to the thousands of pilgrims, tourists, and the curious massed in the immense piazza. The scene before the pope is spectacular: almost the entirety of Rome, from the Villa Medici on the left around an arc to the Janiculum Hill on the right, with Bernini's open-armed forum at his feet, every face in the crowd turned to receive his blessing. Arms raised in the age-old benediction of the Church's first bishop to his flock, John Paul and his congregation communicate.

Above one of the world's most beautiful sheets of water, the jewellike Lake of Albano, lies the small cliff-hanging town of Castel Gandolfo (sometimes spelled as one word—Castelgandolfo) crowning a ridge of the Alban hills just off the Via Appia, twenty miles southeast of Rome. These hills are studded with handsome little storybook towns, many of the steep slopes covered with villas of the well-to-do Romans who can afford the equally steep price of the area's beauty—the region's character has remained this way since Emperor Domitian first built a magnificent villa on these heights. Today, Castel Gandolfo has become the most famous jewel in the Alban crown. In the piazza at the end of its single street, the Corso della Repubblica, two Swiss Guardsmen stand at attention before the portals of the summer palace that is almost a second home to John Paul, the Camp David of the papacy.

The first "palace" to rise on this hilltop site was a defensive castle built in 816 by an aristocratic family named Gandulfi; in the manner of the era, this Genoese clan gave their name not only to the castle but also to the town that slowly built up in its protective precincts. By the time of the Renaissance, Castel Gandolfo had become a duchy in favor of one Bernardino Savelli, whose fiscal fortunes soon sunk to a state that compelled him to forgo ducal dignity and sell his duchy to the government for 150,000 scudi. In 1604, Clement VIII incorporated it into the temporal possessions of the Holy See, and his successor Urban VIII, seeing the possibilities of the site as a retreat from the disgusting miasma that Rome became in hot weather, converted it into a summer residence for himself and his successors. His architect was Carlo Maderno, the same man responsible for much of St. Peter's.

Today, the hundred acres that make up the papal compound, an area nearly as large as the Vatican state itself, legally represent an extraterritorial possession of the Holy See and therefore are not part of the Italian state. Unused from 1870 until the early 1930s, when the Lateran Accord permitted the popes to leave their self-imposed isolation in the Vatican, the buildings had six decades in which to fall apart, left alone by all but the most intrepid of tourists. Pius XI, who was given a choice in the Lateran negotiations as to which of the several former papal villas he wished to serve as his summer residence, had the three primary structures on the property—the main Papal Palace, the Cybo Villa, and the Villa Barberini—entirely restored. The additional work done by his successors to turn it into a productive model farm has given the retreat something of the gloss and function of the British royal family's Sandringham estate. (As is the case with Sandringham vis-à-vis Buckingham Palace, much of the produce served at the papal table in the Vatican palace is grown at Castel Gandolfo.) The Jesuits now maintain the Pontifical Astronomical Observatory facility in the Cybo Villa (the observatory's scientific functions are in the process of transferring, with John Paul's blessing, to the University of Arizona, a move dictated by both its outmoded equipment and light pollution from Rome), and the Villa Barberini is used to house the administrative staff offices.

Although John XXIII visited the villa relatively rarely because of the stress the journey placed on his fragile health, both Pius XII and Paul VI spent their summers at Castel Gandolfo and both died there, and John Paul II has taken even greater advantage than his predecessors of the wonderful and rare privacy it affords. After the newly inaugurated pope encountered stiff curial resistance in getting a swimming pool installed at the Vatican, he had better luck at Castel Gandolfo, where a new fifty- by eighty-two-foot pool was put in for him. Although his courtiers were taken aback at this novel papal activity, not just by the notion of a pope actually swimming but also because of the cost of the pool, John Paul justified the installation on the grounds that it would be "cheaper than having to get a new pope."

Accompanied by a contingent of his Swiss Guard, the helicopter trip to the retreat from the landing pad in the corner of the Vatican gardens is only a short hop. Because of its privacy, John Paul has found the hilltop resort an irresistible escape from the hubbub of his Vatican quarters. The tranquillity of the classically beautiful gardens and the secluded marble rooms of the papal villa provide him with one of the few commodities he treasures—a place and the privacy to be alone.

More than any other pope in history, this pontiff has taken his papacy to the world. The Roman Catholic Church—for that matter, the whole of Christianity—has no more convincing spokesman or salesman, and the extraordinarily charismatic John Paul II seems fully aware of the fact. Like President Ronald Reagan a former actor, the Polish pope has an actor's presence, and like Reagan, knows exactly how best to use it on the international stage, on the center of which he has firmly and without reservation placed Peter's throne.

From the very beginnings of his pontificate, John Paul has openly shown that he would make his person available not only to the tiny fraction of the Church's membership with the means to travel to see him, but also to Catholics on every continent in the world, especially the poor who have historically been discounted in the larger scheme of history. The specifics of his journeys—as of early 1985, there were twenty-four trips abroad as pope, mostly lengthy (210,000 miles have been covered), exhausting, and triumphal—are determined by the Vatican's carefully thought-out diplomatic priorities, both strategic and tactical, but their cumulative effect has been to give the papacy more influence on people and affairs than it has had at any time since the reign of John XXIII. Also John Paul has sought to impress on believers his central message that each local congregation, no matter how far from Rome, is important to the universal Church. John Paul's travels are becoming legion, and one of the most far-reaching in its consequences was his 1979 visit to the United States, today one of the Church's most contentious daughters. It is perhaps the world's major heavily Catholic country that is least understood by John Paul and is certainly the one that appears to understand *him* least.

Any international papal visit becomes a media event, and the three-ring circus surrounding John Paul on these papal progresses unfortunately tends to overwhelm the pastoral significance of the message he attempts to impart—certainly the case with his week-long visit in 1979 to the United States. But even the May 1981 attempt on his life did not slow down the pace of papal visits, although it made the already massive security apparatus protecting him even more visible. (The Canadian government announced it would spend the equivalent of fifteen million U.S. dollars to ensure the pope's security on his September 1984 visit to that country.) He has now planted his familiar kiss on airport tarmacs in countries all around the globe, from poverty-drenched Brazil to the affluence of Switzerland, whose well-fed citizens heard his plea to share their richly abundant material blessings. Only in the somewhat ill-thought-out trip to Islamic Turkey did he find his reception less than wholehearted, though the heavyhanded way in which his Nicaraguan visit was politicized by the hostile Sandinista junta earned his hosts a rare public rebuke.

John Paul's cavalcades through the seemingly limitless masses of people who invariably turn out to see him are conducted in an enormous mine-proof motorized barge with a glass-enclosed platform enabling the pope to be clearly seen, and which is shipped ahead on his journeys as a necessary security expense. His activities range from meetings with heads of state and addressing local episcopal conferences to the gigantic outdoor rallies/masses that have become the hallmark of these trips. Enormously expensive undertakings, the papal journeys resemble in logistical intricacy only slightly scaled-down versions of the visits abroad conducted with such massive complexity by American presidents. The aircraft used by the pope, usually Alitalia but sometimes a national flag line of his host country, such as Aer Lingus or TWA, are luxuriously fitted for his comfort on the grueling journeys. The papal bedroom on the TWA 747 that carried him on the American trip ran the width of the cabin and was decorated with a spotlit crucifix on the bulkhead and his personal coat of arms in the center of the bedspread.

Probably the most personally satisfying as well as the most poignant of John Paul's journeys have been those to his homeland. Today the world's best-known Pole, the pope officially visits Poland as a foreign head of state. But to the solidly Catholic Polish people, they are far more importantly the pastoral visits of a countryman who is also a hero, an internationally influential Pole who has some ameliorating effect on an unpopular government. The primary reason for the Polish government's chary treatment of him—in fact, the primary reason for his importance anywhere in the world—is his ability to reach people's emotions and affect their behavior in ways that no government can duplicate.

But what remains in the wake of the splendid ceremonial and mass goodwill that characterize the journeys of John Paul is the sobering recognition that there still has to be a reckoning with the agonizingly difficult problems that remain unsolved. The pope's heartfelt admonitions to the have-nots of the world to forsake extreme or radical solutions do nothing to alter the fact that the problems they face *are* extreme. The dispiriting fact is that the John Pauline influence fades quickly into everyday reality after the magic and excitement of his presence is gone.

So what of the man himself? Outward appearances seem to mark John Paul II as the supreme spiritual leader of the postindustrial age, a man trying to lead his Church and his worldwide flock on a reasoned and reasonable course. He is unquestionably grieved at the planet's imbalance of abundance and justice but nonetheless steers away from what he believes to be a dangerously liberal course on which the Church had gone theologically adrift. Many of the problems that are the primary concerns of the last decades of the twentieth century—war and peace, civil and human rights, sexual experimentation, abortion and birth control, and, at least for the clergy, ecclesiastical freedoms—became issues that engulfed the Church after the revolutionary floodgates of the 1960s were opened. Paul VI apparently had neither the will nor the ability to redefine orthodoxy as it related to these difficult moral and religious issues, perhaps hoping that the passing of time might help him with his burden. The result was that many Catholics turned away from the Church for answers. John Paul has tried to put his Church back on course, following a conservative path that will return it to its orthodox basics, demanding that it show compassion where possible, but only where such compassion does not conflict with Roman Catholic dogma, something the Church defends as unalterable.

It isn't hard to find criticism of John Paul. Some Vatican observers point out what they see as substantial flaws in the way he administers the Church, namely a too-selective concern with those matters that interest him to the near-exclusion of those that don't, as well as his intensely personal preoccupation with Polish affairs, letting other issues of far more strategic importance to the Holy See slide. Europeans criticize what they see as a pope dangerously exacerbating already overheated tensions between the continent's two competing social and economic systems. Many American Catholics, including a large number of its self-appointed "progressive" spokespeople, feel John Paul is so far out of touch with their country's socioreligious problems—particularly issues related to the status of women in the Church and population control—that he is simply dismissed as "irrelevant." Latin America's "liberation theologists"—those who would tie Marxist principles to the Church on "behalf" of the poor—have found the Church's and the pope's responses to social problems unacceptable to the Third World, which they point out will be home to two thirds of all Catholics by the turn of the century. The Soviet Union regards the pope as such a dangerous influence on its Polish client state—and, by extension, on its entire bloc—that it has almost certainly tried once, through surrogates and within a hair of success, to have him assassinated.

In spite of the sea of difficulty, Pope John Paul II has the attention of the Western world—his office commands it, his personality maintains it. If he is successful in solving even a fraction of the dilemmas facing the twentieth-century Church, it could be a greatly revitalized Church that enters the twenty-first century, a journey he is young enough to lead personally. If he fails, the result will surely be the diminution of one of the world's strongest international forces for reasoned understanding.

4

Princes of the Papacy:
The College of Cardinals

It may be that the Vatican now officially deemphasizes the attribute of princeliness to the members of its Sacred College, but in many nations, their collective eminences, the cardinals of the Roman Catholic Church, are ranked on an equal plane with the highest nobility—are, in fact, held to be the equivalent of "princes." That is precisely what for centuries these scarlet-robed generals of the Church were—princes, living in palaces and presiding over great archdioceses and divisions of the papal administration, surrounded by intricate courts and protocol, enrobed with the majesty of the state as well as of the Church, serving at the right hand of pontiffs, *creating* the successors to Peter. An ecclesiastical power structure has seldom if ever had a more visible guise. Much of this has passed into history, some has remained the same, and this body of men continues to fascinate as do few other institutions.

The College of Cardinals—a "college" only in the sense that its members are regarded as each other's colleagues—has no beginning that can be precisely pinpointed. Since the Church's earliest days, a body of local Roman priests had served as the popes' closest advisers, but in anything like its present configuration and functions the cardinalate's origins are much more recent. These adviser-priests are far removed from the simplicity of the apostles, but a parallel can be drawn between the function the cardinals eventually came to fill and the relationship of the Twelve Apostles to Jesus—namely that of the Church's earliest executive committee.

At the beginning of Christianity, only the original Apostles were considered to have full priestly powers. They were assisted in their clerical functions by lay Church members called deacons. When the fledgling religion started to expand its membership, it became apparent that more men with full priestly powers were needed to get the expanding sacramental work done, duties that were outside the deacons' authority. So Peter's immediate successor, Pope Cletus, ordained twenty-five priests (the word comes from *presbyteri* and means "elder") in Rome. Each was assigned to a different district, or parish, to say mass for groups of people that had grown too large to gather in a single central place, as had been the custom. Two centuries later, in another organizational move, Pope Fabian redistributed the deacons, this time assigning two of Rome's fourteen Augustinian-era districts to each of the city's seven deacons. These deacons—still not full priests—were given the task of teaching catechism, preparing converts for baptism, and otherwise generally helping out with the daily clerical chores in each district.

Over the next few centuries, both the priests and deacons of the city were in turn given assistants, and those who were the head priests and deacons in charge of subordinates became known as cardinals—either cardinal priests or cardinal deacons. The word itself comes from the Latin *cardo,* meaning "pivot" or "hinge," and was used by the Romans in a figurative sense to signify the crucial point of an issue. In the sixth century, the higher-ranking ecclesiastics in charge of parishes or districts, the men around whom the Church pivoted, began to be called cardinals. Another category, the cardinal bishop, came into being in the ninth century.

As the centuries passed and the Church grew at a quickening pace, the position of cardinals both jelled and changed—the original Roman diocesan connotations became merely symbolic, and the popes' highest-ranking advisers were given these titles; the custom of referring to the ordinary workaday priests and deacons in these parishes as cardinals was dropped. By roughly the turn of the millennium, the term "cardinal" had changed entirely from its adjectival sense designating a duty to a noun conferred as a title.

From the eleventh century on, the powers of the members of the now-official college grew rapidly. The majority of the holders of the dignity came to be far more concerned with the vast range of perquisites, then an automatic and highly valued adjunct to the office, than with sacramental or pastoral duties, and were noted considerably more for venality than for piety. It was common for the offspring of the nobility to be granted the Church's highest dignity while still children; little boys so elevated would be dressed in clerical robes for a part of each day as a fulfillment of their office. Perhaps farthest afield from its original function, the office had become optionally nonclerical in that it was conferred without any requirement that the holder be a priest (although marriage was generally not permitted lay cardinals), a situation that lasted well into the twentieth century. Even today, the rank of cardinal has no sacramental basis, being only an advanced episcopal rank signifying increased dignity and power.

The no-holds-barred abuse of cardinalate power was one of the primary causes of the Church's Western Schism in the fourteenth and fifteenth centuries, when the cardinals tried to renege on a lawful papal election, a function that had become their exclusive privilege. When the pope they canonically elected tried to suppress some of their myriad privileges, they retaliated by declaring his election null and void and set about choosing another pope in Avignon (and eventually a third in Pisa), a chaotic web that took forty years to untangle. Into the Renaissance, the cardinalate continued to be the refuge of some of history's greatest and most powerful scoundrels, the Spanish Borgias being prime examples. Alexander VI's son, Cesare Borgia, an occasional cardinal—his father dispensed him from the office so he could marry—is said to have assassinated his own brother, stabbed his father's favorite while the young man hid underneath the papal robes, and engaged in other such sordid deeds as took his fancy. Some members of the College became far better known for their military zeal than they ever were for any religious activities, a zeal often resulting in the wholesale slaughter of "enemy" populations. Cardinal Richelieu and his eager fomenting of the Thirty Years' War with *its* attendant miseries is a well-known example. The general debaucheries of the typical Roman curial cardinal—by now the majority of the college were laity—made the licentious papal court of the sixteenth and seventeenth centuries a subject of international disgust.

A curious position that developed in the Vatican during the sixteenth century was that of the cardinal nephew, the pope's closest adviser and the forerunner of the modern Vatican's secretary of state. Papal nepotism (in Italian *nepoti* means "nephew") didn't start in the sixteenth century, of course, but the paternal instinct among popes to have their closest and therefore most trusted relatives as chief advisers in an often hostile environment reached its height during this period. Some historians have seen a saving grace in a situation that subordinated competence to an accident of relationship in that the generally young nephews perhaps brought a more "youthful" (which is to say liberal) viewpoint to their generally aged uncles, a viewpoint more in tune with what was going on outside the papal palace. The practice indisputably made a significant contribution to art and architecture, for the cardinal nephews generally hurried to complete their own and their families' monuments, not knowing how long they would be in a position to order such items of self-glorification before their sponsor died and with him their privileged status. By the end of the seventeenth century, the position of the cardinal nephew was ended by reforming popes.

After the excesses of the Renaissance, the college gradually became a more respectable body. Its members came to consider spiritual leadership their primary role, rather than the personal corruption, scheming military and political manipulation, and aggrandizement that had been a way of life for a sadly large percentage of their numbers for centuries.

In the twentieth century, the collective international prestige of the cardinals is such that it would be difficult to find a more esteemed group of men anywhere in the world, a status in close keeping with the apostolate after which the office was modeled. The Code of Canon Law—the laws binding on the Church in the same way any legal system is on a nation—states the role of the College of Cardinals very clearly: "The cardinals of the Holy Roman Church constitute the senate of the Roman pontiff and aid him as his chief counselors and collaborators in the government of the Church." In actuality, however, the power of the cardinalate lies in its individual members rather than as a body sharing the authority of the papacy itself. John Paul II has made attempts to utilize the college as a quasilegislative body in the consistorylike "consultations" he has occasionally convoked, but the sessions have inevitably served a more consultory than decision-making function.

Although they are now almost entirely symbolic, there are still three grades of cardinal, jealously guarded by some cardinals: cardinal bishops, cardinal priests, and cardinal deacons. They rank individually from date of appointment in descending order of grade.

In theory, the six cardinal bishops are representative of the seven small "suburbicarian" dioceses, those immediately adjacent to the "urban" diocese of Rome itself. These sees are Albano, Frascati, Palestrina, Porto e Santa Rufina, Sabina e Poggio Mirteto, and Velletri; the seventh, Ostia, is held by the senior of the six in addition to his other see, and he always fills the position of dean of the Sacred College, the highest-ranking cardinal.

Historically the fact that these dioceses are closest to the pope's own has given them their especially illustrious position in the Church, and this honor has lasted into modern times. The cardinal bishops are always members of the Curia—the Vatican government—and thus resident in Rome. In most cases, cardinal bishops are career curialists, rather than having been residential bishops of metropolitan sees promoted to cardinal bishop. Formerly, when a cardinal bishop died, his see generally was filled by the highest-ranking curial cardinal priest, but the practice has been ended, and today the pope's choice of a successor is made without this restriction. Since 1962, even the theoretical responsibility for administration of the suburbicarian dioceses has been withdrawn from the cardinal bishops who hold their titles and given to the working bishops who actually reside in them.

The great majority of the members of the College of Cardinals hold the rank of cardinal priest, a misnomer in modern terms since most of these cardinals are actually archbishops (and a few bishops) of the world's great metropolitan sees. Some are, however, like the cardinal bishops, curialists who have been promoted because of distinguished diplomatic or administrative careers in the Vatican, or else former metropolitan archbishops transferred to Roman curial jobs.

The twenty-five parishes of Rome established by Pope Cletus were the nucleus of the honorary parishes still given each of the cardinal priests as his titular see upon being named a cardinal. (The titles can be thought of as somewhat analogous to those of the British nobility, wherein newly appointed peers are still given titles representative of actual places.) More have been added over the centuries as the total number of members of the cardinalate has increased. The cardinal priest exercises the same theoretical authority in his titular church and parish that he exercises in his own see.

The rank of cardinal deacon is a sort of administrative dignity for the Vatican's newest curial cardinals; many are later promoted to one of the two higher ranks of the cardinalate. The incumbents are fully vested with the supreme accolade of the cardinalate, but have not necessarily been advanced to the episcopate, the highest sacramental dignity in the Church, at the time their appointment is announced. Until canon law in 1917 changed the rules of eligibility to their present form, even being a priest was not a prerequisite for being a cardinal deacon, and thus laymen could and did hold the rank into modern times, although rarely. Pius IX's famous secretary of state, Cardinal Antonelli, was one such example. It was John XXIII who ruled in 1962 that all cardinals must be bishops as well, and in the happenstance that a nonbishop is selected to be a cardinal deacon, he is consecrated a bishop before receiving the red hat of a cardinal. The basis for the titles of the cardinal deaconate spring from the early Church's original seven deaconaries established in Rome's Augustinian districts.

The special category of cardinal *in petto,* meaning "in secret" (sometimes called cardinal *in pectore,* or "in the breast"—the pope's breast) is one of the papacy's oddest phenomena. The pope has the power to create cardinals without actually naming them, a custom started by Martin V in the fifteenth century, undoubtedly on the same grounds that justify the practices today. The seniority of these unnamed cardinals ranks from the moment the pope invokes this arcane privilege, although they have no other perquisites of the cardinalate, if for no other reason than that the person doesn't know he's been made a cardinal. If the pope dies before publicly revealing his *in petto* cardinals, all such promotions are automatically void; no written papal testament or legacy will advance such an unnamed man to the cardinalate.

Today the reason for this sort of elevation is generally political. When the Holy See doesn't wish to rile a Communist state by naming one of its deserving prelates to the Sacred College, the pope can do it anyway without anyone else's knowing. His intentions are to make the name known when the time is "right" to do so. If the cardinal himself dies before being publicly named, it is assumed that he never knew anything about the hidden honor conferred on him by the pope. Frantisek Tomasek of Czechoslovakia was recently elevated *in petto* and only later publicly named. His *in pectore* promotion is now known by the official date of his seniority, which predates his public naming. John XXIII is thought by some Vatican historians to have died with the never-revealed names of three cardinals in his breast.

For four hundred years after the College of Cardinals formally came into existence in the 1100s, its total number of members varied widely, but in 1586, Sixtus V set the maximum membership at 70, a number that supposedly represents the 70 elders named by Moses to help him deal with the Hebrew tribes or, depending on which source you accept, the 70 ancient scholars of Alexandria who, tradition says, translated the Hebrew Bible into Greek. At the same time, the pope made a list of requirements for prospective cardinals. Besides what now seems an obvious prerequisite that a cardinal had to be a person of blameless reputation, then a fairly novel idea, the stern injunction was laid down that he also had to have been born in legal wedlock. Sixtus's rules did not bar those made legitimate by the subsequent marriage of their parents (interestingly, children so born are still barred from succession to the British crown). Furthermore, anyone with children or grandchildren, living or dead, legitimate or otherwise, was out of the running, as was anyone with a brother, cousin, uncle, or nephew who was already a cardinal. This rule grew out of the fact that Sixtus's immediate predecessors had given nepotism an especially bad name. As we've seen, the rules were extended in 1917 to require ordination as a priest and in 1962 to require consecration as a bishop before being made a cardinal. Presumably, today the pope could make a special dispensation waiving any of these rules; in this more enlightened age, illegitimacy is undoubtedly an obstacle that might be overruled for an otherwise qualified candidate.

The college's membership never rose above 70 until the pontificate of Paul VI, but in the years since, the number has been rising steadily. Today it stands at 129*; there are 5 cardinal bishops, plus 2 Oriental rite patriarchs included in this rank, 109 cardinal priests, and 13 cardinal deacons. Since Sixtus V's pontificate, the membership started to become more inter-European and less domi-

*In May 1985, John Paul II increased the total to a record of 152.

nated by the Italians, and since Pius XII's reign, although it still has a disproportionately high percentage of Italians, it has become far more international and even interracial. The Italians lost their majority in 1946 (today there are just over 30 Italian cardinals), while the Europeans are just now losing theirs. The balance will seesaw back and forth for a few years, but the direction toward more non-European cardinals is not likely to change. Today, 23 members of the college are from Latin America, 9 from Asia, 10 from Africa, 14 from North America (the second-place United States follows Italy with 9), 3 from Australasia, and the remainder—62—from Europe; some 50 countries are represented in the distribution. There are still two living cardinals who were named by Pius XII (Guiseppe Siri of Italy and Paul Leger of Canada), 10 by John XXIII, and 94 by Paul VI; John Paul I named none during his short pontificate, and 32 have been named by John Paul II through the spring of 1984. The oldest is Pietro Cardinal Parente at 94; the youngest, Alfonso Cardinal Lopez Trujillo, 49.

New cardinals are formally named and installed to their high dignity in special ecclesiastical courts called consistories. These secret assemblies of the pope and his "senate" are not called solely for the purpose of naming new members to the college, but that is their best-known function as far as the public is concerned. The consistories presided over by John Paul II are the culmination of a long process of reviewing candidates and balancing the considerations of geographical parity. (Some sees almost automatically rate a cardinal, as we'll see in a bit.) Candidates are, of course, given the opportunity to turn down the honor and may do so without any penalty or loss of present position.

While the pope does solicit the views of his top curial advisers on the names of eligible candidates, the final decisions are his alone. At the consistory, he asks the consent of the gathered cardinals—"*Quid vobis videtur?*" or "How does this seem to you?"—but the rite is purely a formality, and no one can gainsay the pope on his choices. He simply states, "By the authority of almighty God, of the holy apostles Peter and Paul, and of our own, we make such-and-such cardinal, in the name of the Father and of the Son and of the Holy Spirit, Amen," and it's done.

A Vatican official delivers a document called a *biglietto* notifying those chosen of the pope's intentions. Assuming that the newly honored agrees to accept the title, he is shortly thereafter invited to

Rome for the ceremony of receiving from the pope's hands the symbols of his new rank, the red biretta and red zucchetto (skullcap). Each will also be assigned one of the Roman parishes as the church over which he will serve as titular pastor. At his own consistory, Cardinal Wojtyla was the recipient of San Cesareo in Palatino, in Rome's oldest section and the neighborhood of the city's aristocracy in the days of the empire.

The public consistory held soon after is an exceedingly impressive show. In addition to the new cardinals, as many as possible of the rest of the college, the Vatican diplomatic corps, and the families of the just-elevated cardinals attend. First, each new cardinal kisses the pope's foot and hand as a gesture of his representation as the vicar of Christ, and the pope then gives each the kiss of peace, which they pass on to each other. Until recent years, the new inductees were dressed in great scarlet-hooded cloaks and the red hat, or *galero rosso,* the supreme symbol of their rank as cardinals, which was touched to their heads for a moment. The hat was never worn again but was placed on their biers at their funerals; afterward, it was hung over the cardinal's cathedral church altar until the hat disintegrated. Today, John Paul's simpler ceremonies reflect his more streamlined way of doing things, with only the new scarlet zucchettos and birettas placed on each man's head. A concelebration of the mass and the singing of the *Te Deum,* the Church's famous anthem of thanksgiving, closes the ceremony.

After this public consistory, there is a third consistory, held in the presence of only the pope and the other cardinals; it includes the ceremony of the pope's opening and shutting each man's mouth as a symbol of the probationary period cardinals formerly underwent. Today it is a reminder that they are expected to be modest in their daily undertakings.

Now that he's finally and fully a cardinal, the new prince of the Church takes on the identity, bearings, and power of an international executive. Even those new cardinals whose status as residential archbishops hasn't been changed find themselves serving on powerful Vatican commissions and boards because of their increased rank. As for the curial cardinals who have advanced, they, too, find the appointment brings a quantum increase in administrative responsibility and, more importantly, authority. It is often said that the 100 United States senators form the world's most exclusive club;

if so, the members of the College of Cardinals run a close second, not to mention that *their* rank is for life.

The external appurtenances of the cardinalate are an important part of the mystique and fascination that this group of men present to the public. Although the custom is dying, the unique and traditional style a new member of the Sacred College uses to sign himself is John Cardinal Smith, not Cardinal John Smith, the reason being that Pope Urban VIII felt the honor of the appointment was so great that the title should become part of the name itself rather than merely an added prefix. The form is becoming unfashionable, especially among the American cardinalate, but it is still used on official papal documents and is seen, for example, in the signature of the Vatican secretary of state, Agostino Cardinal Casaroli. (It should be remembered that residential cardinals are not cardinal *of* New York, for example, but *archbishop* of New York and cardinal *of* his honorary Roman see.)

Further dignity was bestowed by Urban VIII in the unique style of "Eminence" ("Cardinal" is a *title,* "Eminence" is a *style*) he gave the college, distinguishing the members from the lesser usage ("Excellency") borne by bishops and archbishops; cardinals are the only people in the world who are entitled to use this style. Even their emblematic red hats are singular to their rank, with fifteen tassels arranged in triangles on either side as their particular mark, seen on their coats of arms as the "supporters" on either side of the shield. Cardinals are identified with a special color, the famous scarlet red of their zucchettos, capes, and cassock trim. Although cardinals are known in Italy as *porporati,* or "the purple ones," the appellation is inaccurate—purple is used by bishops for their cassock trim and skullcaps, the distinction generally being the only way to differentiate between cardinals and other bishops.

Regulations govern the privileges and perquisites of members of the Sacred College, even down to the specifics of the living arrangements of the curial cardinals stationed in Rome. Although the necessity of living within the confines of drastically reduced financial circumstances has curtailed many of the luxuries that curial cardinals enjoyed up to this century (they were very often related to affluent families and lived in one of the family mansions), their home lives still reflect their exalted rank and are spent in a fair amount of comfort. A few of the highest offices in the Curia include as a perk an apartment inside the Vatican, but such quarters, some within the Apostolic Palace itself, are generally longer on gilded splendor than on modern conveniences. There is also the consideration of an irksome lack of privacy within the papal state's walls. Not only do the gates close every evening at eleven, but also it can be presumed that a record will be kept of one's visitors, all of whom are required to check through both the Swiss Guard and the Vigilance before being admitted.

Outside living arrangements for curial cardinals still tend to be within the Vatican's physical orbit, making getting to and from work easy. Residential cardinals are, in fact, canonically obliged to live in Rome, and technically may not leave the city without papal permission. The Piazza della Città Leonina across from the busy St. Anne gateway is home to several of the Church's princes, all of whom have the right to call upon the papal kingdom's storehouse of spare furniture to help fill their quarters. Sometimes the cardinal's home diocese will also chip in for some of the necessities.

A sort of "family," or court, is allowed: a chamberlain, a gentleman-in-waiting, a majordomo, as well as other domestic servants. A priest, often a monsignor, is generally assigned to act as an ecclesiastical assistant. Although cardinals usually can depend on being assigned two or three nuns from local religious orders to help out with domestic duties, occasionally female relatives act as housekeepers. Each is authorized to have a "throne room" (the now outdated rules majestically specified that it was to be "carpeted in purple") as well as a private chapel. This sort of appurtenance is generally possible in the relatively spacious extraterritorial palaces belonging to the Holy See that are assigned to some cardinals, but for others who have to find apartments in Rome, fitting in a throne room can be a major problem.

The Vatican pays its curial cardinals a salary of about fifteen hundred dollars a month, a pittance if the man's rank and responsibility were compared with his counterparts in the civilian world, but men don't become priests to attain material wealth, not even—in theory—if they reach the Church's loftiest heights. The salary is officially and rather colorfully called the *piatto cardinalizio,* the "cardinal's dish." Expenses are lessened to a degree by many of the perquisites that the title brings. One is the automatic right to hold a Vatican passport, carrying the Holy See's authority and protection with it. The passport exempts the cardinal not only from onerous Italian taxes but also allows the use of the cheaper shopping facilities within the Vatican's walls. "Necessary" transportation is provided by the Vatican's motor pool, which includes a fleet of limousines on call for official duties.

The cardinals outside Rome are generally far better known to the public since they head the world's great archdioceses and are constantly spotlighted by the international media. As has been mentioned, many sees almost automatically carry with them a cardinalate; when a man is named archbishop of one, he can generally expect to be advanced to the Sacred College within a year or two. The cardinalitial archdioceses include Paris, Westminster (London), Milan, Florence, Naples, Toledo, Lisbon, Cologne, Munich, Vienna, Warsaw, Cracow, Buenos Aires, Rio de Janeiro, and, in the United States, New York, Chicago, Philadelphia, Washington, Los Angeles, and St. Louis. Occasionally a glitch will throw off the expected: When Archbishop Montini—later Paul VI—was assigned the Milan see by his mentor Pius XII in the mid-1950s, the red hat was not forthcoming for reasons never explained but often ascribed to papal pique with Montini for having sent Pius a requested report on Vatican finances that cast impolitic aspersions on two papal nephews. Montini was, happily, eventually made a cardinal by Pius's successor, John XXIII, who later remarked that if Montini had been a cardinal on his predecessor's death, he—not himself—would have succeeded Pius to Peter's throne.

In the final reckoning, the primary reason for the College of Cardinals' existence is the perpetuation of the papacy. The fact that its own preservation is accomplished through the popes' naming of new cardinals makes for a very neatly ordered and balanced arrangement.

Although the cardinals have served the Church since its infancy, until responsibility for papal elections was canonically limited to the Sacred College, its actual form was highly fluid. In the Church's youth, the Roman bishops—then the "cardinals"—elected the pope, often in a remarkably offhand way. When one pope died and another was needed, word about the best choice got around, and the consensus possible in a small community would then confirm him as pope without too much time spent on formalities. After

Constantine, the emperors had a say, often a decisive one, in the matter.

As the Church grew more established and ultimately became influential in European king-making, this relatively casual but seldom entirely peaceful process was hedged with increasing political implications, making it ever more difficult to get the Church's elders to settle on one among many candidates, who usually represented competing interests and families. The squabbling among factions led to long lapses in filling the papal throne, and these vacancies meant dangerous power vacuums in what became the most important office in the Western world after the fall of the Roman Empire. Malachi Martin summed it up in his book *The Decline and Fall of the Roman Church:* "There had to a validly elected pope for day-to-day life in Europe to go on . . . without a pope, Europe was impossible."

Ironically, it was the laity who in 1216 took matters into their own hands when the bishops' jealousies threatened the survival of Europe's social order during one of the frequent vacancies in the Holy See. The answer to their impasse was refreshingly guileless: Lock the scoundrels up until they reach a decision. Thus came conclave, meaning "with key," a literal description of the device that changed the way popes were henceforth chosen. The next few conclaves were increasingly severe, the two dozen or so cardinals locked into a single large room. The civil authorities also made sure that they had progressively less food as each day went by without a new pope being named. In one memorable conclave, a cardinal on the verge of death was prematurely shoved into his coffin so the others could get back to their deliberations. The right of every cardinal to vote was considered so inviolable that often the Church's princes were released from jail cells so they could exercise their precious franchise.

Even though the conclave system generally speeded things up, there were still outstanding difficulties facing the Church's electors whenever they were required to fulfill their ecclesiastical duty and fill a vacant Holy See. For centuries, political pressure, not to mention outright threats, remained impediments to the college's independent choice of popes. In fact, the "right" of kings to influence their national cardinals, grandly termed the Right of Veto and considered an inalienable right by Europe's Catholic kings, lasted until the beginning of the twentieth century, when the House of Hapsburg blocked as unacceptable to its interests the election of the favorite, Cardinal Rampolla, to the papal throne. The idea was, of course, for the French to block the Austrians from being elected, the Austrians to keep the Spaniards off the papal throne, and so on. The benefactors of the system were, of course, the Italians. A canon was finally promulgated by Pius X that absolutely forbade governmental influence in the papal electoral process under threat of excommunication for any party caught in the attempt.

Public disorder at the local level—rioting, bloodshed, and murder in the streets—was for centuries a normal accompaniment to any conclave. The civil populace—usually meaning the Romans, since the majority of papal elections were held in Rome—wanted to make their choices known; local bigwigs, both princely and otherwise, usually tried to stir up trouble to influence affairs; and the not infrequent voting deadlocks had a way of making mobs impatient for the cardinals to conclude their business and made it impossible to get anything done when the papacy was vacant. Not until the mid-1700s did civil order become the rule rather than the exception during conclaves.

The most recent major rules overhaul to affect the conclave notably was that instituted by Paul VI that denies the vote to any cardinal over eighty years of age, also the mandatory age of retirement for curial members of the college and the age at which residential bishops are strongly "encouraged" to give up their burdens as well. It is noteworthy, in passing, that Paul himself did not abdicate upon reaching his eightieth birthday, saying, "The father of the family does not retire." Since the Holy Spirit is the hypothetical instrument by which the cardinals' consciences and votes are guided in conclave, it is difficult to understand why the Holy Spirit would abandon the Church's electors precisely at eighty, but age limits are by nature arbitrary. There is no rule, by the way, that prohibits the cardinals from electing a new pope from among those barred from voting because of age.

Before going on, it should be noted that the format and rules for papal elections can be changed by the pope at any time. Most popes do, in fact, add some particular or another to the complicated and mathematically precise procedures that are effected when an election is held, although the relatively major changes like those of Paul are rare. The important point is that the pope's word is final and absolute; there is no earthly authority that can deny him to unrestricted right to change a rule—any rule—governing the Church except those set out in Scripture. In the case of papal elections, Scripture is, of course, silent. The pope could, if he chose, even abolish the conclave system and name his own successor, making the papacy something very closely resembling a hereditary monarchy. There's little doubt that the rebellious Curia would do everything in its power to dissuade such a radical papal mind-set, but it's a scenario that's theoretically possible. And, as an absolute safeguard of the primacy of the bishop of Rome, the cardinals may not modify, annul, or change any of the rules made by the previous pope regarding the election or the conclave.

The modern conclave is one of the Church's most complex and colorful rituals—a spectacle that makes history, often redirects the Church, and invariably focuses the world's attention on the deliberations of the several dozen men who function in the name of the Holy Spirit and acknowledge Jesus Christ as their only authority during the interregnums of the throne of Peter.

The first among many rituals that culminate in the naming of a new pope is the verification of the death of the old pope, and it is traditionally performed by the cardinal *camerlengo,* or chamberlain. This official, today holding what amounts to a largely honorary position, formerly had substantial authority in matters of papal finances. In modern times, he comes into the glory of his office when the Holy See is vacant, at which point he takes official charge of the Sacred College to administer the Church's temporal affairs until a new pope again assumes the responsibility.

In the antique and slightly chilling ceremonial act of verifying that the pope is truly dead, the *camerlengo* must tap the presumed corpse on the forehead three times with a little silver mallet and call out three times, once with each tap, the late pope's prepapal Christian name. When death is thus verified, he immediately continues the ritual by defacing the pope's personal signet ring and seals of office with a pair of silver scissors; notifies all papal officials that forthwith they cease to hold office; seals—literally—the private living quarters; and finally officially informs the world that the pope is dead. Incidentally, because of the macabre pictures published in 1958 of Pius XII on his deathbed, Paul VI later made a rule that no such photos, or tape recordings, can ever again be taken of a pope in like circumstances.

The formidable process of gathering in the Church's princes from their worldwide sees is the next major step in the process. The relative ease of air transportation has, of course, enormously changed what had been up to John XXIII's election an arduous undertaking for the mostly elderly body of cardinals; it wasn't unknown in past conclaves for the journey itself to cause the death of some of the more delicate or aged members of the college. Occasionally a cardinal will die during the conclave, as did an American, Cardinal Mooney, during the 1958 conclave that elected Pius XII's successor. But it should be remembered that eligible cardinals in any condition other than *extremis* are under an absolute canonical obligation to participate in the electoral process, and the penalty for failure to do so can be excommunication.

The conclave itself is held in the Sistine Chapel, depriving Rome's legions of tourists of their number one sightseeing attraction for the duration. This loss is, however, always more than compensated for by the historic atmosphere the city takes on during the *sede vacante,* a time when rumors flow as freely and with as little control as the city's traffic. The game of guessing who will be chosen among the *papabile*—that handful of cardinals generally considered electable—displaces many of the traditional Roman diversions.

Preparation of the chapel and its surrounding salons, corridors, and courtyards in the papal palaces is something akin to creating a convention hotel out of a museum. Each voting cardinal has a bedroom jury-rigged for him, as do the usually two assistants—a secretary and a servant, called conclavists—he is allowed to bring with him into the sealed-off area. The cardinal's quarters are officially called a cell and has been a feature of conclaves since Leo XIII decreed that each elector must have a private room so he can meditate in peace. The quarters are Spartan—a simple single bed, a hardback chair, a *prie-dieu,* a washbowl and pitcher, and a chamber pot. The idea is not to create too much comfort in the hopes that the Sacred College will get its business finished in the shortest possible time. A kitchen staffed by nuns is set up, and the food is delivered to the locked-in cardinals through a revolving pass-through in the chapel's door, which also serves as the sole entry point for medical supplies. In the chapel itself, each cardinal is assigned one of the chairs, set in four rows, two on either side; the traditional rows of canopied thrones were done away with because of overcrowding when the college grew too large under Paul. In front of each is a leather folder, a pen, three ballots, and scratch paper for keeping track of the votes, or doodling.

Nearly three weeks of preparation—including the nine days of the Novendiale masses said as obsequies—separate a pope's death from the preconclave consistory in which the rules of the election process are formally explained to the cardinals and in which they formally swear to abide by them. The cardinal camerlengo, assisted by the marshal of sacred ceremonies, oversees the sealing of the conclave, a thoroughly modern technological process in which they make sure electronic listening devices have not been introduced into the conclave area. Once the cardinals are locked in, they cannot come out except for health emergencies until the new pope has been chosen. The historic cry of *extra omnes*—"everyone out"—coming from the Sistine Chapel signifies the start of the historic deliberations and is the sign that all except the cardinals and their conclavists must leave. When the electors go into their deliberations, they have symbolically become simply priests of the diocese of Rome meeting to elect their bishop rather than princes of the Church gathered to elect a supreme pontiff.

The rules of the process call for a two-thirds-plus-one vote for a winner, a voting procedure that is repeated twice each day—once in the morning and again in the afternoon—until one cardinal receives such a majority. An elector may not vote for himself; if a tally were ever unanimous, the winner would be very embarrassed, not to mention disqualified. If the voting goes on for three days without a winner emerging, a twenty-four-hour break for prayer is called; the senior cardinal deacon also delivers a little exhortation to his fellows in an attempt to break what has turned into a deadlock. After seven more ballots and still no pope, the process repeats, but this time it's the senior cardinal bishop who exhorts. If necessary, the cardinals can, if they're unanimous in their desire to do so, decrease the required two-thirds-plus-one to a simple majority-plus-one as that needed to elect—or even agree to a runoff between the two leading contenders in the last ballot. But generally, when it becomes evident in modern elections that a deadlock between leading candidates from two camps—usually a "pastoral" candidate versus a "curial," or strong administrative type—is causing the logjam, a compromise settles the question.

The actual balloting is done on little slips of paper, printed in Latin with the words "I elect as Supreme Pontiff." Each cardinal enscribes, in a handwriting that is supposed to be as different from his normal hand as possible, the name of the man he thinks the Holy Spirit wants him to vote for; he folds the ballot into halves and drops it into a chalice on a table under Michelangelo's Last Judgment. Ballot-counters called "scrutineers," who were earlier chosen by lot from the college (Cardinal Wojtyla was a counter during the conclave that elected John Paul I), then call out the names on the ballot as each is removed from the chalice. When the necessary majority has qualified one among them to be Christ's vicar, the new pope-elect is immediately confronted by the cardinal camerlengo, who asks two questions.

"Do you, Most Reverend Lord Cardinal, accept your election as supreme pontiff, which has been canonically carried out?" The moment the pope-elect pronounces the irrevocable "*Accepto,*" he is pope. The second question, "By what name will you be known?" is addressed to a man who has already wholly, lawfully, and by a fiat that no power on earth can change, become the spiritual leader of eight hundred million people, and is forever after a man without peers.

No cardinal is obligated to accept the vote of his brothers; any man elected may refuse the honor if he wishes. As recently as 1922, this happened when Camillo Cardinal Laurenti turned down the papacy in the conclave that elected Achille Cardinal Ratti (Pius XI), the cardinals' second choice.

Through the election of Paul VI, after the new pope told the cardinals his pontifical name, the canopies over the thrones lining the chapel were all lowered, except that over the new pope's chair; the act signified the cardinals' homage to their new commander. Since Paul's time, the college has grown so large there is no longer enough space for the canopied thrones in the Sistine Chapel and this traditional nicety.

The crowds that always wait in St. Peter's Square through the ballots share in the college's deliberations via the famous smoke signals emanating from the little stove placed in the Sistine Chapel solely for this archaic ritual. If the ballots to be burned are mixed with certain chemicals (damp straw, formerly the darkening agent, was too untrustworthy), the smoke comes out gray and the crowd knows no one yet has been elected; if the ballots are burned without the chemicals, the smoke puffing out over the roof of the chapel is white, at which signal the masses go communally berserk with the excitement of a new pontifical reign.

Their duty done, the cardinals and the Church can get back to their normal routines. The world's attention will still be focused on the excitement of a papal inauguration and a new reign that will, in all likelihood, bring significant changes to the Church. But the Sacred College sees itself as a continuum, its fraternity replenished by the choice of the one, no longer of the body, who has become its leader. The system goes on.

5

Curia Romana:
The Vatican Hierarchy

Since the eleventh century, the Curia Romana—the Roman Court—has been the bureaucracy that has served the popes as their primary instrument for governing the immense landscape of the Roman Catholic Church. In order to trace the development of the modern bureaucracy more clearly, it is necessary to understand the organization of the Church—the titles, rank, and status that play a part just as vital and as rigorously ordered in the Church as they are in any other complex institution. As is the case with any government, titles and honors flow downward in the Church, so it is appropriate first to describe the mosaic of ecclesiastical rank at its pinnacle.

The papal throne is unique in that the source of its holder's immense authority derives—in the abstract, at least—not from his most important title or most powerful function but from an office that has traditionally taken only a small fraction of the popes' energies. When Peter succeeded as Jesus's vicar on earth, he became *foremost* the bishop of Rome, which meant much the same thing as bishop of the Western world's capital. Today that role remains the well from which all papal authority springs. Simply put, John Paul II is pope because he is bishop of Rome, not the other way around.

During the early days of the Church, up to the fifth century, the title of pope, derived from the Greek *pappas* ("father"), was used for any bishop but eventually was reserved for and universally understood to mean solely the bishop of Rome. Ironically, even today it is not one of the *official* titles of its holder, however. The present pope's ordinary signature is *Joannes Paulus PP. II*, meaning John Paul (in Latin), *pastor pastorum* ("shepherd of shepherds" in Latin) and the second pope of that name. (Incidentally, on the most formal documents, such as papal bulls, the post-nominal number is not used, and is replaced with *servus servorum Dei*—"servant of the servants of God").

An additional title officially belonging to the pope derives from a pagan source of pre-Christian Rome. The ancient priestly cult of pontiffs—the word means "bridge-builders"—were honored with the emperors serving as their titular head, or Pontifex Maximus, as members of royal families still serve as patrons of all different kinds of organizations. When the popes succeeded as Rome's authority, they appropriated the title (Leo I, in the midfifth century, was the first to use it), modified by modern popes in several forms, all considered "unofficial": Summus Pontifex, Romanus Pontifex, as well as Pontifex Maximus. The modern forms—pontiff and pontifical, in English—have come to be universally applied to popes and functions pertaining to the papacy.

A number of styles are used to honor the pope. The most common—"Holiness" (*Sanctitas* in Latin)—is the proper form of address when speaking or writing to the pope. More formal are "Most Blessed Father" (*Beatissimus Pater*) and "Our Most Holy Lord" (*Sanctissimus dominus noster*), usages that have developed over nineteen hundred years of papal history. Ecclesiastics and those at the Vatican ordinarily refer to the pope as the "holy father."

In sacramental terms, the Church has only two classes of fully ordained ministers—priests and bishops. There are many subcategories and honorific and jurisdictional ranks, but as to the administration of the sacraments, the central function of the priesthood, the pope is on essentially the same level of authority as the most junior of the Church's bishops. The sacramental hierarchy of the Church is made up of bishops, priests, and deacons (nuns have no hierarchical status in the Church). Its prelates, the jurisdictional hierarchy, or the public officers of the Church, are the pope, archbishops, and bishops, plus a number of other officers (some of whom may be bishops) with such titles as vicars, administrators, or prefects, included because they have jurisdiction over territories. Members of the Pontifical Household are "honorary" prelates. As we've seen, cardinals are archbishops (or, occasionally, bishops, as in Mainz and Berlin) who have been given the high honor of this added dignity; most serve as residential archbishops in the largest sees, and a lesser number, the curial cardinals, have been assigned to the Vatican to serve as the chief executive officers over its most important bureaucracies. Even residential archbishop cardinals, however, serve on the boards of directors of these bureaucratic departments.

As with the office of cardinal, that of patriarch carries added dignity in the hierarchy of jurisdiction, even though its sacramental character is no greater than that of any other bishop. The term—meaning "chief of fathers"—had its origins in the Eastern Church, where it referred to a sort of episcopal *primus inter pares,* or first among equals. It eventually spread to the Latin Rite and Rome, where the popes added the title of "Patriarch of the West" to their own honorifics. Two European sees—Lisbon and Venice—still officially carry this title for their archbishops (for reasons buried in historical happenstance), but it alone implies no substantive distinction between them and any other residential archbishops. Both the East and West Indies are also still technically Roman Catholic patriarchates. In the eastern Mediterranean, the title of patriarch continues to be used by several Eastern Rite bishops.

Another honorific is that of primate, referring to the residential archbishop—invariably a cardinal—within a country, or sometimes a region, who traditionally commands the most prestige and honor but does not possess any greater authority than the other archbishop or archbishops in his country. Some of the countries that have a primate are Poland, where the archbishop of Warsaw holds the title; France, with Lyon as its primatial see; and Ireland, with Armagh. In Italy, the Bishop of Rome—the pope—is primate. Originally, all of the bishops of a country were subject to the jurisdiction of the primate, who was himself subject only to the Holy See, but the position no longer retains this authority in canon law.

The great majority of prelates are bishops, the pope's lieutenants who possess the highest degree of the Church's holy orders and are responsible for overseeing (bishop comes from the Greek word for "overseer") both priests and the laity. The approximately thirty-seven hundred bishops worldwide are considered the successors to the Apostles, men who have reached the fullness of the Roman Catholic priesthood. Although all bishops are equal with regard to their sacramental authority, they are not equal in the different kinds of administrative jurisdiction they must assume.

The highest episcopal grade is archbishop (about one in every six bishops), a title used in the Western Church since the ninth century and meaning, strictly speaking, a bishop with the title of an archdiocese. Most archbishops have charge of an archdiocese, a unit of the Church that is almost always made up of a group of several dioceses. The archbishop of such an ecclesiastical "province" is called a metropolitan. The pope is the metropolitan archbishop of the province of Rome, just as he is the bishop of the diocese of Rome. More specific to the Curia is the titular archbishop, a man with the rank and title of an archbishop but without any territorial jurisdiction, a fact that technically excludes such archbishops from being prelates in the narrow sense of that term. The titular archepiscopal rank is given by the pope to high Vatican officials as a promotion somewhat analogous to how banks appropriate vice-presidencies. A sort of honorary archbishopric—that of archbishop ad personam—is more in the nature of a personal honor given to certain bishops; it does not imply ordinary archepiscopal authority.

Like archbishops, bishops come in several varieties, and their titles can be even more confusing. The kind most people think of are residential bishops, those in charge of dioceses. From there, matters get somewhat more complex. Since there is no rank available between bishop and priest to which the bishop's (or archbishop's) *sacramental* responsibilities can be delegated, the office of auxiliary bishop was created to help residential bishops get this kind of work done. The archbishop of New York, for example, has ten auxiliary bishops under his authority. The auxiliary has the full sacramental powers of the episcopate, but his is jurisdictionally subordinate to his residential bishop. He is a kind of deputy bishop whose real power, if any, is precisely that which his residential bishop wishes him to have. Much of the diocese's ceremonial work—the confirmations that are held in great numbers each spring, for example—are turned over to the auxiliaries to perform.

Another kind of auxiliary is the coadjutor bishop, also an assistant but of slightly higher authority and who is often named to his post with the firm understanding that he will be the residential bishop's eventual successor. Still another episcopal title is suffragan, which simply means a residential bishop in the ecclesiastical province of an archbishop. All except residential bishops are titular bishops, meaning their episcopal titles are the names of ancient sees that no longer exist as functioning dioceses. A residential bishop is the bishop of, for example, Sacramento, but his auxiliary or coadjutor bishops need to be bishops *of* somewhere, too, so these ancient and obscure sees are assigned to serve as their formal titles. This is comparable to British titles of nobility, wherein one has to be a peer *of* somewhere.

Again more specific to the Holy See itself, curial titular bishops are officers given episcopal rank because of the importance of their positions, or as a reward for long and generally productive careers at the Vatican. Each of the Church's congregations, or ministries, has several of these titular bishops, or archbishops, serving as top officials.

Vicars are bishops' helpers, but for administrative rather than for sacramental purposes; they needn't, therefore, be bishops themselves, although some are. Vicars at the diocesan level are called vicars general, and those with jurisdiction over mission territories are vicars apostolic. The pope has a vicar to run his Roman diocese for him, but in this case the incumbent is always a cardinal, today Ugo Cardinal Poletti. A vicar is also named for the Vatican City.

The rank of monsignor—literally, "my lord"—is one of the Church's less understood stations. It is applied to prelates, not all of whom are bishops, and is also the title given ranking members of the Pontifical Household. In the Vatican specifically and in Europe generally, all prelates except cardinals are referred to as monsignors (as, for example, the Earl of Snowdon is referred to as Lord Snowdon); such is not the case in the United States, where the title is used only in its honorary sense, and where bishops and archbishops are called by their rank. The reason American priests can be monsignors when they obviously are not serving in the Pontifical Household is that this rank includes both "active" and "honorary" members of the household, the latter representing either older priests so singled out for having had successful careers, or younger priests, generally in highly visible administrative posts, who have been marked as comers in the Church. True also at the Vatican, a younger priest with the title is one to watch as a likely future bishop.

In November 1982, John Paul created for the first time in the Church's history a "personal prelature," a type of jurisdictional division authorized by the Second Vatican Council. The prelature was established to make the archconservative Opus Dei organization something on the order of a worldwide diocese. It also created a new principle in the Church's jurisdictional structure. It permitted power sharing between the local diocesan bishops, who have jurisdiction over their own flock, and the new prelate of the Opus Dei, who has far stronger and a far more personal control over his zealously orthodox membership of seventy-four thousand lay Catholics and twelve hundred priests in forty-two countries, who— nominally, at least—also come under the control of their local bishops.

The Roman Curia has, in this generation, ceased being the all-Italian preserve it was for most of the centuries of its existence. Since the restructuring of the Church in the wake of the Second Vatican Council in the mid-1960s, the two-thousand-odd man ("man" is the right word; there are no female curial executives and only a few who can even be classified as officials) institution has taken on the colors of the worldwide membership of the Roman Catholic Church—black African cardinals, bishops from the South Pacific, Chinese monsignori. Over two thirds of its executive membership is now non-Italian, a percentage that nonetheless fluctuates greatly among individual departments. For example, the highly visible and most important Secretariat of State is still largely Italian, while the Congregation for the Oriental Church is far more international. In 1962, twelve of the then sixteen curial departments were headed by Italians; today, sixteen of twenty-two are presided over by non-Italians.

But in spite of the efforts of the past several popes to make it more closely conform to the worldwide racial or national proportions of Roman Catholicism, the Curia still reflects an Italian-style traditionalism, if no longer in national makeup, then in its essential character. Furthermore, the visitor to any curial office hasn't the slightest doubt that he's in an *Italian* office, not some internationalized secretariat where efforts have been made to homogenize the setting. Italian customs and, importantly, the Italian language dominate the Church's bureaucracy.

There is a distinction in definition between the bodies that constitute the Curia itself and the men and few women who belong to them. Not every clerk working in a curial office can be thought of as a *member* of the Curia, a status to which only the higher levels of the bureaucracy belong. Definitions in this area are imprecise, but some sources state that while there are laymen serving as curial officials, only clerics can accurately be called *members* of the Curia. Regardless of definitional problems at the middle levels, there is no doubt that the Curia's executives—those running the prefectures, or boards, of the congregations—are exclusively clerical and almost as exclusively episcopal.

It is not unnatural that the greatest share of administrative control over the Vatican state as well as the Holy See is in clerical hands; to expect otherwise in what amounts to the headquarters of Catholic Christianity would be naïve. But the large majority of the pope's employees are nonpriestly laypersons, the eighteen hundred or so almost exclusively Italian male civilians who perform duties ranging from the governorship of the state to the cleaning of its streets. In 1981, the papal state's quasi-union, the Association of Vatican Lay Employees, formed by a militant minority of employees bent on emulating the labor practices of their fellow unionists on the Italian side of the border, demanded and received recognition for their organization from the pope himself. The association represents sixteen hundred members.

At the top of the Curia, first in precedence and indisputably highest in rank, status, and importance is the Secretariat of State. Its chief official, the cardinal secretary of state, is second in the Vatican only to the pope himself (the dean of the College of Cardinals is second place in *ecclesiastical* status, however), and in the person of sexagenarian Agostino Casaroli, he is the most powerful second-in-command in modern Church history. In April 1984, John Paul gave his secretary of state a handwritten letter charging Casaroli with a "high and special mandate" to represent him "in the process and responsibilities inherent in the sovereignty of the state of the Vatican City," a tacit way of delegating power to the cardinal as the head of the Vatican's temporal affairs. Cardinal Sebastino Baggio was named president of the commission for the Vatican city-state, but the pope made clear that Casaroli is his own chief deputy, ultimately in charge of *all* the workings of the state as well as of the Holy See. He specifically required the commission and its president to report to Casaroli "in all matters that the existing laws reserve to the pope." In this delegation of authority, the noncurially minded John Paul also signaled his clear intention to give up executive concerns with routine temporal matters to concentrate solely on the spiritual side of Church affairs, specifically the serious matter of grappling directly, country by country, with those who oppose or deviate from his vision of the faith. Now a sort of prime minister and chief of staff, the secretary runs an office that supervises the entire Curia, in addition to filling the traditional role of directing the Holy See's diplomatic service. Reports of recent rumblings indicate that the cardinal, after working a quarter century at bridging east-west relations in the Church, has become frustrated with John Paul's hard anti-Communist views, and has been subtly downgraded by the pope as regards influence in internal curial policy. Whether or not the reputed tensions lead to an eventual break, there is little question John Paul recognizes Casaroli's mastery of diplomatic and temporal matters at the Holy See.

The office of the secretary's chief assistant, the *sostituto* (in Italian it means not "substitute" but "deputy")—today Archbishop Eduardo Martinez-Somalo—has developed into one of considerable importance and power in its own right. During the latter part of Pius XII's reign, when he himself filled the role of secretary of state (one he had occupied brilliantly before coming to the papal throne), his state secretariat was run by two highly visible prelates, technically *sostitutos,* but secretaries of state in all but name: Monsignor Domenico Tardini, in charge of the diplomatic side of the department; and Monsignor Giovanni Battista Montini, later Pope Paul VI, in overall charge of the Holy See's internal bureaucracy.

Below the State Secretariat are ten congregations, modern inheritors of ancient names and duties and that are, in effect, the major cabinet-level governmental departments of both the Holy See specifically and the Roman Catholic Church overall. They are, in order of precedence, the Congregations for the Doctrine of the Faith (which is not only in terms of precedence but in fact the second most important department of the Curia), Bishops, Oriental Churches, Sacraments, Divine Worship, Clergy, Religious and Secular Institutes, Evangelization of People, Causes of Saints, and Catholic Education.

Following the congregations in precedence are, first, three tribunals—the Sacred Apostolic Penitentiary, the Supreme Tribunal of the Apostolic Segnatura, and the Sacred Roman Rota, and then three secretariats—those for Christian Unity, for Non-Christians, and for Nonbelievers. A number of pontifical commissions, councils, and committees follow. Next are the offices, familiar because they include the Apostolic Camera, the Patrimony of the Holy See, the Prefecture of the Pontifical Household, Pontifical Ceremonies, and Swiss Guard. The last element of the Curia is the Palatine Administration, composed of the Reverend Fabric of St. Peter's, the Vatican Library, the Secret Archives, the Vatican Press, the Vatican Publishing House, and *L'Osservatore Romano,* the not-quite-official newspaper of the Holy See.

As the supreme head of the Church, the pope is, in the abstract, merely *delegating* authority to his Curia, which has no authority of its own independent of the pope; each department head formally resigns on the death of a pope but usually is immediately reappointed—at least temporarily—by the new pope. The heads of the departments are nonetheless given fairly wide latitude in the decision-making process, if for no other reason than that the pope's time and ability to oversee are obviously limited. Furthermore, no pope can be expected to comprehend anything like all the myriad details that confront the Holy See, although a few—Paul VI, for one—at times seemed to try. John Paul II involves himself more closely in those matters that personally interest him, letting the Curia have pretty much its own head in matters that don't. The pope does lay down broad guidelines to be followed, but the Curia runs less by broad guidelines than it does by the momentum of bureaucratic minutiae.

The curial organizational chart of ranks is finely drawn; spiritual institution or not, there's little its members could learn from anyone as regards the finer points of a corporate pecking order. At the top are the cardinals who head the departments; several are generally assigned to each department's board, and one will be the working head, or prefect. Several archbishops and bishops will be included at the highest level, and together with the cardinals, they compose, in effect, the boards of directors. The heads of the departments generally serve five-year terms before they are replaced, and in a form of curial musical chairs, many are simply reappointed at the end of their term to head some other department.

Grouped just after the cardinals and bishops in the departments are what might be called the executive managers—the secretary, usually a titular archbishop, and his undersecretary. They are followed by what are known as the major officials, whom the pope appoints (a few are laymen, although most nonclerics are lower down the scale). The minor officials are usually divided into three grades, with antique titles such as *minutanti, addetti,* and *scrittori,* describing the original work these levels of assistants performed—drafters of documents, attachés, and scribes—and that today demarcate finely shaded degrees of duty, rank, authority, and privilege.

A curial assignment generally represents, materially speaking, a step up for those priests sent to Rome by their dioceses and orders to staff Vatican administrative positions, although for the relatively affluent American and Western European priests, Roman duty can mean fewer comforts. Diocesan priests are said to be preferred over religious priests (those from orders) in the Curia because they lack the strong loyalties to orders that can get in the way of strong loyalties to bosses. But diocesan or religious, the assignment to the Vatican will almost always be a valuable experience in the lives and dossiers of young *cariera*-minded priests, giving many an inroad on the path to the prelacy. Vatican service, usually begun before the age of thirty-five, can either be a limited tour of duty in a priest's career, or in some cases may mark the beginning of an entire career spent in Rome. This depends to some degree on his wishes but to a greater degree on his talents.

Working conditions for the clerics assigned to curial offices are not greatly different from those for lay employees. Dress often is a black cassock (sometimes seen with every other button unbuttoned), but the black clerical suit has gained considerable ground. The hours naturally follow the somewhat unusual Roman day: a six-hour day that ends at one-thirty, followed by a long lunch, during which time a handful of staffers will stay in the office to keep it technically open. It will not reopen on a full-service basis after lunch, so appointments are inevitably set for mornings. There are very few secretaries, and even relatively high-ranking priests are expected to do their own clerical work. Surroundings in many of the curial departments are Spartan, although perhaps historic, for the troops; red velvet and gilt are reserved for public reception areas and the cardinal prefects' offices.

Diocesan priests serving in Rome are paid a (barely) living salary and are expected to support themselves, although some economies are realized by, for example, lunching at one of the many religious institutions in the neighborhood of the Vatican. Clerics from the United States often live at the Villa Strich, a residence for American priests working in the Curia, and for which they pay room and board. Some religious priests—those from orders—have shared a vow of poverty in addition to those of chastity and obedience taken by their diocesan colleagues and generally live a more cloistered life after work in their orders' Roman residences. An American Maryknoll priest, for example, will receive $125 a month, on which he must pay U.S. income tax, plus room and board, while a Jesuit receives no salary whatsoever. Religious priests are furthermore obliged to give their orders any outside income received, such as royalties from writing. A notable social drawback for the religious clerics serving in Rome is that they rarely are awarded the honorific title of monsignor, although outstanding diocesan priests routinely receive it.

A substantial part of the work of the Curia departments involves inquiries from the 2,408 dioceses and archdioceses and 276 other Church territorial jurisdictions around the world. Since Vatican II, when Latin ceased to be the single official language of the Curia, an attempt has been made to answer this correspondence in the language in which it was written. Documents and inquiries are routed to lower echelons of curial workers to research the facts of the situation and draft replies. (In the sensitive Congregation of the Clergy, the cardinal prefect opens and delegates the mail himself because the extremely confidential matter of priestly conscience on the part of the sender is very often involved.) Replies are more often than not based on a precedent, in much the same way legal decisions are ordinarily reached. At the weekly *congresso,* or staff meeting, the cases are presented in the presence of the congregation's superiors, and opinions are expressed. The cardinal prefect speaks last, either expressing approval or disapproval of the drafter's work and sometimes ordering him to study the problem further. The Church has no desire to rush decisions that can have serious and far-reaching consequences.

In the Congregation for the Clergy, this weekly *congresso* is held in an impressive American-style boardroom in its building on Pius XII Square. The only note giving away its somewhat unusual nature is the small throne serving as a chair for the cardinal prefect. Behind it, high-louvered shutters are thrown back to present one of the finest views in Rome—an unbroken panorama of St. Peter's Basilica with the broad square carpeting its front yard, a powerful symbol that may help the men in the room reach decisions that best serve their Church and the Vatican. Father Vincent Mallon, secretary to the cardinal prefect of the congregation, nicely summed up the purpose of his and the other Roman congregations: "Our job is to assist the Holy Father to keep the barque of Peter in the channel."

One of the most regular tasks performed by John Paul II is the finely timed and orchestrated ceremony of formally receiving newly appointed ambassadors to the Holy See from several dozen countries. Little of substance is discussed at these essentially social first-time get-togethers of the Vatican's head of state and the envoys diplomatically accredited to him. The new ambassadors are no longer expected to kiss his feet, as was once the custom, but behind the bright colors of the swallowtail-coated ushers and the polite murmurs of greeting exchanged between the principals, some of the most important tenets of the Holy See's diplomacy are maintained. The central purpose of Vatican diplomacy is to keep its influence and that of the Roman Catholic Church strong, while ensuring that channels of communication between the Holy See and local governments as well as local churches remain open. In fulfilling what he sees as a vitally important diplomatic mission to promote peace and make himself an international force in ameliorating the world's troubles, the pope's successes in this area have admirably served his Church.

Regardless of the widely held notion that the *state* of the Vatican provides the theoretical framework on which hangs Church conduct of its international diplomacy, the Holy See considers that the right of sovereignty in international law it enjoys to be irrespective of their status of Vatican City as an independent state. During its more than half century without even nominal sovereign land holdings to serve as a "country," it continued to send and receive diplomatic representatives. In modern terms, a limited comparison of the diplomatic role of the Holy See during that period (1870 to 1929) is available: Both the United Nations and the Order of Malta enjoy a similar internationally recognized "right of legation"—neither is a state, yet both are in many respects treated by the international community in ways analogous to that of the papacy. The recent opening by the United States of full diplomatic relations with the Vatican has been characterized as the establishment of formal ties with a "church," and this must be acknowledged. (The ties have been legally challenged in the U.S. District Court in Philadelphia by a group called "Americans United for Separation of Church and State," whose members assert the "unfairness of one faith having a special unique relationship with the U.S. government.") Even though a case can be made that the relationship is with the independent state of the Vatican City, the formal diplomatic letters of credence make no mention of the "Vatican" or "Vatican City" but only of the "Holy See." This convention is, incidentally, followed by the United Nations in its formal references to the papal entity.

The Secretariat of State is more in the nature of a prime ministry than a foreign office (or State Department, in American terms). It sprang from the cardinal nephew system, wherein that high official, related to and thus trusted implicitly by the pope, acted as the papal first minister. When the stigma of nepotism demanded that the position of cardinal nephew be abolished in the seventeenth century, the new office of cardinal secretary of state filled the void.

Today the Secretariat serves as John Paul's chief operational division under the efficient management of Agostino Casaroli, a man whose spectacular rise to his current position of power was based in part on his skillful development of a Vatican *Ostpolitik* for Paul VI. Writer Paul Hofmann correctly referred to him as the "Vatican's Henry Kissinger" during the years he negotiated with Europe's Communist regimes, as well as with Cuba. Casaroli's latest major coup has the establishment of a new concordat with Italy, replacing the one it signed with Mussolini in 1929 and that was the basis for its modern relationship with the Italian state. On February 18, 1984, the cardinal joined Socialist prime minister Bettino Craxi in Rome's sixteenth-century Villa Madama to cosign, with golden pens, the fourteen-article concordat establishing major changes in the relationship between the two sovereign states from those set fifty-five years earlier in the Lateran Accord. The most far-reaching clause declares that the "Italian republic and the Holy See reaffirm that the state and the Catholic Church are, each in its own domain, sovereign. . . ." This is a considerable alteration in the vast powers the Holy See was formerly guaranteed over even civil affairs in Italy and one eliminating Roman Catholicism as Italy's state religion. One article grants parents the right to choose whether their children should receive religious instruction in public schools; another changes annulment proceedings; state subsidies to clergy and Church institutions are replaced with a program partially financed by tax deductions; and the concept of the special "sacred character" of Rome is abandoned. The concordat was formally ratified in June 1985.

Casaroli, as prefect of the Council for Public Affairs of the Church, an independent 1967 creation of Paul VI that serves as a sort of foreign-affairs ministry, must attend to the formal diplomatic relations the Holy See maintains with 116 countries and the Order of Malta. The United States wasn't included in this number before 1983; it had until then sent only a "personal representative of the president." The Vatican does not send a diplomatic representative to the United Nations itself, but it is represented in several of that organization's specialized agencies. Incidentally, the Holy See is generally not the initiator of diplomatic relations with a country; it prefers to wait until it is *asked* to exchange diplomatic representatives. Conversely, the Vatican almost never makes the first move when it comes to breaking off diplomatic relations.

Headquartered next to the Secretariat of State on the top floor of the Apostolic Palace (Casaroli's private apartment is one floor higher in the palace) in some of the best-furnished and most comfortable offices in the Vatican, resides a surprisingly small council staff, including a handful of nuns and laywomen at its lower administrative levels. This staff efficiently serves the perhaps 150 diplomats in the field and runs the council's internal bureaucracy, fulfilling both functions with a justifiably renowned professionalism. Under the day-to-day control of its secretary, Archbishop Achille Silvestrini, the council is divided into three departments for administrative purposes: The first deals with relations with foreign states and matters concerning concordats, or treaties, and functions much like a normal foreign ministry; the second is, in effect, a personnel department handling correspondence with diplomats in the field and recommending clerical candidates for the foreign service (Vatican diplomats are always clerics); and the third is a staff responsible for compiling and translating papal documents that will be sent to the Church's diplomatic missions throughout the world. In light of its

nature as the diplomatic arm of a religious body and because of the
Holy See's limited resources, the Vatican's diplomatic service does
without the normal appurtenances of the world's other foreign services: commercial counselors, cultural officers, intelligence advisers,
and even press attachés.

The Holy See's diplomats, generically known as legates, are divided into several categories of higher and lower rank, in much the
way as secular states divide their diplomatic personnel into ambassadors, ministers, chargés d'affaires, and so on. The highest rank of
legate is the nuncio, derived from the Latin for "announcer." He is a
permanent diplomatic officer with the rank and precedence of an
ambassador and is always accorded the position of dean of the diplomatic corps—the ambassador highest in precedence—of the capital
in which he serves. One notch down, a pronuncio is essentially
equivalent to an ambassador but doesn't have automatic status as
dean, a situation that generally obtains in countries not
predominately Catholic. Internuncios are the equivalent to ministers, legates who have been accredited to a government to foster
goodwill between it and the Holy See; they are also sometimes
charged with fulfilling missions of a more delicate, personal nature.
Apostolic delegates are the Holy See's representatives in some of the
capitals without official diplomatic ties with the Vatican, of which
there are currently sixteen. Hypothetically, their mission is strictly
limited to the country's Church, as they do not serve in a diplomatic
capacity. However, before official diplomatic ties linked the United
States and the Vatican in 1984, the apostolic delegate in
Washington often, though unofficially, dealt directly with the U.S.
government on a wide range of matters relating to the Church and
the Holy See. Finally, a pontifical representative is a legate assigned
specific missions to local churches.

If it is true that members of the Vatican diplomatic service are
receiving the finest diplomatic experience available in the world, so
then are the representatives of foreign states assigned to the Vatican
likewise in a position to gain inordinately useful experience in their
assignments. Vatican diplomatic duty usually represents a plum
post in each country's foreign service because of the opportunity it
affords to observe closely the skilled functioning of the supranational
Holy See. The Vatican no longer accepts ecclesiastics as representatives, and currently there are no women in the role of a head of mis-

sion to the Vatican. Furthermore, the Vatican generally will not accept ambassadors who are at the same time accredited to Italy (although exceptions are sometimes made). Diplomats assigned to the Holy See do not actually reside within the Vatican City itself because of its size, but even though living in Rome they enjoy the customary diplomatic immunities afforded by the papal state as though they were on Vatican territory.

Representatives of the Holy See serving abroad as legates have more or less work to do depending largely on the size of the Catholic population in the country to which they have been assigned. The traditional "first class" nunciatures are Paris, Lisbon, Madrid, and Vienna, both because of their historical importance and their countries' large Catholic majorities, but today Washington or Warsaw is likely to be at least as important. Diplomatic relations have been established by the Holy See with governments of several Communist countries, including Yugoslavia and Cuba, but not so far with the Soviet Union or China, although Cardinal Casaroli has stated that "indirect contacts" have been achieved with the latter. Neither have ties been made with Israel or Jordan, the Vatican stating that relations can only come after "further resolution of the region's problems."

Vatican legations are invariably small, usually no more than two or three accredited representatives in each. The head of mission generally will be a prelate and probably will have studied his craft at the Pontifical Ecclesiastical Academy, the principal training school for the service. Italians still make up the great preponderance of Vatican diplomats serving abroad, but a man of any nationality could be sent to any country; the first postwar nuncio in Bonn was a former American archbishop, Aloysius Muench of Fargo, North Dakota. There is, for that matter, no rule barring an American from being posted as the Vatican pronuncio to Washington (currently an Italian, Archbishop Pio Laghi, fills the role). Nuncios and pronuncios are formally accredited to heads of state, but the larger share of their duties involve Church business with local bishops. Vatican diplomats are, in effect, the primary liaison officers between the Holy See and its worldwide episcopate, although since Vatican II and the subsequent strengthening of national episcopal conferences, this traditional intermediary role has been somewhat eroded.

The modern successes of the Vatican's diplomatic service are very much in keeping with the mellow glow of its reputation from past centuries. Two notable examples of this excellence are the finesse with which it has handled the Church's delicate adversarial relationship with the Polish Communist government, and the groundwork for finally opening full diplomatic relations with the United States, an achievement that would have seemed very unlikely not many years ago considering traditional U.S. hostility to the notion. In keeping with the practice of quiet excellence, there seems little doubt that the Holy See's international representation will continue to garner the respect of the world community.

The congregations of the Church, most of which are settled comfortably in the Fascist-era office complexes at the end of the Via della Conciliazione, are powerful bureaucracies making daily decisions that will bear on the lives of millions of Catholics—and not a few non-Catholics—around the world. Like the permanent civil service bureaucracies in any government, the Vatican's ministries have long successfully resisted too-strong winds of change, even sometimes those that blow from the Apostolic Palace itself.

An idiosyncratic mix of modern high-tech corporate efficiency and medieval theocracy, these highest branches of the Roman Catholic corporate organization chart are to a large extent intertwined through the multiple memberships of their directors on many governing boards, putting the congregations under the effective control of a relative handful of powerful curial cardinals. Cardinal Casaroli, for example, serves not only as secretary of state but also heads the Church's Council for Public Affairs (as its prefect) and serves on two of the congregations' boards and those of a number of the lesser secretariats and commissions; other cardinals are members of the governing councils of even greater numbers of the Church's administrative bodies. While this sort of interrelated work undoubtedly provides for a better grasp of the Church's big picture and maybe even for quicker decision-making, it also opens it to charges of autocracy, today an ironically uncomfortable jab at a newly image-conscious institution that in the past had never pretended to be anything *but* an autocracy.

Of the ten sacred congregations, eight are located in the two matching office buildings at the end of the Via della Conciliazione and one in its own building in the Piazza di Spagna. The tenth and most senior has its headquarters in the old palace in the Largo

Sant'Uffizio, to the left of the St. Peter's Square colonnades, outside, but an extraterritorial possession of, the Vatican state. Founded in 1542 as the Congregation of the Holy Inquisition of Heretical Error, its purpose was to serve as an agency to combat heresy. It later changed that designation, too redolent of the physical excesses for which it and some of its branches were once notorious, to the less ominous-sounding Congregation of the Holy Office (at the same time merging with the old Congregation of the Index), the name by which its headquarters building is still known. Its latest postconciliar transformation is to the Congregation for the Doctrine of the Faith, still dealing with doctrinal matters of faith and morals and "dogmatic errors contrary to Catholic teaching." Since 1969, the lay thirty-member International Theological Commission—set up to represent the spectrum of Catholic thought but now dominated by the center and right of center—has assisted the congregation in its deliberations.

This most traditionally secret of all Vatican departments is still perhaps most widely known for the famous Index, the list of books once proscribed for Catholics under penalty of excommunication, a "guide" that today only requires the exercise of "prudence"; the congregation still sees to it, however, that all books sold at, or distributed from, churches have the approval of competent ecclesiastical authority. An example of the sort of doctrinal decisions now being made by the congregation was the recent move to deny to the radical German theologian Hans Küng the right formally to continue to designate himself an expressly *Catholic* theologian, a relatively mild form of censure compared with some acts of the past. Its latest international notice has come from its announced plans to inquire into the possible heresy of the Reverend Leonardo Boff, a forty-six-year-old Brazilian priest from São Paulo and theology lecturer at the Brazilian Catholic University of Petropolis, who seeks to reconcile the Church's traditional teachings with Marxist revolutionary theory in spite of direction to the contrary. The act earned the priest a sharp rebuke from the congregation in March 1985, the Church taking the view that Boff's teachings "endanger the sound doctrine of the faith."

After the relative liberalism of the Pauline years, the Congregation for the Doctrine of the Faith has taken a turn right to a more conservative stance under John Paul II. But even John Paul's conservatism is strongly condemned in some quarters as too liberal, most notably by the ultrarightist Archbishop Marcel Lefebvre, who accused the "suppressed" congregation of allowing the free spread of "heresies" in a 1984 open letter to the pope in *The Wall Street Journal*. Even though the brand of traditional Catholicism espoused by Lefebvre is not likely to become the Church's norm again, the congregation has the same standing orders from the Apostolic Palace shared with the other curial departments: to direct its primary efforts toward the restoration of Church discipline. The new head of the congregation is Cardinal Joseph Ratzinger, a former archbishop of Munich and an outspoken opponent of "liberation theology." The cardinals opposition to liberation theology is based not, he explains, on its use of Marxist socioeconomic theory, but because it injects social theory "into the fundamental postulates of the gospel" and "raises social theory to the level of theology." In this, Ratzinger is very much in tune with the pope, who has stated that "the solidarity of the church with the poor . . . cannot be dictated by an analysis based on class distinctions and class struggles." Ratzinger has publicly stated that the Church's current crisis came as a result of Vatican II, whose reforms passed from "self-criticism to self-destruction." With the prefect's views reflecting so accurately those of his pontiff, Ratzinger's role in the hierarchy is bound to be a powerful one.

The Sacred Congregation for the Bishops, formerly the Sacred Consistorial Congregation and founded in 1588, does the work of screening episcopal candidates vetted by local nuncios and apostolic delegates (except for those to missionary countries, about 20 to 25 percent of the total) for the pope's approval, as well as the more mundane task of setting boundaries for newly established dioceses (two new ones were created in Florida in the summer of 1984) and coordinating relations between Rome and the various episcopal conferences around the world. It also has the incidental responsibility for the romantically named Apostolate of the Sea, ministering to merchant seamen and those involved in the maritime industry.

The congregation's prefect is considered by many to be the most powerful curial position after the cardinal secretary of state. In a surprise move in the spring of 1984, the pope named to the post sixty-two-year-old Cardinal Bernardin Gantin, from the People's Republic of Benin, an important step in the John Pauline agenda of internationalizing the hierarchy. The first black African to head a congregation, Gantin most recently earned John Paul's trust for his successful presidency of the Pontifical Council "Cor Unum" and the Pontifical Commission "Justice and Peace" (see below), *and* for his theological conservatism. Known and respected by John Paul since their meeting at the Second Vatican Council, Gantin, six-feet, two inches tall and distinguished as one of the Vatican's friendliest and most engaging personalities, shares the pope's rejection of the Marxist mystique of "anthropocentrism"—the theory that the universe is man-centered. Gantin's appointment marked the first time in the Vatican's modern history that bishops of the world were chosen without Italian traditionalism being the dominant force. Parenthetically, the congregation's second-in-command is also a Third World prelate, Archbishop Lucas Moreira Neves of Brazil.

The Congregation for the Oriental Church, a nineteenth-century creation of Pius IX, deals with more than twenty Eastern Rite churches and their 11 million members; the seven Oriental patriarchs are included on its governing council. Its prefect is Cardinal Wladyslaw Rubin of Poland. The Congregation for the Sacraments and Divine Worship was a 1975 creation by Paul VI from two older departments and was on April 5, 1984, divided by John Paul II into two separate bodies, the Congregation for the Sacraments and the Congregation for Divine Worship. The two primarily concern themselves with liturgical books and reform and with matters of priestly ordination. Included in this latter role is the tricky question of releasing priests from their vows, an issue not treated as liberally by the present pope as it was by Paul VI, who granted thirty thousand dispensations in the mass exodus of the years following Vatican II. The new proprefect for both congregations, Archbishop Augustine Mayer of West Germany, is known to frown on the sort of innovation that became nearly daily occurrences during the height of the Church's period of liberalization. One of the thorniest issues facing Mayer will be the implementation of new Church guidelines for the mass in Latin, the so-called Tridentine rite, recently allowed but only under extremely limited circumstances.

Until recently the Congregation for the Clergy had as its prefect an American cardinal, John J. Wright, onetime bishop of Pittsburgh, and consequently came to have a particularly close relationship with the American Church. The congregation was founded

in the sixteenth century as the Congregation of the Council as a vehicle to implement the reforms of the Council of Trent. Today it
covers three broad areas: the overseeing of pastoral norms for the
clergy—clerical garb, fasts and abstinence, mass obligations, and
stipends; catechetics—the review and approbation of national catechism taught outside of parochial schools; and administration—
diocesan and parochial finance, and pensions for diocesan clergy. An
archconservative Italian cardinal, Silvio Oddi, a staunch backer of
Opus Dei, heads the congregation. His orthodox views were recently reflected in a retreat he held for priests, the participants hearing from the cardinal that priests "do not need the love of a man or a
woman to achieve a complete personality," and that "it is a sad and
serious error to insinuate that a priest requires the love of another
mortal to achieve maturity."

The Congregation for Religious and for Secular Institutes' primary involvement is with the tens of thousands of men and
women—priests, brothers, and nuns—who live in religious
communities and have sworn vows of poverty, chastity, and obedience. Now involved in a consuming and far-reaching struggle with
many of the 120,000 women religious in the United States over
feminist issues, the congregation is faced with openly rebellious sisters who no longer accept Vatican control over the minutest details
of their lives. Ironically, many believe the rapid decline in the number of nuns has been accelerated, at least in part, by the easing of
traditional discipline, now being unilaterally brought about by the
religious orders themselves after being triggered by conciliar-
inspired reforms. The congregation is the Vatican's front line in
dealing with these explosive issues, and its defense of John Paul II's
belief that religious sisters must lead lives of cloistered prayer and
contemplation is sure to keep the congregation in turmoil and severely try the management skills of its new proprefect, Archbishop
Jean Jerome Hamer of Belgium, formerly an official of the Congregation for the Doctrine of the Faith who bears a reputation as a conservative, if not as a hard-liner.

One of the Vatican's most powerful departments—its cardinal
prefect is sometimes called the "red pope"—was long known as the
Propaganda Fide, or the Congregation for the Propagation of the
Faith. Since the Nazi lexicon irremediably stigmatized the connotation of "propaganda," it was felt necessary to change its name to that

of the slightly less pithy but more acceptable Congregation for the Evangelization of Peoples. New name or not, its main role is still to oversee missionary activities and Christian life in areas where the Catholic Church's domain is minimal. Until 1908, the United States was included under the aegis of the Propaganda Fide, even though it had, of course, by that time long since ceased to be anything like a missionary country. The congregation also deals with the appointment of bishops in missionary areas. It is the only one of the congregations located at some remove from the Vatican, in its own Renaissance palace in the Piazza di Spagna, near the Spanish Steps in the heart of Rome's tourist area. John Paul's recent choice to head it as proprefect was the archbishop of Dublin, who was at the time Dermot J. Ryan.

The final two congregations are those for the Causes of the Saints, which prepares the groundwork for the beatifications and canonizations of the Church's saints, and that for Catholic Education, formerly the Congregation of Seminaries and Universities, an expansion of its area of responsibility to cover all orders and degrees of Catholic education, including seminaries. The former is headed by Cardinal Pietro Palazzini, like Oddi, a strong Opus Dei supporter; the latter's prefect is an American cardinal, William Wakefield Baum, a former archbishop of Washington, D.C. and now the highest ranking American of the Vatican.

Immediately below the Sacred Congregations in curial precedence are the three tribunals, all ancient Vatican departments whose shared function is primarily the administration of justice. The first is the Sacred Apostolic Penitentiary, an office whose head was first mentioned in the twelfth century as the "cardinal who hears confession from the pope." It has evolved into a tribunal adjudicating issues of favors, absolutions, dispensations, and the use of indulgences. It would, for instance, deal with the issue of a priest requesting absolution after having been automatically excommunicated for "attempting" a marriage as no such marriage can be considered valid by the Church. The Supreme Tribunal of the Apostolic Segnatura is a sort of Vatican Supreme Court, although *any* decision made by *any* Vatican body can be altered or voided by the pope. Made up of six cardinals, the court reviews questions of procedural error for the other two courts, particularly the Sacred Roman Rota.

Unquestionably the best known of the Vatican's courts and the one that most affects the lives of ordinary Catholics is the famous Sacred Roman Rota, often incorrectly termed the Holy Roman Rota. Before 1870 it served as the Tribunal of Appeal for the Papal States, a function that their absorption into the Italian kingdom obviated. The Rota's primary area of care today is its well-known review of requests for marriage dissolutions, cases upon which it sits in judgment. In the canonical eyes of the Roman Catholic Church, there is no such thing as a valid "divorce"; for a Catholic to be allowed remarriage, proof must be presented to the Rota's three-man judicial panels that an ecclesiastically acceptable impediment to his or her first marriage existed in the first place, which is to say that no *valid* marriage ever took place. The problems inherent in this position based on the Church's inviolable marriage sacrament are obvious, painful, and—because petitions are backlogged from Catholics all over the world—inevitably protracted. Twenty-one prelates serve as the court's justices.

The three Vatican secretariats are essentially postconciliar creations (although the first was founded in 1960) in that they are consultative bodies whose main purpose is the establishment of "dialogue," a catchword of the Vatican II reforms. The most important, the Secretariat for Christian Unity, has two main sections, one for establishing "dialogue" with the various Western Christian denominations and the other to achieve the same thing with the Eastern and Orthodox churches. Union is the long-term goal, but a kind of union that at heart presupposes some form of Roman control. The secretariat's most publicly visible achievement has been laying groundwork for rapprochment between Rome and the Anglican Church.

Paul VI established the other secretariats—those for Non-Christians, concerned with "dialogue" rather than proselytization and led by Francis Arinze, a fifty-two-year-old former archbishop of Onitsha, in Nigeria, and for Non-Believers, which does the same thing with atheists and is under Archbishop Paul Poupard. These are considerably smaller and have less to show for their efforts, partly because of their somewhat vague purpose. Separate commissions for Judaism and Islam are subordinate to the Secretariat for Non-Christians.

Following the secretariats in precedential order are the large number of pontifical councils, commissions, and committees of the Curia, many of which are Pauline creations to implement the recommendations of Vatican II. The Council for the Laity is charged with promoting the religious activities of the lay members of the Church and is one of the few curial departments with lay members at its executive level, including several women; it is under the presidency of Cardinal Eduardo Pironico. Another with civilians, including women, is the Pontifical Justice and Peace Commission, under the presidency of the former archbishop of Marseilles, Cardinal Roger Etchegeray. Etchegeray's commission started out in 1967 with its basic concerns in the area of economic aid to the developing nations from the developed nations but is now involved with human rights and the peace-*cum*-antiwar movement, a subject closely supported by the pope himself.

One of the most visible departments of the Curia is the Pontifical Commission for Social Communications, whose personalities and functions we'll look at more closely in the next chapter; the commission serves basically as the Holy See's public voice. The Pontifical Council "Cor Unum" (One Heart), also under Etchegeray's presidency, serves as the coordinating body for the distribution of funds to the various Catholic charities and aid organizations; among its many international members is the American Catholic Relief Services.

A dozen or so more bodies follow under this category: the Committee for Historical Sciences, the Commission for Sacred Archaeology; the Commission for the Interpretation of the Decrees of the Second Vatican Council; the Council for the Family; and the Council for Culture. The *Annuario Pontificio*—the Vatican directory (see the following chapter)—lists each body along with its governing members.

What are now termed the "offices" of the Curia have names with more historical associations than the group of new departments we've just looked at. The Apostolic Camera was founded in the eleventh century (under the papal *camerlengo*, or chamberlain, hence the name) to administer financially the temporal goods of the Holy See and of the Curia. Today the responsibilities of the Apostolic Camera are the same but in a very much more limited way, coming into effect only during a papal interregnum.

The Prefecture for the Economic Affairs of the Holy See, a sort of Vatican Treasury Department and reporting directly to the pope, supervises the activity of the Church's financial bodies, including the powerful Vatican Bank; it also has the authority to tax them. Its prefect is Cardinal Agostino Casaroli, the Vatican secretary of state. (More on this office later.) The administration of the Patrimony of the Holy See, a 1967 Pauline creation, and now headed by Cardinal Agnelo Rossi, is one of the Vatican's main policymaking bodies for finances.

The largest of the offices in terms of staff, the Prefecture of the Papal Household, the Casa Pontifica, was the result of another 1967 reorganization of three considerably older Vatican departments: the Sacred Congregation for Ceremonial (the downgrading of the Holy See's ceremonial activities since Vatican II is reflected in the demotion of this congregation from a full congregation to simply part of an office), the Office of the Majordomo, and the Office of the Maestro di Camera. Besides control over the papal household and ceremonials, the prefecture is responsible for the pope's many and logistically complicated journeys abroad. Papal audiences as well as the establishment of relative precedence of the Vatican's departments and individuals are under its area of authority, as is the Swiss Guard.

Visible at the pope's right hand at nearly every public event he attends is Archbishop Jacques Martin, the prefecture's highly experienced prefect. Another of its chief officials—also one of the Vatican's most recognizable "faces"—is Monsignor John Magee, secretary to Paul VI, John Paul I, and John Paul II and now master of pontifical ceremonies.

The final category of the Vatican's departments is the Palatine Administration, technically outside the Curia and answerable only to the pope. The Vatican Library, the Secret Archives (which is literally owned by the pope, and admission to which is therefore accounted a personal concession from him), the Vatican Printing Plant, the Vatican Polyglot Press, and *L'Osservatore Romano* are under the aegis of this department and will all be discussed in the next chapter. Perhaps the Palatine's best-known responsibility is the Reverend Fabric of St. Peter's, the governing body that cares for the basilica around which all else in the little state lies in shadow.

6

Affairs of State:
The Vatican at Work

At the same time that the daily throngs of tourists are being immersed in the splendor of St. Peter's Basilica, a far different, intensely purposeful world inhabited by technicians, scholars, clerks, bureaucrats, postmen, bankers, priests, nuns, and soldiers exists nearly unseen behind walls rarely broached by the Vatican's temporary visitors. It is the marbled and ecclesiastical quiet of the Holy See's bank and the scholastic collegiality in the Vatican Library and the Secret Archives, a tone of secular sophistication in the offices of Radio Vaticana and *L'Osservatore Romano* and of close-to-the-vest discreetness in the Pontifical Commission for Social Communications—a mix of impressions that mark the papal kingdom's unique status as a sovereign religious state. A look behind the walls at some of the functions that are the cogs and gears of the Holy See may lead to a better understanding of the Vatican and its purpose.

Father Lars Rooth, head of English programming for Vatican Radio, struck me as typical of the kind of priest sent to work in the Holy See. Highly articulate, courteous, slightly preoccupied, he periodically cracks tiny in-jokes illustrative of the institution for which

114

he works, as when he smilingly refers to the station's collection of the pope's recorded speeches as the "papatheke." Rooth, a Jesuit, speaks a virtually unaccented somewhere-American English that belies his Swedish nationality and native tongue, the sort of linguistic skill that serves as a superb and typical qualification for employment at Radio Vaticana, the multilingual worldwide voice of the Roman Catholic Church.

The headquarters, administrative offices, and main studios of Vatican Radio are in a 1930s-style white marble office complex in the Piazza Pio at the river end of the Via della Conciliazione, just across from the ancient Roman imperial mortuary, Castel Sant'Angelo. But the physical extent of Vatican Radio is the greatest of any of the Holy See's services: The offices of the director are in the Vatican grounds in a sixteenth-century villa that housed the observatory before it was moved to Castel Gandolfo, while the transmitting facilities are ten miles northwest of Rome at Santa Maria di Galeria, near Lake Bracciano, in buildings that were inaugurated by Pius XII in 1957. The skein of lattice towers and rotating antennae at Santa Maria, the largest in the world when they were built and later upgraded in the 1970s, is set on property ten times larger than the Vatican state itself and was accorded extraterritoriality and diplomatic immunity in a 1951 agreement between the Holy See and Italy. The station has been under the direction of the Society of Jesus since it was founded; its current director is Jesuit Father Roberto Tucci, who, incidentally, also occasionally acts as John Paul II's tour manager.

At three-thirty in the afternoon of February 12, 1931, Pope Pius XI broadcast the station's first message on transmitters built by Marconi himself; a pope's voice—quoting in Latin from the Bible, "Listen, heavens, while I speak; earth, hear the words that I am saying"—was, for the first time, heard all over the world. (Latin started as the station's main language and remained as such until 1960.) By the time Europe became entangled in its second war of the century, the Holy See's station was broadcasting regular programs on an international scale, and equally importantly, the Vatican's Secretariat of State was keeping in instant communications with its many diplomatic representatives around a divided world. During the six war years, Vatican Radio spent a large part of its efforts broadcasting humanitarian inquiries seeking after missing civilians, soldiers, and prisoners; in all, 1,240,728 such messages were transmitted.

Constant postwar growth and modernization—it is now on the verge of adapting its operations to both an expanded television capability and to computerization—has today put the station among the most powerful in the world, as well as among the most influential. Newer, farther-reaching transmitters have been donated to the Vatican from many countries, and the staff of nearly 350 administrators (of whom the 35 or so Jesuits are the power elite), producers, performers, technicians, and clerks from 35 countries create a weekly broadcasting output of 470 short (usually no longer than 15 minutes) programs, an average of 70 every day. The majority—259— are beamed within Europe in the station's main languages: Italian, Spanish, French, German, English, Portuguese, and Polish, also the languages of the routine daily news programs. The regional-language programs go out in 36 languages, everything from Latin, Albanian, and Slovenian to Amharic, Tamil, and Malayalam.

Every other continent also receives its share of the shortwave Vatican programs, a mix of papal events and ceremonies, liturgy and religion, news and music, and—the station's spectaculars—special direct transmissions of the pope on his travels. Heavy emphasis is put on broadcasting to Communist countries and to other states that enjoy little or no religious freedom—the area in the Piazza Pio building containing the program offices for the Eastern European languages is called the "Iron Curtain corridor." A late-evening mediumwave show (broadcast off the largest mediumwave antenna in the world), following the daily rosary, is called "With You in the Night" and specializes in "light" music, which might mean anything from American Dixieland to Tom Jones warbling "Delilah." Studio "A"—the station's FM broadcasts—were the first in Rome when started in 1974 and now are sent out stereophonically.

Under Lars Rooth's production direction, the English-language programs, including a daily feature show with heavily Church-accented news, are among the station's most important efforts because of English's lingua-franca status in many parts of Africa and South Asia. What is called the "general" English section aims at the British Isles as its main target and, secondarily, the United States and Canada, where the same show arrives as an early-evening program, and finally to Australia, where it is picked up in the morning.

An "English for Africa" section develops special shows for that continent. The Indian office is responsible for fifteen minutes of English in its daily mix of Tamil, Hindi, and Malayalam. The station's well-researched justification for including Malayalam with the two far more prevalent Indian languages is that fully 38 percent of the subcontinent's Roman Catholics speak the relatively little-known language.

L'Osservatore Romano—"The Roman Observer"—serves a similar mission as a print medium for the Holy See that Vatican Radio fills as the broadcast voice of the papacy. The paper's offices are located in the Street of the Pilgrims in some of the least prepossessing quarters in the least prepossessing part of Vatican City, a condition that seems not inappropriate for the clattering composing machines and presses that run off the eight different editions informing a very influential segment of the world's population of the Vatican viewpoint on matters ranging from the pope's appointments to the publication of new dogma. The offices are a warren of poorly lit and vaguely dingy rooms populated mostly by clerics. But the slightly sleepy and underpopulated atmosphere aside, *L'Osservatore Romano* can hold its own for cool authoritativeness with any paper in the world.

L'Osservatore Romano isn't really a *news*paper, at least not in the sense of, say, *The New York Times,* and makes no attempt to cover the same territory as that reported by Rome's numerous dailies. Founded in 1861, it began as an independent complement to the official government newspaper in what would still be for a few more years the Papal States; Marcantonio Pacelli, vice minister of the interior under Pius IX and grandfather of Pius XII, was one of its four layman founders. Pope Leo XIII finally bought the publication for the Holy See in 1890. But from its beginning the Church was its de facto sponsor, and thus the paper was always vested with, at the very least, semiofficial status. For only one month since its founding has it had to suspend publication, during the crippling 1870 invasion of the papal capital by troops of the Italian monarchy.

Throughout the paper's history, its loyalty has been only to the Holy See and to the reigning pope, not to partisan interests on any side of the Continent's disputes. During World War I, when its circulation reached an all-time high of 120,000, it maintained what the Vatican called a "balanced" position in a conflict that was lacking the sharp black-and-white moral tones of the next war, when the papacy clearly came down morally on the side of the Allies. With the rise of Italian fascism, when *L'Osservatore* was seized from newsdealers and burned in the streets by Mussolini's black-shirted goons, Pius XI's famous encyclical letter *Non Abbiamo Bisogno* was published condemning this and other anticlerical attacks. On the issue of Italian and German fascism, it took an equally denunciatory stand.

By the time World War II started, *L'Osservatore* was the only free paper in any Axis-controlled territory. With a 1939 circulation of a hundred thousand and with many more anxious to read a non-Fascist account of world events, its growth was curtailed only by the limitations of its physical plant. When after the actual start of hostilities the danger to its workers became too intense to continue to criticize Axis policies, the publication accepted caution as the better part of valor and confined itself mainly to religious news until it and Rome were liberated in 1944. The day after the Allied troops entered the city, the front-page headline spread across eight columns was, with typical careful sanguinity, concerning a religious ceremony, with a few lines detailing the military situation quietly buried on the back page. But with its caution it had survived a quarter of a century in a sea of totalitarianism.

The circulation of the daily Italian edition of *L'Osservatore* has fallen to about fifty thousand today, but the paper's influence far exceeds its modest size. Smaller weekly editions that have been intermittently inaugurated since 1949 in English, French, Spanish, Portuguese, German, and Polish (the latter started in February 1980), together with the Italian daily edition (on Sundays, an illustrated tabloid-style paper, *L'Osservatore della Domenica,* is published in Italian), are read by top churchmen, politicians, and leaders of opinion in nearly every country in the world; even the Kremlin has a subscription. International reporting and analysis of Vatican news is often taken directly from *L'Osservatore's* sedate columns.

In appearance, the Vatican newspaper might be termed "dignified." The Italian-language daily is printed in a large, old-fashioned format resembling the kind of national journals of opinion that expect their views to be taken seriously. Its masthead, one of the most cleanly elegant in the world, includes the two mottoes *Uniquicue Suum* ("To each his own") and *Non Praevalebunt* ("They shall not prevail")—references to and reminders of the 1870 loss of papal independence to the insurgent Italian state. The generally eight-page Italian-language daily edition, costing five hundred lire (about thirty cents) in 1984, exhaustively reports the pope's activities, prints the verbatim text of his speeches, discusses international events bearing on the Church, and quietly reports—more in the nature of commentary than of news—on the international political scene. The front-page column "Nostre Informazioni" is the Holy See's daily bulletin board and the only part of the paper it terms "official." Although it has no foreign correspondents, *L'Osservatore* can depend on the Church's many international sources, particularly episcopal, for its overseas information. There is relatively little advertising, and what there is leans to the very conservative, both visually and in content (e.g., "Desire Priesthood? Write . . .").

The smaller weekly foreign-language editions are substantially different from the Italian daily. Little more than compendiums of the pope's speeches from the prior week, they do not carry any substantive political comment, other than, of course, what can be deduced from the papal addresses. Since the public utterances of *this* pope are rarely simple homilies composed principally of generalities, instead almost always being carefully crafted although subtle expressions of John Paul's philosophy, these translated editions do, however, have a substance and value beyond what they might present at first glance.

After it came under direct Vatican ownership, the administrative control of *L'Osservatore* was assigned to the Salesian Congregation of St. John Bosco, and it together with the Vatican Press are subject to the direction of the Palatine Administration, an extracurial authority directly responsible to the pope. The lay general director and editor-in-chief is the widely respected Professor Valerio Volpini, who heads a staff that includes a ten-man editorial board, three of whom are priests. The editor of the English-language weekly is Father Lambert Greenan, a Dominican from Ulster and one of the Vatican's most knowledgeable officials, as well as one of its most waspish commentators in off-the-record private conversations with importuning writers.

Closely tied to *L'Osservatore Romano* under the direction of the Palatine Administration are the Vatican Polyglot Press, whose facilities actually print the paper, and the Vatican Publishing House. The appropriately named Polyglot—"many-tongued"—Press, located in the Street of the Pilgrims, is the Vatican's official printing facility and can print material in thirty languages. Founded by Sixtus V in 1587, the press is one of the world's oldest. A multilingual facility equipped with various Oriental fonts was instituted four decades after its founding to serve the needs of the Oriental Church, and the two were merged by Pius X under their current name. The press's main contemporary function is printing the writings of the official Church authors.

Next door to the buildings housing *L'Osservatore Romano* and the Vatican Polyglot Press is the Vatican Publishing House. The legend "Libreria Editrice Vaticana" on a book's title page is a virtual guarantee of the highest qualities of the publishing industry. Some of the periodic publications issued by the Libreria are the *Acta Apostolicae Sedis,* the official Vatican bulletin of record containing papal encyclicals and acts, documents assuming the effect of canon law three months after the date of their publication; *L'Attivita della Santa Sede,* an annual pictorial yearbook describing the activities of the pope and the Vatican; and the Vatican's "bible," the *Annuario Pontificio*—the Pontifical Directory.

Arranged in neat little rows on shelves in many of the offices of the Curia are the scarlet-bound and gold-embossed copies of the *Annuario,* with something of the place in the Vatican that *Burke's Peerage* occupies in Buckingham Palace. A special white leatherbound copy is ceremonially presented to the pope each year. Edited by the Central Statistics Office of the Church, published by the Vatican Publishing House, and printed by the Vatican Polyglot Press, the diminutive but exhaustive—almost twenty-one hundred pages—guide to official Roman Catholicism is a terrific read for anybody interested in the minutely arcane intricacies of the Church's organization. One prerequisite is a working knowledge of Italian, however, the linguistic *sine qua non* of Vaticanology. Until the early 1960s, major language translations in the back of the *Annuario* deciphered some of its critical explanatory passages, but this thoughtful touch has been inexplicably dropped (really inexplicably—nobody I spoke to was able to come up with even a clue). Today's *Annuario* is a descendant of the *Notizie* that the Holy See first published in 1716, which after a few stops and starts metamorphosed into the *Annuario Pontificio* in 1860, then to the *Catholic Hierarchy* in 1872; assumed by the Vatican Press as an official publication in 1885, it had its 1860 title restored in 1912.

Since 1924, the book has ceased to be "officially official," but it is nonetheless still an indispensable source for episcopal biography, who the Church considers to have been true popes, the names and positions of every member of the Curia, and a thoroughly fascinating trilingual (modern Latin, classic Latin, and Vulgar Latin!) listing of the thousands of ancient sees from which titular bishops take their titles. At about forty dollars in the Vatican Publishing House's bookstore, the *Annuario* is a terrific buy as one of the best and most substantial souvenirs available from a visit to the papal state.

From the utilitarian thumping of the printing presses in the business quarter, a three-minute walk through the Belvedere archway into the great private courtyard of the old palace will bring the seeker after knowledge to what is internationally judged by scholars to be one of the world's foremost treasuries of the written word. The Apostolic Vatican Library houses the Holy See's accumulated heritage of writing dating from the earliest centuries of the Church. It is a relatively small collection of primarily ecclesiastical works—over half a million volumes, seven thousand incunabula (books printed before 1500), and sixty thousand manuscripts—compared with some of the great national and university libraries of Europe and America. It is not among the world's hundred largest libraries in size, but it is a collection of great value and rarity, primarily because of its incomparable manuscripts. Today the Vatican Library is a merger of reliquary and research facilities, a sometimes exasperating and seemingly impenetrable place for those more accustomed to the democratic openness of the United States' libraries, particularly the Library of Congress. But it is, nonetheless, a remarkably useful key to understanding the frame of timelessness that infuses and characterizes the Vatican.

First the notion—general in Europe—of a library as primarily a place where books are *preserved* is the Vatican Library's principal *raison d'être,* rather than the American concept that at least as important should be its function as a research facility. In consequence, *relatively* less consideration is given to the pure convenience of researchers at the Vatican Library. For example, for those without knowledge of Italian, anything like efficient use of the facility or even communication with the staff is exceedingly difficult, although

I was told plans are "being studied" to compensate for this Italian bias.

A request to carry out research is directed to the library prefect's office. Assuming the applicant is a qualified, bona fide postgraduate student or professional writer who can adequately justify a need for utilizing the Vatican collection—those "noted for their titles and publications" are given preference because of space limitations—a permanent or a temporary admission ticket will be issued. This is flashed at the Swiss Guard and at the Vigilance officer upon entering the papal state through the St. Anne Gate, tantalizing the devil out of the tourists. One is also given a three-page "rules for study" (again in Italian only) outlining the Library's dos, don'ts, and regulations.

Change comes slowly to the Vatican Library. Decades-old photographs of the magnificently vaulted main reading room show the same little boxes of pasteboard placards on the desks that are still used by researchers to mark the place in the shelves where a book is removed. The computerization that has transformed many great libraries has yet to make a dent here. But the sense of slowly moving time is appropriate for an institution that had its official founding five hundred years ago and that has in its collections precious documents from papal libraries dating back to the fourth century.

Many of the earliest acquisitions were once lost primarily as a result of political upheavals, and were dispersed all over Europe during the medieval centuries, only to be reassembled slowly and painstakingly over later centuries in the modern Vatican collection. The famous fresco depicting Sixtus IV nominating the kneeling Bartolomeo Platina as prefect of his new Apostolic Library on June 15, 1475, is probably the most exact pictorial record of the founding of this institution. Though now displayed in the Pinacoteca museum, it was painted for the original library by Melozzo da Forli as a reminder of its unique papal beneficence. Sixtus's newly established library was the direct result of the efforts of one of his near-predecessors, Nicholas V, who had accumulated what was for the fifteenth century a considerable collection of books. Nicholas intended to make the library available for research and to his Curia, and above all he wanted the books safe from any more of the sorts of misadventures that had dispersed so many of the papal collections in the past.

Sixtus had studied at universities in Paris and Bologna as a young man and knew the needs of scholars from experience; also he was a member of the Franciscans, an order for whom the preservation of the written word was a passion. So Sixtus thus formalized what Nicholas had begun by creating a modern library with research facilities and a formal lending system. A century later, Sixtus V built a new home for the library, the architecturally controversial first arm to cross the Belvedere courtyard, reducing it from one magnificent esplanade to two merely grand spaces; this wing, although substantially remodeled, still is the heart of the library.

Three hundred years after its founding, the library—as well as the papacy—was to endure a nearly fatal blow, ironically from an invader who considered himself a model of modern enlightenment. Having been immensely enriched by many bequeathed and purchased collections, the Vatican Library was an irresistible target of plunder for Napoleon, who saw the rich mass of manuscripts and books as a worthy addition to France's national library. Sharing the fate of many other European libraries that came under the emperor's disposition, the Vatican collection's finest elements—including all manuscripts older than the ninth century and many of those with the finest illuminations—were packed up and in 1797 sent off to Paris. This was also the fate of the pope himself, who was, with very little more ceremony, dispatched to a French prison. Most of the items were eventually returned after the 1815 fall of the empire. Since that time, the Vatican Library has been enlarged with the addition of several more invaluable collections, including the Borghese manuscripts (part of the ancient papal library dating from the "Babylonian Captivity" in Avignon), the Barberini Library, the Borgia manuscripts, and the library of the noble and also pope-producing Chigi family.

After Sixtus IV's initial efforts, the library ceased to be a research facility freely open to scholarship. That it is today accessible to scholars is owed in great part to Pope Leo XIII, who opened the papal collection with his famous if somewhat ingenuous comment that "the Church has no secrets," at the same time instituting reforms to update both the collections and the mechanics for their use. In 1911, Achille Ratti became vice-prefect (and three years later advanced to prefect); when he was elected to the papal throne in 1922 as Pius XI, a new golden age for the Vatican Library was inaugurated, with valuable collections bequeathed from all over Europe to the librarian-pope. Under Pius's direction, the great librarian Eugene Cardinal Tisserant (who as dean of the Sacred College and *camerlengo* was one of the most powerful members of the Sacred College until his death in the early 1960s) ordered improvements in the reading rooms, modernized the cataloging, and installed a new system of steel shelving—eventually to extend seven miles—taking as its model those used at the U.S. Library of Congress and the libraries of Columbia University and the University of Michigan. Many of these improvements were made with funds from the Carnegie Endowment for International Peace, to which hundreds of American public libraries also owe their existence. The reign of Pius XII saw a milestone for the library as well as the Holy See itself when the first women other than nuns to work at the Vatican were hired as catalogers.

When the neutral Vatican state became a sanctuary for politically hounded refugees during World War II, its library also became a refuge for some of the greatest book collections in Italy. The most valuable incunabula and manuscripts of, among others, the Victor Emmanuel II Library; the National Library; the Frascati Library founded by a Stuart, Cardinal York; the Library of the Institute of German Studies; and the Library of the House of Dante were offered a safe haven in the Vatican from danger both from bombings and from surging armies that threatened their existence. The most dramatic of all these wartime "guest collections" came from the birthplace of the Order of St. Benedict. On October 14, 1943, two German officers of the Hermann Göring Division warned the abbot of Monte Cassino that he should remove everything of value from the world-famous abbey, because its commanding mountaintop location in the line of the advancing Allied army put it squarely in a war zone, subject to destruction. The Benedictine monks hurriedly built packing cases, and, not far ahead of the shelling that turned the abbey and its mountaintop into a sea of rubble, the treasures—works by Seneca and Cicero, the writings of Augustine, forty thousand parchments—were transported in trucks, first to the Castel Sant'Angelo and finally to the Vatican.

So important and central to the Holy See is the library that its "protector," who holds the title of librarian of the Holy Roman

Church, is almost always a cardinal, though at this writing there is a partial exception to this near-rule. An Austrian Salesian and canon lawyer, Archbishop Alfons Stickler, the library's longtime prefect, was promoted in late 1983 to the position of prolibrarian of the Church ("pro" literally means substitute, and in this sense means the holder of the title doesn't yet have sufficient rank to bear the title proper; Stickler was made a cardinal on May 25, 1985). The archbishop is assisted by a senior library staff of thirty-eight, including eight priests.

On February 7, 1984, Pope John Paul II inaugurated and blessed a steel and aluminum vault newly constructed below the library courtyard as a refuge for the rarest and most valuable of the library's treasures. There they will be kept, permanently out of circulation and out of reach of the institution's students and researchers. But these rare manuscripts are being withdrawn for their own preservation, and exact facsimile copies, printed by German laser technology, will serve as their surrogates in the future.

Hollowed out of the basement in the small courtyard, the new vault, officially called the Manuscript Depository, eventually will hold seventy thousand of the library's most precious codexes, manuscripts, and incunabula. Nearly seventy thousand linear yards of shelving are covered in neutral surfaces of polished aluminum, a material that was chosen for its ability to resist any conceivable infestation of parasites or seepage of water, two of the greatest dangers, along with handling, threatening the documents in their old home. A rolling cylindrical edge on the shelves allows the heavy volumes, some of which are enormous, to be slid out without causing them damage. The vault itself will have almost thirty-five hundred square yards of air, changed three times every hour, and maintained at 10 degrees Celsius, with a precise humidity of 55 percent. Behind a foot-thick door in the corner of the depository is a vault within a vault, a heavily grilled area where the rarest, most precious, and most fragile of all the Holy See's documents will be kept in even more guarded isolation.

These manuscripts are for all practical purposes hereafter off-limits to actual use. But the library's authorities reason that their importance to future generations as its heritage from the past outweighs any considerations to the present. The point that the Holy

See would like to see understood is that it is making an attempt within the bounds of economic reason to guard forever a highly important part of the world's memory.

The Vatican Library's twin institution—closely linked to but separate from it since the seventeenth century—is the Secret Vatican Archives—the correspondence files of the papacy and probably the most important archival treasury in the world. Confused by the public with the better-known library, the archives—officially the personal property of the reigning pope—is not merely a closed repository preserving the past but a functioning arm of the Church, its thirty miles of bookshelves constantly being enlarged and serving as a window open on the history of Christianity and European civilization. No one—not even an inside expert such as Monsignor Charles Burns, an official in the archives for nearly a quarter century—knows all that they contain, so vast is the quantity of material that has still been neither cataloged nor inventoried.

I sat with Monsignor Burns on a drizzly autumn afternoon, with the gloomy Roman sunlight dimly refracting through the high windows in the archives' reception room. The Scottish-born priest and paleographist started his Vatican career in 1962 as a *scrittore,* or writer, in the archives, being promoted to full *archivista* six years later. Burns told me the qualifications scholars are required to meet to be allowed use of the archives, rules similar to but somewhat more rigorous than those required for admittance to research at the library. About two hundred permits are granted each year for the archives (as opposed to perhaps twenty-five hundred annually for the library). Bona fide scholars, both priests and laymen, must present proper letters of introduction from their bishops or a head of a major library or cultural organization, understand Latin, be students of paleography—the science of interpreting ancient writings—and, as Burns put it, have "proper appreciation and come without preconceived ideas." An archives regulation first written in 1927 and still in effect says, "Whoever for his own convenience . . . habitually troubles archivists, scriptors, and ushers will render himself unwelcome," giving the staff a sort of catch-all rule to remove anyone who isn't living up to his exalted surroundings.

The archives staff tries to be impartial in granting permission to use the material, but it understandably doesn't want people consulting the Church's records solely to "prove" their theses, often to the detriment of the official position or teachings of the Holy See. An applicant's final permission is granted only after an interview with the prefect himself (in May 1984, the pope named Father Joseph Metzler, a sixty-three-year-old Oblate priest and Church historian, to the post), and because of the archives' status as the property of the pope, this permission is theoretically considered a personal papal concession, with all the import inherent in such a privilege.

The Secret Vatican Archives are still an object of popular speculation, thought by many to contain politically explosive and even lascivious material exposing the peccadilloes of the high and famous, the latter idea perhaps connected to the fact that the annulment records of the Holy Roman Rota and findings of the Congregation of Rites dealing with beatification and canonization are kept there. The papers that make up the bulk of archives' historical collection include, among many others, the minutes of consistories and conclaves; material recording the activities of the Inquisition and the Avignon episode; and extremely rare documents on the Church's nemeses, from Barbarossa to Luther to Calvin to Napoleon; all of this is stored in boxes (called "registers") along the thirty miles of shelving. One popular story, usually dismissed as hogwash, says the archives' most secret safe contains the third of the three early-twentieth-century prophecies of the Portuguese peasant girl of Fátima, the first two supposedly confirming the two world wars, while the third is said to be the date of the third—and last—worldwide Armageddon.

Much of the political material in the archives pertaining to the Holy See during the last millennium has been published with the Vatican's permission, and unquestionably larger quantities— including diplomatic registers on modern leaders, both statesmen and tyrants, with whom the Vatican has been obliged to deal—are yet to be released for study. Since material must be seventy-five years old before being made available to researchers, records documenting the still-controversial actions of the Holy See, especially those of Pius XII during World War II, will remain off-limits at least until 2020, unless a release is authorized sooner by a reigning pope. Obviously, though, a pope isn't *required* to release anything—ever.

Although the Secret Vatican Archives contain papers documenting the central government of the Roman Catholic Church back nearly to its beginning, very little remains from before the reign of Innocent III at the end of the twelfth century. Constant wars and sackings, papal dislocations, and the fact that highly fragile papyrus was routinely used by the papal chancery until the eleventh century have taken an enormous toll on the Church's earliest records. Innocent began the shift of the Curia into the safety of the Vatican from the Lateran and moved the Church's archives along with it, but losses continued, especially during the confusion of Avignon, although much that was disbursed during the medieval centuries eventually found its way back to Rome. During the 1527 sack of Rome, the most valuable papal documents—diplomas of sovereigns and records of the privileges of the Church—were stored in Castel Sant'Angelo and thus survived the depredations visited on the Vatican itself.

Though the random papers that had accumulated by the beginning of the seventeenth century might be considered a treasury of the Church's most valuable historical documents, they still didn't constitute a central archives in the modern sense. Paul V finally issued a papal brief on January 31, 1612, establishing a true combined archives for the entire government of the Church, located in and an administrative part of the Vatican Library, this over the objection of some of the curial department heads who preferred keeping their records to themselves. In 1630, it was officially separated from the library under its own governing body and prefect, and the "Secret" in its title would remain very much the archives' condition until the end of the nineteenth century.

Just as with the library, the archives' greatest modern loss was to Napoleon, whose covetousness knew few bounds. He hauled them off to France in 1810, hoping to merge all the national archives he had stolen into one gigantic collection. Again as with the library, some of the material stayed in Paris after Napoleon's fall, although most was ultimately returned to Rome.

At the same time that Leo XIII made the Vatican Library accessible to the public in 1881, he also opened the Secret Archives to scholars of all countries, both Catholic and otherwise, explaining to his incredulous Curia that "the Church's one desire is truth." Leo put some provisos on his generosity, most importantly limiting access only to material orginating before 1815 (the seventy-five year rule is now in effect), the still-secret remainder to be kept *sub clave*.

Leo also decided that the archives should permanently enjoy the status of having a cardinal at their head and gave the post of archivist of the Holy Roman Church to historian Joseph Hergenroether. (In July 1984, Pope John Paul II appointed Prolibrarian Stickler to the post of proarchivist.) Three years after opening the archives, Leo founded the Vatican School of Paleography and Diplomatics, institutions that still grant diplomas in those disciplines; Pius XI later added a course especially for the training of professional archivists.

The greater danger to the archives today is from time. The documents contained in the vast Vatican collection are made of organic materials, and over time they have been injured by both fungus and mishandling of the weakened sheets, the latter one of the reasons such extreme caution is taken by the staff in limiting access to them. The Vatican Archives have nothing to protect themselves against the imponderable factor of war, certainly nothing like the mountain caverns of Utah in which the geneological records of the Mormon Church are safely buried. Many of the books in the Vatican Library have been microfilmed and are stored at St. Louis University, thanks to funding from the Knights of Columbus, but so far no significant parts of the archives have been duplicated. And they continue to grow, particularly with collections from papal offices and military corps suppressed in recent years, including the Apostolic Chancery, the Apostolic Datary, the Noble Guard, and the Palatine Guard.

Because so much of the archives' records are still unexamined, it can reasonably be said that much material explaining the history of Western man is there to be uncovered. Today probably the most important center of historical research in the Christian world, the protection of the archives should be seen as the responsibility of all mankind.

After Monsignor Burns finished his discourse on the archives, we went into the small court of the library, where he bought me a coffee from one of the peculiar Italian espresso vending machines found in the less gilded corners of the Vatican. As we drank from the jigger-sized plastic cups, the archivist told me of ideas under discussion to modernize the rather cumbersome mechanics for using both the library and the archives, including a proposed multilingual visual presentation to ease the considerable Italian-language bias. But whatever changes come, they will be made only after the most min-

ute and painstaking scrutiny of their long—very long—range effects. It wouldn't do to be hasty in dealing with the collected
wisdom—and folly—of two millennia of Western experience.

Skirting the unfamiliar back side of St. Peter's Basilica, the walk
from the Courtyard of the Belvedere to the Palace of St. Charles
takes about five minutes, a time span that delivers the traveler from
the hushed scholarship surrounding the Vatican's written treasures
to the offices of one of the most contemporary functions in the papal
kingdom, the Pontifical Commission for Social Communications.
Located in St. Martha's Square, the prettiest in the Vatican and
happily removed from the inelegant commotion of the St. Anne
area—the three gasoline pumps on the sidewalk, the only ones in
the Vatican, are the single jarring notes—the windows of the nineteenth-century building look across the formal little greensward to
the weathered walls of the basilica rising a few yards to the north. If
you're planning to write a book about St. Peter's, film a television
program on the Sistine Chapel, have yourself accredited to the Vatican press corps, or request an interview with the pope, it is the kind
people in St. Charles's Palace to whom you would turn. Except perhaps for the last item, liberal assistance will very likely be forthcoming. The stately tone exemplified by the marble floors and high ceilings of the commission's headquarters might be momentarily upset
by an agitated television crew looking for a piece of camera equipment that has gone astray, but the mood of these offices struck me as
purposefully serene, as might be expected in a place whose focal
point extends considerably beyond that of most public-relations
services.

The immensely difficult task of trying to communicate the actions, views, and motivations of the Holy See to a world increasingly
disinclined to view the Church in a largely unquestioned vein is the
primary role of what amounts to the Vatican's channel to the outside
world—if you will, its public-relations department. A slowly built
accretion of tentative measures to deal with the twentieth century's
information explosion, the commission originated with Pius XI's
1936 encyclical *Vigilante Cura,* a document that first delineated Roman Catholic norms on motion pictures in an attempt to address
and reckon with what had become one of the most important social
phenomena in history. Twelve years later, Pius XII went a step farther and set up an experimental commission to study the subject,

calling it the Pontifical Commission for Didactic and Religious Motion Pictures, a body that in 1952 had its name trimmed down to the Pontifical Commission for Motion Pictures, its basic function being to study and keep the Holy See informed on films as they related to faith and morals. In 1954, the commission had its charge extended to radio and television, and a few years later, John XXIII made it a permanent office of the Holy See under the direction of the Secretariat of State, requiring all curial departments "to ask the opinion of this commission before they order or permit anything that concerns motion pictures, radio, and television." In 1964, Paul VI gave it its present title, adding responsibility for the daily and periodical press, the latter more broadly covered by a subordinate press office set up in 1968, one that had grown out of a press center set up for the hordes of journalists who descended on Rome for Vatican II. This last move gave the organization something of the appearance of the cart leading the horse, with the Sala Stampa della Santa Sede—the Holy See's press office—nominally only a branch of the commission but certainly the largest element, and the most visible as far as the public is concerned.

John Paul's fellow Pole, Archbishop Andrzej Deskur, was for many years the commission's president (the pontiff did his friend, a stroke victim, honor by bestowing on him the title of president emeritus of the commission), but in 1984 the pope surprised the Curia-watching world with his appointment of an American, forty-eight-year-old Monsignor John Foley, to serve as the commission's new president, with the rank of archbishop. (Foley was also named president of the council for the administration of the Vatican Television Center.) Until his promotion, Foley had been editor of Philadelphia's official archdiocesan weekly, the *Catholic Standard and Times,* and he is expected to bring some welcome New World candor to the traditionally stuffy—and, many journalists complain, excessively secretive—Vatican news operation. On his appointment, Foley promised that a primary aim of his commission will be to "clear away obstacles" to the reporters' "getting the truth" about the Church. The commission's permanent secretary and the man often quoted in the world press as the "official Vatican spokesman" was until recently Father Romeo Panciroli (in late 1984, he was assigned to a diplomatic post in West Africa), a soft-spoken but thoroughly efficient administrator who also served personally as the director of the press office and who, incidentally, published in 1971 a splendid book on the Pontifical Apartments, a volume now long out of print and considered a collector's item.

One of the highest-ranking women in the papal state is on the Social Communications Commission staff. Dr. Marjorie Weeke is the person most responsible for magically removing the innumerable bureaucratic obstacles to getting behind at least some of the Vatican's abundance of closed doors. She came to the commission in the early 1960s, and while observing from a front-row seat the tumultuous changes that have transformed the Holy See, she has advanced to the rank of minor official of the second grade, a rare station for a woman in an overwhelmingly male-dominated bureaucracy. A multilingual American married to a Danish national, Weeke has raised a now college-age son while holding down a position that has allowed her a range of experiences from working with Gregory Peck when he was doing a film based on the wartime Vatican, to easing the way for a Japanese film crew recording the restoration of the Sistine ceiling, to simply becoming an indispensable source of assistance and expediter for media people who've run aground on the shoals of the Italian language. Signora Weeke, as she is called by her mostly Italian colleagues, jokes about some of the correspondence she routinely handles, such as the constant stream of importunate letters asking "to interview the pope," as though that represented a perfectly reasonable and easily manageable request. But a fair measure of authority goes with the job, too, such as arranging for the rare and logistically complicated closing of St. Peter's Square one predawn morning so that Gregory Peck could complete one of the key scenes in his movie.

The more than three hundred correspondents who make up the working press don't use the commission's offices in St. Charles's Palace, having been provided with a modern facility a few doors down the Via della Conciliazione from St. Peter's Square, just outside Vatican territory. Not surprisingly, the Holy See's press office has far more the atmosphere of Roman flutter than do the other Vatican offices with their air of stately imperturbability. Inside double glass doors, tables are piled with the Holy See's press releases and the latest acts of the curial congregations, and across the usually busy lobby is a station where earphones for the multilingual translating facilities are handed out. A corridor leads to a large reporters' room equipped with a bank of telephone booths and a long center typing table on which correspondents can bang out their copy.

The central auditorium is the scene of the weekly press conferences, held daily during special events, such as episcopal synods, at which time the number of reporters may double. A huge overly saccharine religious painting decorates the front of the hall behind the speaker's platform. The room is equipped with television and radio facilities, and in each armrest is a jack for the earphones issued in the lobby. The listener can dial any of the Vatican's official languages—Italian, German, French, Spanish, or English (no Polish—yet). Glass booths in the rear of the room house the intensely concentrating translators, a few of whom are fluently trilingual.

In an institution that has to defend its more controversial stands as often as the Vatican, the press office is heir to a large measure of controversy. Much of the press's dissatisfaction predictably comes from the perception that the Vatican discloses very little of its inner workings, a perception that is, in fairness, probably shared by the press corps covering governments in most if not all of the world's capitals. But speakers at the press conferences can tend to be ecclesiastically vague, sometimes answering questions in a sort of prelatial double-talk. When a cardinal was pointedly asked by a reporter, "What good are the [episcopal] synods?" the fifteen-minute nonanswer responded not at all to the admittedly impertinent question. Another query, on contemporary Judeo-Christian relations, elicited a homily more specific to biblical conditions two thousand years ago. An inquiry about the status of women in the Church brought forth from the cardinal speaker a nice but utterly irrelevant essay on Esther.

The Holy See's attitude that that works best which works privately doesn't go very far in assuaging reporters anxious to report what is *really* going in pontifical councils. In a way, of course, this implies a certain tribute to the Catholic Church, particularly during the current reign. What was an institution that for centuries existed but for its own members is today expected by even non-Catholics to take a leading role in helping solve the problems of the *whole* world. How it is perceived to discharge that responsibility depends in no small measure on the face it presents to the world through its Social Communications Commission.

. . .

Julius II, that Renaissance superstar of the papacy, is owed an enormous debt of gratitude by the Corps of the Pontifical Swiss Guard—the Cohors Helvetica—because it was he who did an inestimable honor to the Swiss-German cantons of Zurich and Lucerne when he contracted with them for their best soldiers to become his personal guard. That Julius's move very neatly squelched the political game of footsies the Swiss were playing with France, actions that could have had untoward consequences for Swiss-papal relations, must have added an extra bit of sweetness to the Pope's pleasure during the reception he gave to the first 150 Guardsmen who arrived in Rome on January 21, 1506, a date still commemorated by the little military organization as its official birthday. Led by their first two commanders, Peter Hertenstein and Gaspar de Silinon, the band of Helvetian mercenaries marched into the city through the Porta del Popolo and proceeded noisily to St. Peter's Square to receive from the soldier-pope Julius his solemn pontifical blessing bestowed from the balcony of the thousand-year-old basilica.

The new papal life guard had been in their post a bare two decades when they came close to being wiped out. In the horrendous sack of 1527, German and Spanish imperial troops, also mercenaries, had beaten the papal armies back to Rome, where the strengthened Swiss Guard made a valiantly heroic stand to save the pope, Clement VII. In a breakthrough into the Leonine City, the imperial troops butchered 150 of the Guards in St. Peter's Square, on the steps of the basilica, and at the church's main altar itself. This, however, gave another group of 42 Guards a chance to form a protective ring around the foolishly dawdling pope and run at top speed with him, an attendant holding up the papal train, down the Passetto and into the safety of Castel Sant'Angelo, a race during which many in the rear were killed by the campaign-maddened marauders hired in the name and cause of Emperor Charles. The Swiss commander and his wife were, meanwhile, caught, tortured, and murdered in their apartment. The date—May 6, 1527—is still remembered as the most solemn holiday in the calendar of the Guard, the annual date of a special service of commemoration on which new Guardsmen are formally sworn into the corps.

Today's descendants of those early papal defenders serve a dual purpose for the Holy See. Essentially it is a police force charged with the infinitely serious duty of protecting the life of the pope, but it is also a symbol, one accentuated by its theatrical medieval costumes and colorful ceremonial display mirroring the continuity of the Holy See itself. A sad but indisputable reality is that for all its modern training in crowd control and the martial arts, the Guard can no longer guarantee the pope's safety even on the territory of the Vatican itself, a fact tragically demonstrated when two nearby Guardsmen watched helplessly as John Paul II was seriously wounded by Mehmet Ali Agca in St. Peter's Square. The protective line they and their civilian counterpart, the Office of the Vigilance, draw around Vatican City and its head of state is a precariously thin one that still must depend in large measure on the universal respect that keeps the papacy *almost* inviolate from serving as a target of international political terrorism.

The Swiss Guard is the last of the three military units that retained a ceremonial existence after the nineteenth-century end of the temporal power of the papacy. In the same spirit of cautiously leading his Church into the modern world that had prompted him to pare down so much of its pomp and circumstance, ceremonial he felt had played an overly prominent role at the Vatican, Paul VI in 1970 decreed the dissolution of the Pontifical Noble Guard and the Palatine Guard of Honor, two magnificently ostentatious and totally ceremonial bodies that had long since ceased to have the real police responsibilities that the Swiss Guard had maintained after 1870. The Pontifical Noble Guard, founded in 1801 as a papal bodyguard, was, in relative precedence, the highest-ranking armed force of the Holy See until its disbanding. Composed solely of officers (probably the only such military body so constituted in the world), its only requirements for admission were that its members be scions of Italy's princely nobility (the commandment was traditionally from a noble Roman family) and that they be available to fulfill ceremonial duties, under the immediate direction of the majordomo, around the pope's person during the high Vatican solemnities when their presence was needed to add the requisite flash. With gaudy uniforms and fantastic great horsehair-plumed silver helmets, the corps never had any difficulty in attracting recruits. The Palatine Guard of Honor, a half century younger than its noble counterpart, was Pius IX's merging of two much older papal military units, the Milizia Urbana and the Civica Scelta. Ranked lower than the Swiss Guard, it was really the last of the regular army of the Papal States. After

1870 it became solely a ceremonial unit, open to any Roman and serving the same general purpose as the Pontifical Noble Guard. During the final days of Mussolini's state, the Vatican permitted the Palatine's recruitment of hundreds of Romans anxious to avoid service in the dying Fascist military services.

The "Switzers" are the last of the military units that went to battle for the popes and protected their state during the centuries of temporal papal power, and today their place in the scheme of things seems secure from any future papal streamlining. The Guard is restricted to healthy, "unblemished," Catholic, male Swiss citizens who have honorably completed their Swiss military obligation; they may be speakers of any of Switzerland's four languages, although the corps is overwhelmingly dominated by Swiss-Germans, with only a few Swiss-French and Swiss-Italians. (There are also one or two Romansh speakers from Ticino, an area that had formerly been barred from providing Guardsmen because it had at one time been part of Italy; a change of the Guard's constitution in 1959 was required to allow Ticinese to enlist.)

The command structure of the roughly hundred-man corps is headed by the captain commandant, who holds the Guard rank of colonel and is by virtue of his position automatically a member of the Pontifical Family and a gentleman of His Holiness, two ceremonial titles that carry a *very* considerable amount of social status in the Vatican. The role of the captain commandant has the curious and extraordinary history of having been virtually the fiefdom of one Swiss family since 1652—eleven of the twenty commanders since that time have been named Pfyffer von Altishofen, the last captain commandant (1972–82) having been one Franz Pfyffer von Altishofen. (He was preceded over the centuries by his ancestors Johann, Ludwig, Franz, Johann, Franz, Jost, Franz, Karl, Martin, and Heinrich.) The colonel today is Roland Buchs, who is served by three subordinate officers, a chaplain, twenty-three noncommissioned officers, two drummers, and about seventy Guardsmen, called halberdiers ("halberd-bearers") for the spiked axes-on-poles they carry. These halberds sometimes are still called into service, although it's not the sharp end that's used today. When overexcited spectators get a little too insistent on approaching the pope on ceremonial occasions, the Switzer first digs his elbows into the offending pilgrim's ribs, and if that doesn't do the trick will bang the bottom of the halberd on his toes. More is rarely needed.

Recruitment into the Guard has to be carried on somewhat sur-
reptitiously. The Swiss Constitution forbids its citizens to serve in
foreign military units, on pain of losing citizenship, but makes an
exception for the not-really-foreign-military Swiss Guard on the
proviso that no open recruiting be carried out in Switzerland itself.
Most of the informal persuading takes place when Guardsmen go
home on vacation and ask their friends—the Guard comes from a
remarkably homogeneous middle-class background—if they
wouldn't like to have a little adventure, see Rome, and maybe even
get a foot up on heaven. Once a qualified young man takes the bait,
he goes for an interview at the Guards' Vatican headquarters, and, if
accepted, is signed up for a two-year hitch. (After a year of good
contract, his train fare will be refunded.)

A Guardsman may freely leave the service after a three-month notice is given, but most stay for the full two years. Those who remain
for eighteen years will receive a pension equal to half their salary
(now about three hundred dollars a month for a starting halberdier),
and two thirds after twenty-five years; after thirty years, the pension
equals full active-duty pay.

The Guard's home is the barracks just to the left inside the St.
Anne Gate, an old but modernized and comfortable building that
compares very favorably to the memories I would imagine most ex-
GI's have from their own military days. A large central courtyard
has recreation areas at its corners, and the two-man rooms in the
long wing on the far side, along the Vatican wall, are tolerably comfortable. A watch office/orderly room is immediately inside the main
gate. Just outside and around the corner toward the basilica, wonderfully tucked into the shadows at the base of the Apostolic Palace
complex, is the little church that serves exclusively as a chapel for
the Guard.

Most of the young bachelor Guardsmen remain fairly isolated
from their Italian environment, although one of their first requirements on enlistment is lessons in the Italian language. I didn't ask
whether they take a special course in courtesy, but the fact remains
that every one I encountered was remarkably polite, a trait that is in
noticeably short supply among the world's security forces. Very
identifiable around the Vatican precincts because of their clean-cut
Swiss good looks and usually German speech, they are expected to
keep a low profile, remembering, as their rule book puts it, the
"uniqueness of their position." As for all Vatican residents, the gates

are shut at eleven, and for a Switzer to be admitted later involves the embarrassment of having to ring the night bell to get in.

Unquestionably the best-known facet of the Guard is its wonderful uniform, popularly said to have been designed by Michelangelo but now thought not to have been. Some attribute the colorful dress to Raphael, which is even less likely. It seems that the Guard was wearing something very similar to the present uniform when the first members arrived in Rome, but it's possible that one of Julius's genius artists added a fillip or two to the basic outfit.

A large costume room in their barracks is littered with sewing machines, bolts of the bright blue and red fabric that makes up the halberdiers' dress uniforms, and the various accouterments and gewgaws—neck ruffs, feather plumes for their dress helmets, white dickies for their nondress blues—that tie the corps to its Renaissance origins. Another good-sized room in the barracks—the armory—is lined with rows of three-hundred-year-old cuirasses, the ceremonial breastplates symbolic of the Middle Ages. Very few of the Guards wear the famous slit-trousered dress uniforms on ordinary guard duty; most are dressed in the sleeker but equally antique nondress uniform of blue tunic and knickers topped with a big floppy beret. It looks really quite snazzy in a timeless sort of way, which is an effect much prized at the Vatican.

The absolutely basic role of the Guard is to protect the person of the pope, in the fulfillment of which they are assigned to stand duty outside his bedroom at night and to man the corridors of the Pontifical Palace. Their other posts in the papal state are at the St. Anne Gate, the Arch of the Bells (in both locations they are backed up by the officers of the Vigilance), and, because of long tradition, at the foot of the Scala Regia, leading up to the papal quarters from St. Peter's Basilica. A detachment accompanies the pope almost everywhere he goes, within or without the Vatican, and all papal processions in the basilica and ceremonies in the square or in the audience hall include a contingent of fully uniformed Guardsmen armed with their halberds.

Less colorful and far less benignly historic-looking are the Vatican's civilian force, the Vigilanza—Office of the Vigilance—the modern successor to the Pontifical Gendarmerie, which performed police duty in the last years of the Papal States (their name wasn't to take its modern form until Paul VI's reign); some of the members of the Vigilance are former members of the Palatine Guard of Honor who switched to the civil force when that corps was disbanded. The officers who patrol the grounds of the Vatican (other than St. Peter's Square, which is guarded by the Roman police) belong to the Vigilance, and members of the force assist the Swiss Guard in protecting the person of the pope. In 1981, they gained some attention in the American press for arresting comedian Don Novello, who as Father Guido Sarducci, the cleric *manqué* of *Saturday Night Live,* showed up in St. Peter's Basilica wearing a priest's cape (his spaghetti-plate hat, cowboy boots, and pink sunglasses probably were his undoing), a matter not taken with any noticeable degree of humor at the Vatican; he was released after being held for six and a half hours.

One more function of the Holy See should be included to clarify how the popes have been able to serve simultaneously as head of the whole Church and as bishop of their own Roman see. Since the Church's early centuries, it has been a fact of their unique role that the popes' wider responsibilities very often precluded their being able to attend personally to the effective religious governance of Rome, a duty that always has been, after all, the theoretical base of their universal authority. All too often, the moral and political degradation in which the city so continuously wallowed was largely the result of the popes' unavoidable preoccupation with much bigger fish elsewhere. Vicars—substitutes for bishops, as the pope is Christ's vicar, or substitute, on earth—had sporadically been appointed to act in the pope's name, but it wasn't until Urban IV appointed Tommaso Lentini as permanent vicar of Rome in 1264 that the office become a stable element of papal administration.

Today the vicariate of Rome is the Chancery of the Diocese of Rome, the office that manages the religious affairs of the city of which John Paul II is bishop. The vicar general—always a member of the Sacred College since a decree of Paul IV in 1558 to that effect—is the substitute bishop, acting under his own full episcopal authority but in the name of the bishop-pope (authority that, incidentally, is not automatically terminated during a vacancy in the Holy See). In effect, the principal de facto religious administrator for Rome is a cardinal, just as the largest and most important Roman Catholic archdioceses around the world are headed by cardinals.

Cardinal Ugo Poletti, vicar general of his Holiness and justice ordinary of the Roman Curia, has his administrative headquarters in the refurbished sixteenth-century Lateran Palace (moved in the late 1960s from the Palace of San Calisto in Trastevere, Rome's supposedly Bohemian quarter), adjoining the Basilica of St. John Lateran, the cathedral church of the city and the site of papal coronations until the end of the Papal States. Poletti himself lives in quarters adjacent to the palace.

The organization of the vicariate resembles a smaller version of the Curia. A vice-regent, Archbishop Giovanni Canestri, is Poletti's second-in-command, with a group of titular bishops acting as auxiliaries. The diocese is divided into five parts, with the vice-regent having special responsibility for central Rome, and with the other four districts—Appio, Tiburtino, Cassia, and Magliana—each assigned to an auxiliary bishop. Although Vatican City is technically part of the Diocese of Rome, it nonetheless has a separate religious administration under its own vicariate; Petrus Canisius Jean van Lierde, titular bishop of Porfirione, has been vicar general since the reign of Pius XII. Lierde's jurisdiction covers the extraterritorial exclaves of the papal state, but the Basilica of St. Peter's is under yet another separate religious authority.

In keeping with the strong pastoral reputation he made when cardinal in Cracow, John Paul II has made special efforts in his pontificate to visit as many of the parishes in his diocese as possible, with frequent Sunday visits to its churches. The pope is well aware that church attendance in his and other dioceses in industrialized Italy has fallen precipitously in the past twenty years, as well as have both priestly vocations and building of new churches. That there are parishes in Rome with twenty-five thousand inhabitants and only two priests belies the assumption that the city is awash in ecclesiastica, a myth perpetuated mainly by the sea of domes in the historical city center. John Paul's going directly to the people of his own diocese—as he has to the people of the world—has the very serious pastoral purposes of trying to reverse this trend away from religion and to revitalize his Church. Added to the almost unbearable burden of the other demands on his energies, it seems utterly remarkable that the indications are that he is succeeding.

7

Splendid Solemnity:
Ceremony in Peter's Kingdom

Monsignor John Magee, a soft-spoken, dignified Irish priest, was onetime private secretary to Paul VI, John Paul I, and John Paul II, posts in which he held enormous influence and experienced the intricate workings of the Vatican from its epicenter. Today he is the man in control of the pageantry and spectacle surrounding the Holy See, the single facet of the papacy seen by the overwhelming majority of the people who come in contact with it. Vested with the lyrical title of master of pontifical ceremonies, Magee has the ultimate responsibility for orchestrating the fantastically intricate rites, formalities, and sacramental observances that have John Paul II and, very often, a large part of his court as their focal point. Based on customs some of whose origins are lost in time but whose essentials have remained unchanged for centuries, the ceremonial side of the Holy See has quite consciously been developed over the centuries to capture the attention of the Christian world and emphasize the gravity and splendor of the papacy. The priority assigned to this side of papal life reflects an institution that understands full well the symbolic power of ceremony—that the heady layer of solemn splendor is a vital and indispensable part of Roman Catholicism's appeal.

141

John Paul II's public life is primarily a Joseph's coat of many colorful stripes made up of the ceremonial, from the Good Friday torchlight processions through Rome's ancient precincts to the Holy Thursday washing of the feet in St. Peter's Basilica, but the most numerous and familiar ceremonies are the endless audiences in which he must participate. Categorized by type according to the importance or the business of the visitors, the true private audiences, those in which the pope actually engages in personal conversation, are quite a different matter from the mass tourist happenings that the weekly general audiences have become in the age of jet travel. In the narrower meaning of a personal encounter with the pope, an audience can be defined as a formal presentation, granted as a ritualistic courtesy, or, more substantively, as an opportunity for a visitor—one usually of considerable station—to have a hearing or discussion with the head of the Church.

The official audiences are among the most ritualized tasks on the pope's nonliturgical schedule, the times when the diplomatic pomp of the papacy is put on display. Reserved almost exclusively to visiting heads of state or other persons of extraordinarily high rank, numerous elements of the Curia and the Papal Household enter into the planning and execution of this highest category of audience in terms of precedence. Official invitations and acceptances are dispatched through the cardinal secretary of state's office to the foreign ministries of the visitors' countries, and the intricate quadrille that makes up the biggest part of the visit, a formula based on rules that have the object of ensuring that all such visitors are given exactly the same degree of reception, is orchestrated by both Monsignor Magee and Bishop Jacques Martin, the longtime and highly skilled prefect of the Papal Household.

The ceremonies are, of course, extremely formal, and they differ in some details according to the occasion. The guests of honor invariably arrive weighted down with all the decorations appropriate to their exalted stations in life, the women in the long black dresses they think papal etiquette requires, arms covered as papal etiquette does demand, tiaras flashing, and veils flowing. After exiting their limousines and receiving a courtly reception in the Courtyard of St. Damase, the guests together with their retinue are conducted by a knot of prelates and Swiss Guardsmen to the third floor of the Pontifical Palace. The party—except for the principal guests—is ushered into one of the large salons, most likely the Clementine Room; the guests of honor themselves are then taken by an escort of prelates along the corridors overlooking the courtyard and into the formal Papal Library directly beneath John Paul's private apartment.

There presentations are made to the pope, and a brief private meeting is held. After a photo session and an exchange of gifts—most likely items with religious significance (books are often the papal gift)—the pontiff and his chief guests will be joined by the larger party, each of the two principals then reading a short speech. The essentials are the universal stuff of official state formalities, but the halberded Swiss Guards and corps of robed prelates, the supranational nature of the Holy See, the setting suggestive of a higher authority, and, above all, the unique white-robed figure of the Supreme Pontiff combine to make official audiences at the Vatican far more memorable affairs than those in other, less exalted surroundings.

A variation on this kind of audience is the reception accorded an official "pilgrimage" group, often led by a prominent figure, sometimes a head of state. Such an audience was granted in October 1983 to a delegation from Liechtenstein headed by Franz Josef II and Georgina, the pocket principality's reigning prince and his princess consort. The logistics involved on an occasion of this sort can rival those of a small amphibious landing, the majority of complications inevitably arising out of the exigencies of modern security considerations. For the Liechtenstein mass visit, one for which it appeared that half the Alpine homeland might have been emptied, elaborately crafted identity badges with the Liechtensteinian national emblem had been issued to ensure against interlopers. The principality's command post—the center of intensive preaudience planning—was set up at the fashionable Hotel Victoria on Via Campania, just off Rome's expensive Via Veneto.

On the morning of the audience, the Liechtensteiners—who had been dispersed to hotels all over the city—were instructed to assemble at the obelisk in the center of St. Peter's Square, where they were marshaled into a huge line and taken to the Vigilance security entry point set up beneath Bernini's colonnade in the shadow of the palace. Each of the prosperous-looking pilgrims, some elaborately done up in their national costume, and a group that included members of the principality's Parliament and a good part of its media were subjected indiscriminately to the inelegant scrutiny of an electronic bomb wand, with all purses carefully sifted through. The few people without one of the official badges gummed up the flow a bit, as did a number of probably guileless tourists who tried to join the interesting-looking line but were politely turned away. After being passed through the checkpoint, each of the pilgrims were directed into the St. Damase Courtyard, up the regal marble flights of the Audience Stairway, and finally into the Clementine Room, there to await the papal appearance.

The royal family leading the delegation went through none of this, of course. The reigning prince and his huge family arrived at the palace by limousine after their countrymen had all been assembled in the Clementine Room, and with state pomp were ceremoniously ushered to a section near the papal throne in the front of the hall, the prince and princess's gilded chairs nearest that of the pope, where the ordinary people of Liechtenstein could proudly observe and remark on the much-beloved Princess Georgina's easy grace. Something over an hour of waiting passed, during which time the television lights (this was being televised for whoever was left back in the homeland) were turned on for a while and then turned off again, windows were opened and then inexplicably shut, both temperature and humidity rose to tropiclike heights, and a dirndl-clad woman fainted from the effects of the crush.

At last a four-man contingent of Swiss Guards marched into the room and performed a little drill-like maneuver, a signal that the pope probably was close behind. Another few minutes passed, and the papal party entered, with the slightly hunched-over pope surrounded by the usual *cordon sanitaire* of prelates, officials, and gentlemen ushers. The dark-suited, grim-visaged security men were every bit as obvious as those who surround the U.S. president, being the only ones not looking at the pope.

Both prince and pope read lengthy speeches in German, the latter's addressed to "Your Serene Highnesses and dear brothers and sisters of the Principality of Liechtenstein." After the formalities, John Paul, preceded by his Swiss Guards, walked down the salon's central aisle, greeting as many of the Liechtensteiners as he could reach. Photographs were then taken of the beaming royal family gathered around the beaming pope, after which the papal party left, leaving the princely family around the throne for more photographs, presumably for family albums.

Although by this time some of the hundreds of Franz Joseph's subjects were more than ready to take their leave, especially those in the rear who had missed most of the action up front, two Swiss Guards blocked the single exit. Even after the royal family departed, the ordinary people still weren't allowed to leave, the Guardsmen apologetically explaining something about necessity of a diplomatically graceful limousine departure for the principals. After another half hour, the crowd was finally allowed to start down the Audience Stairway, but—again in an attempt to slow things up so the official party could complete what had become a seriously overlong exit— only one flight at a time, the whole descending mass of people being brought to a forced five-minute halt behind the Swiss Guards every time another landing was reached. The whole affair may have been memorable for people who admittedly have few chances to see an enthroned pope in his own palace, but it can only be hoped that the magic of John Paul's presence exceeded the less than magic realities of this particular papal encounter.

At the opposite end of the scale from the semicarnival atmosphere of these kinds of official audiences are the private audiences, personal, off-the-record interviews granted either to very important people, or people with very important information—cardinals, religious leaders, occasionally heads of state who wish to have substantive private talks with the Roman Catholic leader. A variation is the special audience, also meetings in which the visitor can be assumed to be of some importance, with the difference that the audience really is private, not even reported in *L'Osservatore Romano,* as are all other official appointments on the papal calendar.

An odd concomitant of the audiences for dignitaries is the venerable custom of tipping the lower-ranking functionaries who participate—even peripherally—in the formalities. After the talks, the principal who has been received by the pope sends an aide with cash-filled envelopes to distribute among the attendants and aides who populate the background of these rites. Gratuities are not, of course, given to the prelates in the papal party or to the Swiss Guardsmen, but to forget the *pourboire* for the others is considered graceless.

A common kind of semiprivate papal audience, one often held in the Apostolic Palace before the reign of John Paul II and treasured as the highlight of a lifetime by the Catholics so honored, was the *baciamano,* or "kissing of the hand." The relatively small number of people (usually highly placed lay Catholics who came with a recommendation from their local bishop) who could be accommodated at these much-prized encounters would be conducted to one of the Noble Apartments in the Apostolic Palace and there lined up to await the pope, who would pass down the file of people offering either a handshake or allowing his ring to be kissed, and exchanging perhaps a word or two before gliding on to the next person. The pontiff would give each visitor a small medal, reaching over his shoulder to an aide and being smoothly handed the little tokens one at a time for presentation. Many of the guests would bring items to be blessed, sometimes taking advantage of the occasion and holding up a sackful of rosaries over which the pope would make a quick sign of the cross. The *baciamano* presentations often followed general audiences in St. Peter's, but those held in the Apostolic Palace itself were considered to be more "important." Today John Paul II still receives special guests for this kind of personal presentation after general audiences, but the palace *baciamano* is a thing of the past.

To most people today, a papal audience means the general audience, occasions Romans associate primarily with monstrous traffic blockages, especially in the vicinity of the Borgo. The superstardom of John Paul II has turned what used to be a merely crowded semireligious service into something on the scale of a weekly Rose Bowl. In winter the audiences are held in Nervi Hall, but during the rest of the year, St. Peter's Square is transformed into a huge outdoor arena, set up with an ocean of chairs divided by traffic aisles forming popemobile lanes, the whole oriented toward a large portable throne backed by the towering granite of Maderno's façade.

Although the pope doesn't appear until noon, by nine o'clock hundreds of tour buses from all over Italy and Europe have packed the Piazza Pio XII, spilling well down into the Via della Conciliazione and lending the occasion its characteristic odor of diesel fuel. An army of peddlers hawking everything from rosaries to pizza do a brisk trade around the edge of St. Peter's Square, maintaining the carnival atmosphere all through the pope's coming lecture, which the most distant elements of the throng haven't a hope of hearing clearly anyway.

By way of opening ceremonies, a speaker of each official Vatican language gives a short introductory address about the general meaning of the audience. A contingent of Swiss Guards then marches into the square, halberds at their shoulders. The signal that the pope is on the way is the distant increasing swell of cheering that marks the appearance of the white popemobile a it comes rolling into the square through the Arch of the Bells. From most vantage points, all that can be seen of the pope is his head, floating surrealistically along the top of the crowd. Since the assassination attempt in 1981, the white vehicle moves along at a startingly brisk clip, looking very sassy and impressive as it follows the cleared pathway marked by the sturdy wooden crowd-control barriers. Thousands of the visitors stand on their chairs for a better look as the mass pandemonium picks up, but for my audiences I thought the most excited participants were the groups of enthusiastically waving and cheering nuns, who appeared to represent nearly every major ethnic group in the world. Many were dressed in elaborate habits—one group with white crossed helmetlike hoods worn over their wimples stood out particularly—an indication that the North American and European nuns who have opted for lay street dress have not been universally followed by their Third World sisters. Blue-uniformed medics of the Order of Malta, the papal state's official first aid corps, are seen every little while running through the crowd with a body on a stretcher, someone who has in all likelihood merely been temporarily felled by the Roman summer heat, the extreme crowding, or both.

The pope first circumnavigates the far edges of the square, generously giving even those who aren't "officially" in the audience—those without tickets and thus without seats—a chance to see him at fairly close quarters (at Easter 1984, for the first time a giant screen was erected to make these proceedings more visible). He is then dropped off at a point a few yards from the throne in front of a group of high dignitaries, both prelates and lay guests, whom he slowly walks through, greeting and shaking hands, and finally mounts the stairs to his gold chair under its gunmetal gray steel templelike canopy. Aides fuss around a bit, putting a red cloak over the papal shoulders if there's a too-cool breeze, adjust the microphone or a sleeve hem, and hand the pope his speech.

John Paul will give his major talk in Italian, a language he does remarkably well with but one that obviously and understandably does not come to him as easily as his own. He gives the homily bent over on what looks to be a very comfortable throne chair, reading the prepared text word for word, with no improvisations, few gestures, and rarely raising his eyes from the sheaf of papers. The usually highly complex (not to say obscure) sermons can range from an exposition of the opening chapters of Genesis to remarkably frank discourses on sexuality and probably go flying over the heads of most of his audience.

After the main talk is completed, the pope says a few words of special greeting in several languages, identifying from a prepared list the major pilgrim groups in the audience by name, each of which causes a little cheer to go up as the pope's eyes try to find the source of the sound. On a few particularly loquacious occasions, John Paul has extended greetings in forty-five languages—an onerous task for both pope *and* audience. The pope ends with Polish, when the papal shoulders drop noticeably, his voice changes to a far more natural tone, and the words come very much faster—the lifting of the linguistic strain is unmistakable to those sitting in the seats nearer to the throne.

The entertainment section of the day's festivities follow, perhaps a troup of circus performers or a visiting group of Polish pilgrims singing a folk song, one in which John Paul probably will half join. The memory of a large contingent of sub-Saharan Africans holding up spangled umbrellas and doing a sort of yodel in the pontiff's honor was not one to be soon forgotten. The audience ends with the presentation of gifts to the pope, fancy grocery baskets of local produce, hand-carved crucifixes, presents that sometime appear to be longer on kind thoughts than on artfulness. John Paul leaves after a selected few—perhaps diplomats or other officials—are allowed the *baciamano*, visiting prelates have been said good-bye to, and a last walk around the periphery of the innermost seats. During his leave-taking, the frenzy on the part of some in the inner circle of seats reaches an astounding pitch—elegantly groomed men and women throwing *hauteur* to the wind as they climb their chairs to reach out for the pope, nuns trying to touch his face, knots of people rushing from one side of the enclosure to the other hoping to get another chance to come for a moment into the magic of the papal orbit. John Paul II seems far more like Lyndon Johnson than he does to any of his predecessors in this form of physical closeness—"flesh-pressing," as Johnson used to call it—that he allows himself in crowds. As I watched this at close range, it struck me as amazing that no injury has come to the pope from these well-meaning but temporarily delirious admirers. This overenthusiasm is known to give those charged with his protection a fair amount of concern as well as they continually look for ways to protect John Paul better in the largely public life he leads.

If it seems impious to include the masses celebrated by the pope in a discussion of Vatican ceremonials, it should be remembered that these solemn tableaux are an infinitely more elaborate matter than those masses carried out by less exalted celebrants. Admittedly, the central act of any mass—the Roman Catholic Church's basic act of homage—remains precisely the same whether the pope or parish pastor is the officiating priest, but at no other time are the glory and the pageantry of the papacy so evident as when a pontiff assumes the high altar of St. Peter's. Papal masses are rarely "ordinary" in the sense of being without a special or commemorative purpose; probably the most famous example is the midnight mass celebrated every Christmas Eve, and televised by satellite around the world. But the fact that the pope shares the same common duties as any other priest was demonstrated by a special matrimonial mass he solemnized for some three dozen couples on a Sunday morning in the fall of 1983.

Although the group wedding had originally been planned as an outdoor ceremony in St. Peter's Square, chilly weather led to moving it inside the basilica, and the church began to fill with the thousands of invited guests hours before the time set for the pontifical nuptial mass to begin. As is now routine whenever pope and public come into contact, armed guards searched everyone, causing a temporary gridlock at the grilled gates opening into Bramante's portico. But once inside, the attendants—some in dark blue suits, other wearing the gray dovetailed coats of the Corps of Gentlemen Ushers of His Holiness—showed traditional weddinglike courtesy in leading guests to their assigned sections of seats. Choice sections to the side and rear of the altar under the bronze canopy were saved for press, diplomatic corps, and prelates, with a small section of upholstered chairs directly in front for the ranking members of the Curia and other bishops. A crescent-shaped double row of seats extending to either side of the central aisle was reserved for the brides and their bridegrooms. It was easy to feel the frustration of the people seated behind the massive pillars supporting the dome, eliminating their chance to see the pope say mass.

A flurry of lay officials, priests, Swiss Guards, and security men approaching the altar signaled that the ceremony was about to get under way, and an audible murmur filled the building as the first of the bridal couples started down the longest church aisle in the world. About a quarter of the brides were in some sort of regional wedding costume; one—obviously wearing her mother's, or perhaps grandmother's, dress— had a sleek satin deco look; a good part of the remainder, influenced by the recently wed princess of Wales, were almost lost in massive bubbles of puckered satin. Considering the solemn singularity of the occasion and the distinction of being married by a pope, both brides and their grooms displayed an admirable and fittingly Italian composure.

When all the couples were seated in their semicircle of chairs, the basilica suddenly and overwhelmingly was transformed in what surely became one of the magical moments of a lifetime for those fortunate enough to experience it. Coincidental with the distant applause that started from the rear of the nave, heralding the pope's arrival, massive banks of enormously bright lights changed what had been merely a bright interior into a sea of white light, throwing every detail of St. Peter's baroque ornamentation into a knife-edged relief. The massed voices of dozens of choirboys rang out at the same moment, and everyone in the congregation instantly stood, many applauding and cheering with vigorous and quite unself-conscious gusto. The Swiss Guard drew its collective self to attention, halberds at the ready. Even the smoke from censers curling up in fragrant wisps to the under side of Bernini's canopy lent a note of being outside of reality. The pope, accompanied by his personal escort of Swiss Guards and followed by a procession of scarlet-robed prelates, slowly, majestically, and smilingly made his way down the long aisle, accompanied every foot of the way by the cheers of a congregation gone gleefully mad. It was a moment that could extinguish the heartiest flames of cynicism.

The pope's homily—spoken partly in German, in recognition of those in the wedding group from northern Italy whose native language it is—was being both broadcast live over Vatican Radio and televised, the camera operators perched on the little balcony midway up the pillar of St. Longinus. The papal homily reminded the couples of the deeply held John Pauline belief that they must "discern the rhythms of human fertility and regulate . . . parenthood according to these rhythms." The pope then left his throne and went down to the arc of about-to-be husbands and wives, accompanied by an assistant with a silver tray sparkling with golden wedding rings, and there personally officiated over the individual exchange of vows of each of the couples. The pledging of troths was heard by the congregation over loudspeakers, the same loudspeakers that had a few minutes before carried the request to the assembly not to stand on their chairs to improve their views. One of the couples was Gypsy, a thoughtful and needed papal reminder that that much-maligned group is as deserving of the pope's blessings as any other. After giving each bridal pair a copy of *Familiaris Consortio,* an apostolic exhortation dealing with marriage and the family that he himself had written in 1980, John Paul returned to the high altar to complete the service with the celebration of the mass. An hour after the ceremony ended, the pope was at his window in the Apostolic Palace, giving his traditional Sunday blessing to a whole new crowd that filled St. Peter's Square from one far colonnade to the other.

Twice in each pope's reign, the most memorable and eloquent of all papal ceremonies are held—one a celebration of a pontificate's beginning, the other a series of obsequies to mark its end. The inauguration and funeral of a pope may be separated by a wide spectrum of emotions, but both are marked by ancient rites and the spectacle and pomp of which the Vatican is a bottomless reservoir. The inauguration ceremony of Paul VI was the last of a Roman pontiff to be distinguished by an actual coronation—the crowning of the new pope with the familiar triple tiara. After Paul started the dismantling of papal ostentation, symbolized by retiring the *sedia gestatoria,* abolishing the Vatican's ceremonial guard corps, and streamlining a bloated papal court, his successor was moved to reduce his ritual enthronement to a relatively simple ceremony symbolically confirming his accession to Peter's throne.

Before the reign of John Paul I, the formalities of inaugurating popes, were, quite pointedly, centered around the coronation, the element of the service so symbolically important that it had remained virtually unchanged since a crown was placed on the head of Leo X in 1513 with the words, "Receive the tiara adorned with three crowns and know that you are father of princes and kings, victor of the whole world under the earth, the vicar of our Lord, Jesus Christ, to whom be glory and honor without end." The pontifical tiara was regarded as a potent symbol of the primacy of the papacy since the Church's earliest days as an outlaw sect, and the crown continued to be thought of as the most exalted of all the ornamental symbols of the office down to the modern era, an extraliturgical headpiece that continued through Paul VI's reign to be worn by the popes once each year in commemoration of the anniversary of their coronations.

The tiara had its origins in the *phrygium,* a sugarloaf-shaped bonnet that was held as an emblem of liberty in ancient Rome and would again be famous as the revolutionary symbol of eighteenth-century France; it and the episcopal miter (described later in this chapter) may come from the same common ancestor, the two simply having taken separate paths in the course of their eventual development. The high-pointed cap was probably first used in an actual coronation ceremony by Nicholas II in the ninth century, and sometime during the next two hundred years it was decorated with a metal circlet, or crown. The appearance of the second circlet is known with greater certainty: Boniface VIII at the end of the thirteenth century enhanced the by-now hefty headdress with a second crown. Within a few years, the third was added, creating the basic form of the triple tiara worn through the reign of Paul VI. The three tiaras have been explained as representing any number of things, from the continents (Europe, Asia, and Africa) known at the time the third circlet was added, to the "militant, penitent, and triumphant" Church, to the popes' roles as priest, pastor, and teacher. "Fillets" (also called "lappets," or "infulae"), two decorated ribbons thought to have originally been used to tie the whole affair under the chin for stability, have hung down from the back of the tiara for at least a thousand years.

By the time John Paul I acceded to the papacy, the triple tiara had long since ceased to have any symbolism as a sacramental emblem, if in fact it had ever had any concrete place in liturgy. Over many centuries, the headdress had become a massively and ostentatiously bejeweled ornament in the manner of the crowns used in the coronation of Europe's secular monarchs. When Cardinal Montini was elected pope in 1963, the Vatican treasury contained four usable papal tiaras, including one that had been given to Pius VII by Napoleon, and used by John XXIII at his coronation. The new pope, Paul VI, was presented with a modern brushed silver model by his former archdiocese of Milan; he later donated the protohightech ornament to be sold for charity, and it is now on public display in the undercroft church of Washington, D.C.'s National Cathedral of the Immaculate Conception.

Probably because of the nonreligious significance of the papal crown, John Paul I felt it was opportune to drop the formality of coronation from his installation as pope, a token he hoped would emphasize the pastoral papacy message he meant to convey. Many doubt that the more traditional and conservative John Paul II would have taken the same course had he followed Paul directly, but John Paul I's action set a precedent so close in time to John Paul II's own inaugural mass that he undoubtedly felt obliged to follow it. With the coronation now abandoned in two pontificates, there is little likelihood that the triple tiara will ever again figure in the ceremonies marking the beginning of a new pontificate.

The inaugural mass of Karol Wojtyla as Pope John Paul II took place in gray Roman sunshine on the morning of Sunday, October 22, 1978. Invited to witness the ceremony, the second papal inaugural attended by many of them in less than two months, were the major and minor leaders of both the temporal and secular worlds— the presidents of Poland and Italy; monarchs of Spain, Luxembourg, and Monaco; the U.S. president represented by his Polish-American security adviser Zbigniew Brzezinski, House Speaker Thomas "Tip" O'Neill and his wife, and Luci Baines Johnson Nugent (Walter Mondale had been Jimmy Carter's deputy at the inaugural for John Paul I); and hundreds of Catholic and non-Catholic prelates, including Dr. Donald Coggan, the first archbishop of Canterbury to be present at such a function since the Reformation. In addition to the official guests, St. Peter's Square was packed well past overflowing with a crowd estimated at three hundred thousand people, including a delegation of two thousand of the new pope's fellow Poles, and the television and radio crews positioned on top of the colonnades brought the ceremony live to another seven hundred million people in nearly every country of the world.

When the clock on the façade of St. Peter's struck ten—the unprecedentedly early hour was a gesture made deliberately by the Vatican so as not to interfere with a popular soccer game scheduled for that afternoon—a procession of white-mitered cardinals, walking two by two, emerged from the basilica to mark the opening of the ceremony. The new pope appeared at the end of the procession, uniquely identifiable by his gold miter and crucifix-topped staff that had belonged to Paul VI. The miter, incidentally, carried a reminder of the coronation that had formerly been at the center of the occasion: The triple tiara—still chief symbol of the papacy—was embroidered on each of the fillets that hung down from the back of the papal headdress.

The most historical part of the rites, now its central ceremonial act as well, was the investing of the pope with the pallium—a simple yoke-shaped woolen band marked with black crosses—as a sign signifying his role as the bishop of Rome; as an archbishop, Karol Wojtyla had first received this symbolic mark of rank, but now a new pallium, symbolizing the heavy yoke of duty he would bear, was placed around his shoulders. The *obbedienza,* or homage, was received from each of the cardinals as they knelt before him and received the kiss of peace. The most poignant moment of the day came when John Paul first embraced and then unexpectedly kissed the hand of his former mentor and now subordinate, Poland's primate, Cardinal Stefan Wyszynski. With each of the cardinals, he exchanged a few words, and he helped some of the older members of the Sacred College to their feet after their homage.

The mass itself was the last part of the service, one concelebrated by the entire body of cardinals but with only the pope and his old friend from Warsaw, Cardinal Wyszynski, at the altar. The pope's homily, addressed from the throne and spoken in Italian from a text he held in both hands (the news on the Italian television that evening proudly stated that he had made only three "minor" mistakes in pronunciation), was a heartfelt and ecumenical plea to "open the frontiers of states, economic and political systems, wide realms of culture, civilization, and development." A long section in his native Polish was followed by shorter greetings in the nine other languages John Paul speaks with greater or lesser degrees of fluency: English, Spanish, Portuguese, German, French, Slovak, Russian, Ukrainian, and Lithuanian.

After his message, the mass continued, with two hundred priests distributing the communion wafers all over the square. But at its end, John Paul broke with tradition and went down to the crowd,

The magnificent dome of St. Peter's Basilica rises above the crowd in
St. Peter's Square.

Plan of the Vatican City State

1. St. Peter's Square
2. *Piazza Retta*
3. St. Peter's Basilica
4. Swiss Guard Barracks
5. St. Anne Gate
6. Church of St. Anne
7. Street of the Pilgrims
8. Belvedere Palace
9. Post Office
10. Vigilance Office
11. Bastion of Nicholas V
12. Courtyard of Sixtus V
13. Papal Palace (Papal Apartments)
14. Courtyard of St. Damase
15. Belvedere Street
16. Sistine Chapel
17. Courtyard of the Parrot
18. Courtyard of the Borgias
19. Courtyard of the Sentinel
20. Borgia Tower
21. Courtyard of the Belvedere
22. Vatican Library
23. Courtyard of the Library
24. *Braccio Nuovo* (New Arm)
25. Courtyard of the Pine
26. Vatican Museums
27. Museums Main Entrance
28. Pinacoteca
29. Maintenance Shops
30. History Museum
31. Casino of Pius IV
32. Vatican Radio
33. Ethiopian College
34. St. John Tower
35. Helicopter Landing Pad
36. Railway Station
37. Government Palace
38. Mosaic Studio
39. Church of St. Stephen
40. Tribunal Palace
41. St. Martha's Square
42. St. Charles's Palace
43. St. Martha's Palace
44. Sacristy of St. Peter
45. Office of the Scavi
46. Square of the First Roman Martyrs
47. Church of St. Mary Pieta
48. Paul VI Audience Hall
49. Palace of the Holy Office
50. Bernini's Colonnade
51. Information Office
52. First Aid
53. Arch of the Bells

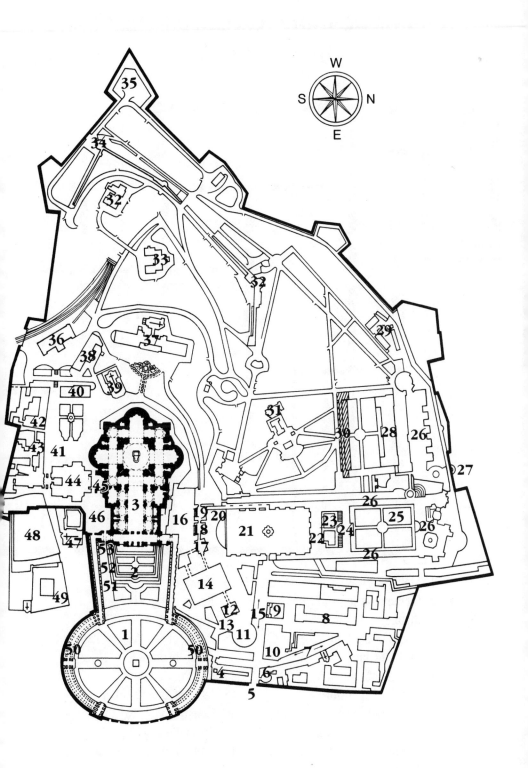

Pontifical Audience Apartments in the Apostolic Palace

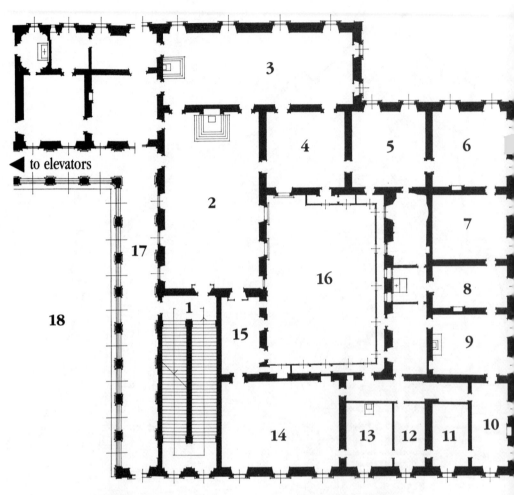

to elevators

1. Main Stairway
2. Clementine Room (with throne)
3. Room of the Consistory (with throne)
4. Antechamber
5. Room of St. Ambrose
6. Room of the Sculptors
7. Room of the Popes
8. Room of the Painters
9. Room of the Evangelists (with throne)
10. Room of the Redeemer
11. Room of the Madonna
12. Room of St. Catherine
13. Room of Sts. Peter & Paul (with throne)
14. The Pope's Library
15. Library Antechamber
16. Courtyard of Sixtus V
17. (part of) Raphael's Loggia
18. Courtyard of St. Damase

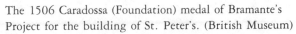
The 1506 Caradossa (Foundation) medal of Bramante's Project for the building of St. Peter's. (British Museum)

A fourth-century goldglass bowl depicting Sts. Peter and Paul. (Metropolitan Museum of Art)

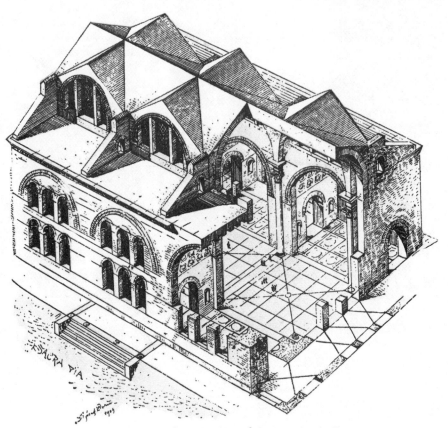

A reconstruction of the Basilica of Constantine in Rome.

Bernini's Baldacchino in St. Peter's Basilica. (Alinari—Art Reference Bureau)

An aerial view of St. Peter's Square, with the Vatican City State and Rome in the foreground. (Alinari—Art Reference Bureau)

HIEREMIAS

The prophet Jeremiah, one of Michelangelo's monumental frescoes in the Sistine Chapel. (Alinari—Art Reference Bureau)

Pope John XXIII at a papal audience. (National Catholic News Service)

Pope John Paul II arrives at St. Peter's Basilica to deliver his World Day of Peace address January 2, 1985. (United Press International)

first to a section of physically handicapped pilgrims and then to the two thousand delirious Poles who looked as though they might in their enthusiasm break down the wooden barriers and engulf their most famous native son and now, because of circumstances unimagined a few days earlier, expatriate. After the exhausting service, lasting four hours, John Paul finally took his leave from the cheering masses and went back to the Apostolic Palace, appearing in the famous window until he closed the public part of the day by telling the crowd, in Italian, "We really must finish now, it's time for dinner."

The opposite side of this ceremonial coin is the melancholy time that bespeaks the end of a pontificate. Generally preceding a papal inaugural by several weeks, the *sede vacante* is a minutely regulated interlude marked by the gathering in Rome of the Sacred College to conduct the election perpetuating the institution at the head of the Church. Earlier we saw the immediate activities carried out at the bedside of a just-deceased pope—the ceremonial tapping of the forehead, the calling out of his Christian name, the breaking of the signet ring, the sealing of the papal apartments. The *camerlengo* of the Holy Roman Church, the most important functionary in the Vatican during this interlude, now begins the preparation for the funeral. Both it and the *novendiales,* the nine days of ritualized mourning, must be concluded so that the conclave can begin in not more than eighteen days, the maximum allowed in the most recent papal ruling governing the subject.

In modern times, popes have been embalmed, except those who have specifically forbidden their remains to be subject to the two-hour process of first draining the corpse and then injecting a succession of fluids into it to harden the organs and give the body a firmer texture and more "natural" hue. After this procedure, the corpse, dressed in the scarlet chasuble proper to papal mourning, a white miter placed on the head and red slippers on the feet, is taken to lie in state, first on a high sloping catafalque in the Sistine Chapel, and later before the main altar in the basilica. The body of Paul VI, who died at Castel Gandolfo, was also exhibited there for two days before his body was returned to Rome. Numerous funeral masses will be held in the deceased pope's memory in preparation for the final and grandest service, one that has been for the last two deceased popes conducted in the open air of St. Peter's Square.

The funerals of Paul VI and John Paul I displayed very contrasting moods: that of Paul somber but not the stuff of tragedy in light of his long pontificate and not unexpected death, while John Paul's, coming only four weeks after his inaugural mass, was a far sadder affair, a rain-soaked square mirroring the tragedy of a far too early end to his promising pontificate.

In outward appearance, the two funerals didn't look greatly different from the inaugural service we've just described, with masses of invited guests; the colorfully caparisoned foreign heads of state and government; and the long lines of cardinals, cloaked now in blood-red chasubles of papal mourning rather than the festive gold robes worn for an inaugural. The body at the center of the mass, still dressed in its scarlet robe, was sealed in three coffins, one inside the other, simple containers of cypress, lead, and elm. Distinguished by the lighter scarlet chasuble marking his office as head of the Sacred College, the dean led his fellow cardinals around the altar in a requiem mass of resurrection, and the service was closed by the carrying of the casket on the shoulders of twelve frock-coated pallbearers into the basilica and down to a prepared sarcophagus in the Sacred Grottoes. The college then dispersed, but only for a short time, knowing it would meet in a few days to choose a new successor to Peter, break the vacuum in the leadership of the world's oldest office, and begin the process anew.

Early in his papacy, John Paul II made it clear that the disregard of conventional clerical garb is a matter of substantial concern to him when he warned his priests that the trend toward dressing in a manner indistinguishable from "civilians" would no longer be tolerated, asserting his orthodox belief that "people need signs and reminders of God in the secular city, which has few reminders of God left." True enough, but reversing the strongly entrenched drift to mufti was greeted in some of the more liberal quarters of the Church with a massive lack of enthusiasm.

But at the center of Catholicism, clerical dress is still very much part of the texture of orthodoxy. Granted, Rome is no longer the rich sea of ecclesiastical costume that it was even through the post-World War II era, but it still presents the most concentrated cross section of Catholic priestly garb in the world, the details of which have been little written on and only vaguely comprehended outside the clergy. To help differentiate the multigarbed mosaic of the Holy See, herewith is a primer on some of the intricacies of ecclesiastical raiment.

Still the single most distinctive feature and the mark that most readily identifies any Catholic priest is his clerical collar—the "Roman collar," a name referring not to its place of origin but to the Church that first made it the badge of its priesthood. The origins of this now simple emblem are historically cloudy, but some sources trace its descent from the wide lay collars that in one degree of exaggeration or another survived as part of masculine dress down to the late nineteenth century. Over the past half millennium, men's collars had gradually become lavishly extravagant decorations, those peaking in the early sixteenth century made of expensive lace and dropping over the shoulders of many of their more voguish wearers, a category that inevitably came to include a large number of priests. Up to this point, priestly street dress, differing little from that of the laity, had been codified only in generalities: that it be in conformity with interior holiness and that it be *decens*—free of both prideful elegance and sordid negligence, the garments "neither too long nor too short." Prior to the Council of Trent, 1545–63, the matter was left for the most part to the discretion of the cleric, the tonsure—shaved crown—the sole required priestly mark. Seeing little good coming from anything representing a deviation from the status quo, particularly gaudy lay-influenced fashions, Pope Urban VIII issued a decree in 1624 forbidding the wide lace collars for clerics, requiring that they keep their neckwear simple, one version that explains the beginning of what eventually resulted in today's so-called Roman collar and the start of the papal-mandated wearing of a distinctive, nonliturgical mark of priesthood.

A different and more complex course of development for the collar has been put forward by other historians, one that sounds equally plausible and that traces its origin to the original form of the amice, a still-used liturgical vestment that took a divergent path to its modern style. The ancient amice was a strip of linen cloth, usually decorated with embroidery to mark its religious significance. Wound around the neck and tucked inside the collar of the cassock, the upper part was raised over the head until after the priest donned all his other vestments, when it was thrown back over them to form a protective collar. According to this line of descent, the strip eventually was abbreviated into a plain linen collar worn alone and held in place with a white tie. In the sartorially extravagant Tudor period, the collar and tie were transformed into a neckcloth with long bands hanging down in front, bands that eventually became distinctive clerical tabs that at one time were universally recognized as a mark of the clergy. The tabs disappeared in due course, although they're still seen on the court dress of French judicial officers, leaving only the collar, a mark which today has become a stylized white strip, often made of plastic and usually worn under a black collarless shirt, notched in front.

Whatever its provenance, at today's Vatican this collar, worn with a plain black suit—black became the required color for the diocesan clergy in the sixteenth century—and a black or dark gray clerical shirt, has become the standard working costume of priests of every rank, including the Curia's prelacy. Until recent years, the cassock—the *vestis talaris*—was the normal utilitarian work uniform, but a liberalization of the clerical dress code under Paul VI has made its wear on Rome's streets a relatively uncommon sight, although the pope's immediate retinue is still ordinarily seen in the gownlike dress. But it is still the garment the public most closely associates with the priesthood. Sometimes called by the French *soutane* (meaning "beneath," since during mass the garment is worn under the sacramental vestments), the cassock is not itself a vestment but simply the clerical equivalent of a suit, and in some predominantly Catholic countries still is commonly worn on the street. A T-shirt and black trousers are worn under the cassock, and a cincture, or girdle, a wide waist sash—black for ordinary priests—with long fringed ends hanging from the left hip, together with the clerical collar showing under the notched neck, are the only additions. Very wide cuffs are turned back almost up to the elbow, and the front is fastened with about thirty very small buttons.

As clerics rise in rank, their cassocks take on special decoration marking their new stations. Those worn by monsignors and bishops have purple piping, representing the color of the robe worn by Jesus after his scourging, along the front edge and at the top of the cuffs; the buttons are covered with purple fabric; and the sash worn with it is purple. Bishops (but not nonprelatial monsignors) add an "ordinary" pectoral cross, hung around the neck on a chain, and often lifted and attached to one of the cassock buttons by a little hook to keep it from flying out when the wearer bends over; what is called a "pontifical" pectoral cross, hung by a colored cord, the color determined by the wearer's rank, with a tassel in back, is used with "choir" dress and sacramental vestments.

A garment often confused with the cassock is the simar, which is a form of cassock with an added capelet attached to the collar that covers the shoulders. The wearing of this garment is restricted to the pontiff, the episcopate, and to monsignors, with very few other minor exceptions; ordinary priests are not allowed to wear it. Besides the small buttonless cape, a simar is distinguishable from an ordinary cassock by half sleeves over the top part of the regular sleeves; they reach from the shoulders to just above the elbows and are slit in front and fastened with a row of buttons. A sash and Roman collar complete the outfit, just as they do with the cassock. Bishops and monsignors wear a simar trimmed with purple piping and sash, and for cardinals red is used. For both, the simar itself is black. Those entitled to wear it can, if they wish, substitute a plain cassock for it, except the pope, who could but doesn't (see later in this chapter). The great sweeping unlined silk cape, called the *ferraiolo*—one of the most beautiful garments ever designed and much seen on Hollywood's celluloid cardinals—is a sort of formal evening cloak worn as an outer wrap but is now rarely seen; again, these capes followed normal clerical colors.

The pope alone wears a white simar, the only street dress normally used by him except for outerwear, which is either a red woolen two-tiered cape edged with gold or, less formally, an ankle-length white double-breasted dress coat. The pope never wears an ordinary cassock in public. White has been reserved for the popes' use alone since the Dominican monk Antonio Ghislieri came to the pontifical throne as Pius V in 1566 and refused to give up the white of his Dominican robes for the red that had been the usual papal color to that time. The hoary legend that the pope's simars are made only from the wool of virgin sheep *may* once have been the case, but today they are less dramatically woven of ordinary wool, with the warm weather version made of linen. The outfit is trimmed entirely with white watered silk, except for the gold fringe and gold-embroidered papal coat of arms at the end of the sash. Popes complete their dress with red leather loafer-style shoes, or special velvet slippers with their personal crest embroidered on the instep. Pontiffs used to have a cross on the insteps of these slippers, and clerics were through the reign of Pius XII expected to kiss that cross on greeting their supreme leader.

Three kinds of headdresses are worn with either the cassock or simar: the low-crowned hat with a broad, upturned brim, worn by all clerics including the pope; the biretta, worn by all clerics except the pope; and the zucchetto, or skullcap, worn by the pope and the episcopate. The first, a street hat—priests are not, like soldiers, *required* to wear a hat outdoors—is rarely seen in the United States but is still fairly common in Rome. The papal model, often seen on John Paul in cooler weather when he is traveling, is red with the sweatband and edging decorated in gold.

If you can't conjure up a biretta, think of Barry Fitzgerald in *Going My Way* and it'll probably come to you. One of the oddest pieces of ecclesiastical dress, the biretta is meant to be worn on the street as well as during parts of the mass, but this has been a sometime thing since the relaxations of Vatican II, especially for ordinary priests. Originally a soft, brimless cap, it got its distinctive indented folds by several figurative centuries of being pinched between the fingers when being put on and taken off; the folds, or "horns," eventually became an integral part of its style and were sewn right into it and stiffened with cardboard inserts to make convenient handles. There is no horn on the left side, except for those worn (rarely today) by priests who have a canon law doctorate from a university authorized by the Holy See to give the degree; the four-horned biretta is never worn liturgically, however. Three-horned birettas are said to represent the Trinity, four horns symbolizing the cross. Birettas are topped by either a pompom for the rank of archbishop and below, or by a small twisted knot for cardinals; their color follows normal hierarchical divisions: scarlet for cardinals, purple for bishops, black for ordinary priests. The pope never wears this type of hat, and those who do must take it off in his presence.

The zucchetto, a skullcap originally designed to cover the tonsure that was an early mark of the clergy, is made by sewing together eight triangular wedges, often leather covered with fine silk. Rarely used except by prelates and the pope, it is worn on the back of the head, either alone or under the biretta or miter, and again follows ecclesiastical colors: purple for bishops, red for cardinals, and white for the pope. The pope never removes his zucchetto except during the most solemn parts of a mass.

One other type of head covering, one that may be worn solely by the pope but has rarely been in recent times, is the camauro, an extraliturgical item of dress often seen in the portraits of Renaissance popes. John XXIII was a great admirer of the little red velvet sheepskin-lined cap that comes down over the ears. Velvet is, incidentally, also authorized only for papal use. The camauro is thought to be the original primitive shape of the biretta, which may explain why the pope doesn't wear the latter. No pope since John has publicly worn a camauro, possibly because they look ridiculous, like a kind of clerical nightcap.

The ordinary dress of prelates is completed with two pieces of jewelry reserved to their rank. We've already mentioned the pectoral cross, an official ornament of office that has come into use only since the seventeenth century. The cross should, according to the old rules, be made of gold and decorated with gems, but the gems are often omitted today, possibly because of their somewhat elitist connotations. A relic of a martyr sometimes is contained in the center of the cross. John XXIII's preferences ran to the heavily decorated baroque, and his favorite pectoral cross perfectly mirrored his tastes. About seven inches long, the extremely intricate filigreed ornament was set with knuckle-size diamonds, an astonishingly large one in the center, and was hung from a heavy and beautifully crafted gold chain sturdy enough to anchor a small yacht. The crosses Paul wore were considerably simpler, and John Paul I's simpler yet. The understated and nonjeweled pectoral cross John Paul II used when he was consecrated bishop in Cracow in 1958 still is often seen on him.

Since the sixth century, bishops have worn a ring to mark their consecration to the Church's highest sacramental office. Hollywood costume dramas still like to show the bishop holding out his hand to have his ring kissed by the faithful, a custom taken as a sign by some Protestants of the "degeneracy" of the Roman confession, but in fact this act has become another tradition pretty much eclipsed by the new ways of doing things. A handshake is preferred today. In any event, the ring is still worn, on the third finger of the right hand. A bishop can choose any stone he wishes except a sapphire, which is reserved for cardinals. Paul VI wore a plain silver ring, identical copies of which he gave to every bishop in the world. Both John Pauls have worn simple wide gold bands, the present pope's—the same worn since his episcopal days—shaped on top in the form of a cross. The fisherman's rings of the popes have on their node a small image of St. Peter fishing from a small boat; this is the official seal ring of the pope and is defaced on his death.

Now for the more complex and regimented part of the dress of the Catholic priesthood—the sacramental vestments, raiment never worn as mere street dress but instead reserved exclusively as ceremonial components of the liturgy. In the matter of episcopal vestments, there are complicating factors, such as the distinction between choir dress and pontifical dress; the former is used when a bishop officiates or is present at liturgical ceremonies, the latter are the more formal garments worn in the celebration of mass at his own cathedral or at a church in his diocese. There are also territorial restrictions on these vestments—certain items, for example, may not be worn outside the bishop's own diocese. But here we'll stick to the main elements represented at the Vatican, with digressions only as necessary.

In the same way that the ordinary ecclesiastical dress worn by priests is essentially a distinguishing mark to set them off from the laity, their sacramental robes are primarily meant as a subtle way of increasing devotion in both those who see them and those who wear them, and, secondarily, as symbols of the elements of Christianity itself. The Church divides the main outer vestments into four colors to mark different parts of the liturgical year or the purpose for which the mass is being offered: white to represent purity—Jesus, the Virgin Mary, angels, saints, as well as for funerals; red for fire and blood—the Holy Spirit, Pentecost, martyred saints; green for growth and the triumph of life over death, the "ordinary" color used at various times in the year when no special mystery or person is commemorated; and violet for penance, such as that represented by the seasons of Lent and Advent (black is no longer used). The minor vestments, usually meaning those worn under the major vestments, are always white.

Briefly, the principal vestments, those worn by a priest at mass, are the amice, alb, cincture, stole, and chasuble; added at certain other religious services are the cope, humeral veil, and surplice. The five principal mass vestments are worn over the basic cassock; the first to be put on is the now optional amice, the white linen vest tied around the shoulders with strings. Another long linen gown, called an alb, goes over this, and then the cincture, a kind of belt, is used to tie the alb around the waist. The maniple is an ornamental napkin or handkerchief—representative of one that once served a practical purpose—draped over the priest's left arm. The stole, the primary and indispensable mark of the clergy and the clerical state and used by priests in nearly all religious functions, is a long, narrow strip of cloth hung around the shoulders and neck; for accuracy's sake, the stole sometimes is classified as an insignia rather than a vestment. Finally, covering all the rest is the most conspicuous item of ordinary sacramental dress, the chasuble (from the late Latin *casula*—"little house"—because it forms a "shelter" for the priest), the poncholike garment that is thought to be descended from the ancient Roman toga. Hanging over the shoulders and coming down on both front and back to about knee level, the back of the chasuble sometimes is decorated with a large Latin cross.

The cope (the word has the same derivation as cape) is very much like the chasuble but doesn't have the significance as a mass vestment. Originally essentially a clerical raincoat, it is today used for administering sacraments, in processions, and at funerals. The flap that decorates its back is a vestigial ornament of the original hood that came up to cover the wearer's head, a covering later replaced by the biretta. The cope is held together in front with a fastener called a morse, of which only prelates are allowed a jeweled model. The humeral veil is a scarf worn around the celebrant's shoulders at the benediction of the host, and the surplice—a corruption of the Latin *superpellicium,* or "dress worn over furs"—is only a variation of the alb with a slightly different liturgical significance, mainly worn by priests assisting the main mass celebrant.

A number of special additional vestments used by bishops are generally distinguished by the fact that they are, in light of the added dignity and vastly increased ceremonial involvement of the episcopate, a good deal richer and more elaborate than those used by ordinary priests. Even the vestments that the episcopate shares with priests are often made with greater decoration and in finer fabrics, and although some of the more elaborate items have been dropped in the wake of Vatican II, a cardinal fully garbed in the ceremonial dress of his Church is still one of the world's principal sumptuary sights.

The choir dress of a bishop (these items are the same for archbishops and cardinals, differing in some cases only in the color indicating their rank), meaning that which is used at liturgical ceremonies where he is not the principal or the celebrant, includes two special garments over his cassock. The first is the rochet, a surplicelike coat made of linen, the hems generally ornamented with lace; hanging to the knees, the fringe edge of the cassock sash shows below the bottom of the surplice's lace hem. Over the cassock is the mozzetta, which is a small silk cape fastened at the breast and coming down to elbow level. The *cappa magna,* or great cape, a longer, hooded version of a cope, was once worn at very high and solemn functions but now is rarely seen. With choir dress, the pectoral cross changes to its "pontifical" version, being hung on a striped silk cord instead of on a chain.

There are two additional items peculiar to the episcopate, together considered the hallmarks of this rank. First is the crozier, a pastoral staff used as a kind of prelatial scepter and symbolic of the bishop's duties as shepherd of his flock. (During lengthy ceremonies, the crozier makes for handy support in addition to fulfilling its spiritual significance.) A stylized and often magnificently enriched version of a shepherd's crook, the crozier also is officially a sign of the bishop's own jurisdiction and thus is not ordinarily used outside his diocese. Bishops in Rome never carry croziers in religious ceremonies partly in deference to the fact that the pope does not use this version of the emblem, using a crucifix-topped staff instead.

Related to the crozier in that the two are used nearly at the same times and for the same purposes is the most recognized episcopal symbol of all, the miter. It is a ceremonial headpiece made of two triangular sections sewn down the sides, which when squeezed together make an opening for the head. Redolent with history and centuries of liturgical symbolism, the miter's origins go back to the earliest years of the Church, and its antecedents can be traced even farther, to the headdresses worn by the kings of Persia and Assyria many hundreds of years before the beginning of the Christian era. As a definite mark of episcopal office itself, it dates only from the thirteenth century, however. The headdress evolved its distinctive cleft shape gradually, from the low, concave type associated with medieval bishops to today's higher, much more pointed model. The two horns are supposed to symbolize the Old Testament and the New Testament, Scriptures the bishop is charged with explaining to his flock. The miter worn by the pope is given the additional symbolic value of a protective helmet whose purpose is to guard the pontiff against the enemies of truth.

Depending on the occasion, bishops use three different kinds of miters. The "precious" miter, generally made of golden cloth, is ranked highest and is worn only for the most solemn ceremonies. Next is the "gold" miter, made of white silk embroidered with gold thread, and the workaday model in terms of solemnity. Finally, the plain white "simple" miter is reserved for Good Friday and funeral offices. The spectacularly high, oval miters, now less seen than before Vatican II, are called "Italian miters." (The headdresses worn by Eastern Orthodox bishops and shaped like imperial Russian crowns are the equivalent of miters in that Church.)

Other than a difference in color and trim of some of the vestments, there is little distinction between the liturgical dress of cardinals and archbishops and that of the rest of the episcopate. The single sign of the higher dignity accorded to archbishops over bishops is their right to wear the pallium, the simple band of white wool worn over the chasuble and that is presented to its recipients by the pope, tying its wearer symbolically to the Church's first bishop. In shape, the pallium is a narrow circular band fitting over the head, with two handle-shaped pendants, each about a foot long, which hang down in front and in back and whose tips are black; there are six black crosses embroidered on it, one on each quadrant of the circular neckband and one on each of the pendants.

Nobody knows for certain the origin of this now especially sacred symbolic vestment, but there is evidence that something very much like it was worn by Greek prelates as early as the fourth-century Council of Nicea. The pallia are now made by the Benedictine Sisters of St. Cecilia in their Roman convent in Trastevere, and once each year the pope goes into the Confession of St. Peter's to lower a freshly woven batch down into the recessed site of St. Peter's grave. After this requisite blessing, each new residential archbishop (titular archbishops do not wear the pallium) must formally ask the pope to send him one within three months of his promotion. It is worn only within the archbishop's province and only on certain days and at pontifical masses and is handled with extreme care and reverence, often being kept in a special glass case. It will eventually be buried with him.

Until recently, when the custom was dropped, cardinals were given one item of ceremonial dress by the pope unique to their rank, but that they never actually wore after receiving it from the pontiff's hands at their election consistories: the red hat with a great wheel of a brim, so closely associated with the cardinalate that to "receive the red hat" was synonymous with being named to the Sacred College, an emblem which was taken home solely to be used for symbolic display. Decorated with the heraldic symbol of the rank of a cardinal—a pendant on either side made up of fifteen red tufts (the hat is, in fact, an integral part of a cardinal's coat of arms, as we'll see later)—the *galero rosso* would after its owner's death be hung from the vault of his cathedral church, there to remain until it literally fell apart from age.

The vestments of the pope are not substantially different in kind from that of lesser bishops, but their color, richness, proportions, and details always permit the wearer to stand out in any kind of ecclesiastical ceremony. As we've seen, the ordinary, nonsacramental outfit for a pope is the white simar, with a white watered silk sash edged and decorated in gold, and a white zucchetto. For the more important or solemn of his private audiences, the pope will wear a linen rochet edged with lace and over it a scarlet mozzetta (or small cape), satin in warm weather, and, if he wishes, velvet edged with ermine in cooler weather. A red silk stole, the red almost hidden under heavy gold embroidery and ending with wide gold fringing, is worn on especially important occasions over the mozzetta. The stole, filled with religious symbolism, is omitted when receiving a non-Catholic state visitor, such as the British monarch.

The pontiffs' formerly enormously complex and lavish sacramental vestments have in recent years been considerably simplified. For example, the falda and the fanon, two items once reserved exclusively for the pope, are no longer seen. The former was a long white linen skirt worn under the chasuble; the falda's amplitude required assistants walking with the pope to raise the front and back of the garment so the wearer wouldn't get tangled up and trip on it. The fanon, an almost equally cumbersome thing, was a sort of double mozzetta worn over the chasuble like a cape.

The chasubles worn by the current pope are not cut much differently from those of other bishops but are nonetheless clearly distinguishable by their brightness in a group of similarly robed bishops. The papal pallium is decorated with four little jeweled daggerlike devices inserted through special loops on the black crosses; the golden skewers represent the stickpins that centuries ago held the pallium to the vestments. The papal miter, now often a relatively simple white silk model decorated with a gold embroidered flowering-vine motif, may be replaced with the aptly named "glorious" miter, encrusted with jewels and the first miter worn by the new Pope John Paul II as he left his election conclave. As mentioned above, the pope does not carry a crook-topped crozier, instead using a silver-gilt crucifix on a staff for the same sacramental purposes.

Not vestments, but certainly very much a part of the papal ornamental scene in years past were two items that have now been retired. The *sedia gestatoria,* the portable throne that bore aloft the pope on the shoulders of the *sediarii,* has been abandoned with apparent permanence by John Paul II. And the *flabella,* the huge peacock-feather fans that always lent a Byzantine flavor around the papal throne and in processions, were at one time actually waved to keep insects away from the communion wafers. They had a bit too much of the royal secular past about them to fit comfortably into a post-Vatican II setting.

A final note on the subject of clerical dress and sacramental costume concerns their availability and cost. Across the Tiber from the Vatican, in the tight little Via Santa Chiara behind the Pantheon, is the unpretentious but highly respected ecclesiastical tailor Gammarelli's, responsible not only for the pope's clothing but also for that of a good part of the prelacy of Rome. One afternoon I visited Gammarelli's, where a hugely friendly clerk of Savile Row mien and excellent English (he volunteered that he owed his ability in his English to his Scottish wife) discussed his shop's trade with me.

When a bishop is appointed in Rome, I learned that he very often makes a visit to this establishment—curial and papal tailors for almost two centuries—his first order of business. The firm presents their new client with their catalog, an old, well-thumbed, and beautifully colored tome illustrating the ideal of how the newly nominated bishop is going to look in the principal outfits of his higher rank. Some of the more arcane or preconciliar items can now be safely dispensed with, but the wardrobe is still going to represent a considerable investment for just the essentials. A watered silk moire biretta is a relative bargain at 26,000 lire (just over $15), but a black cassock with red piping will cost about $120, a surplice Vaticana a few dollars less, and a purple episcopal simar a few dollars more. Chasubles can go from a low end of $40 up to a high of $750.

A finely cut black mohair suit is about the same price as a cassock. His new excellency can figure on spending well into the four figures, American.

Before leaving the shop, a bit of interesting sartorial lore was imparted to me, which the salesclerk evidently found to be slightly short of *lès papauté*. Ready? The hot-weather simars run up especially for the pope no longer have the formal double half sleeves. They are now omitted in consideration of John Paul's comfort.

It has been long and amply demonstrated in those countries that still award them that the prospect of a knighthood can go as far in prompting a virtuous public life as can the promise of earthly riches or a heavenly reward, but only two major conferrers of this antique kind of honor remain in the world—Britain, for the service of the state, and the Vatican, for the service of the Church. Both well understand that the status the attribute accords has value far out of proportion to the effort it takes to award these symbolic tokens of recognition, and neither is likely to give them up anytime soon.

In recent times, the Vatican's knighthoods have been awarded to non-Catholics, even to non-Christians, but today the higher degrees within the several orders are generally—and understandably—reserved for Catholics. The conferring of pontifical knighthoods to women is known to be under study by the Vatican, but a decision whether to institute such awards has yet to be reached. The clergy and the religious—both men and women—are excluded from membership in all the papal orders of chivalry.

Five functioning orders of pontifical knighthood, generically the Ordini Equestri Pontifici—the Pontifical Equestrian Orders—have survived into modern times, although the two highest ranking are now rarely given. The Supreme Order of Christ, approved by Pope John XXII in 1319, and the Order of the Golden Spur, sometimes called the Golden Militia, restored in 1905 after a lapse of several centuries, have in recent pontificates been awarded primarily to Christian (because of the particularly strong religious nature of the two orders) heads of state, and only for what the Vatican considers to be extraordinary reasons. The actual conferring is done in ceremonies reserved for very important celebrations, the pontiff always being personally present. Members have run from Prince von

Bismarck, initiated by Leo XIII, to Charles de Gaulle honored by John XXIII. An indelicate controversy embroiled the issue of papal knighthood when the exigencies of politics prompted Paul VI to give the Golden Spur to the shah of Iran—definitely neither Catholic nor even Christian.

Both orders are composed of a single class, members of either of which can be recognized not only by their distinctive insignia but also by special and quite lavish court costumes peculiar to the orders, costumes that not all new members bother to buy. The Supreme Order of Christ is the higher ranking of the two. King Denis I and Queen St. Isabella of Portugal originally founded it as a bulwark against Moorish invaders of their country, the pope agreeing to be its patron. The Golden Spur has hazier origins, believed to be buried in the knights of Emperor Constantine. The members' gilt spurs—presented at their dubbing ceremonies—were the symbols of their high rank and of the office they held. One of history's most colorfully malignant Militiamen was Benito Mussolini, ritually honored by Pius XI for concluding the Lateran Accords. The Duce's more illustrious predecessors included Mozart and Donizetti; a later knight was King Hussein of Jordan, made a member in 1964, before Paul VI strictly decreed Catholics only in the future.

The Ordine Piano—the Order of Pius—named for both Pius IV and Pius IX (who reinstituted it in 1847), was the last pontifical knighthood that conferred actual papal nobility (in differing degrees) on its members; Pius XII suppressed the privilege in 1939, making the honor representative simply of "personal merit and worth." (The former conferring of nobility on its members derived from the statutes of the older Pian order.) Today it has four classes: Knight of the Golden Collar (usually given only to heads of state and sovereigns), Grand Cross Knight (an anomalous exception to the male-only rule—the Pian Grand Cross, generally reserved for ambassadors to the Holy See, was given to Her Excellency Lombe Chibesakunda, ambassador to the Vatican from Zambia, when she left her posting in 1981), Commander (in two divisions—those with and those without star), and just plain Knight.

The Orders of St. Gregory the Great (dating from 1851) and St. Sylvester (1841) have similar subcategories. The Gregorian order is generally awarded to worthy civil servants, the Sylvester to other worthy laymen.

Though not ranking as knighthoods, the two surviving papal decorations function something like the American Medal of Freedom—the Cross Pro Ecclesia et Pontifice and the Benemerente make for highly valued pontifical recognition. The Pro Ecclesia et Pontifice ("For the Church and Pontiff") started out as a token of commendation for those who had helped Leo XIII with his jubilee celebrations, and, like the Benemerenti, is today given as a sign of the pope's gratitude for some special service to the Church; many religious brothers and sisters receive the medals.

One final papal distinction is the Golden Rose, the highest honor bestowed on Catholic female sovereigns; the last to receive it was Grand Duchess Charlotte of Luxembourg. The Golden Rose is also given to shrines, particularly those dedicated to the Virgin.

Two other orders of knighthood, military rather than pontifical, are closely associated with the papacy and the Church, the first under the protection of the Holy See, the second a nominally sovereign body but also a religious order under the authority of the Vatican's Congregation of the Religious.

The Equestrian Order of the Holy Sepulcher of Jerusalem is possibly the oldest religious knighthood in the world (its inception vis-à-vis the Order of Malta is disputed; the latter order was instituted earlier but approved—by Paschal II in 1113—later). Founded in 1099 to "preserve and protect" Jerusalem as the cradle of Christianity, the Holy Sepulcher was conceived in the Holy Land by a knight named Godfrey of Bouillon, the leader of the First Crusade. The original body of knights who formed the crusade was broken into four divisions, determined by the individual missions they were assigned: the Knights Templar to guard the temple; the Knights of St. Lazarus to care for lepers; the Hospitallers of St. John of Jerusalem to care for the sick, the poor, and strangers in the city; and the Knights of the Holy Sepulcher—under Godfrey—to stand guard around the tomb held to be that of Christ.

Reorganized twice in the nineteenth century, once by Pius IX and later by Leo XIII—one of the changes made by Leo XIII was to allow female members, called Matrons of the Holy Sepulcher—the now honorary society has the distinction of having a cardinal as its grand master—appropriately Cardinal Maximilian de Furstenberg, the last European noble to have been promoted to the Sacred College. Besides a self-imposed charge of preserving the holy sites of

Christianity, the order works very industriously and with notable success to promote loyalty not only to the reigning pope but also to the institution of the Holy See. Its seat was transferred in 1945 from Jerusalem to Rome's Monastery of San Onofrio, on Janiculum Hill, but the official headquarters is in the Vatican and thus under pontifical protection. The ten thousand Knights of the Holy Sepulcher, organized in lieutenancies and delegations, are divided into five classes, whose members wear formal floor-length white capes, the left breasts marked with the famous five-cross emblem, an insignia representing Jesus's five wounds. None of the knights takes priestly vows, although their head—the grand master—is always a cardinal and is named by the pope.

"You were born as 'Hospitallers,' and this original name of yours has lost nothing of its relevance." So spoke Pope John Paul II at the June 1984 audience he granted the members of the Sovereign Council of the Sovereign Military Hospitaller Order of St. John of Jerusalem, of Rhodes, and of Malta—universally abbreviated to the Order of Malta. With headquarters in the extraterritorial Palazzo Malta in the Via Condotti, the Rodeo Drive of Rome, the organization is a diplomatic curiosity, being recognized as the world's only landless sovereign "nation" by upward of forty-five Catholic and non-Catholic countries (the United States is not one of them), mostly in Latin America and Africa. One small division of its ten-thousand-strong international membership, comprising only about thirty knights but representing many of the organization's full-time administrators, has taken individual priestlike vows of poverty, chastity, and obedience, and as "professed" knights (designated Knights of Justice and called "Fra") come under the authority of the Church's Sacred Congregation for the Religious, the curial department in charge of monks and nuns. Conversely, as a sovereign entity exchanging ambassadors with the Holy See (sovereignty that resulted in the first place because of its recognition by the Holy See), the order deals as an equal with the Vatican's Secretariat of State. In its role as a sovereign international entity, it mints coins, prints stamps, and issues passports to its diplomats—envoys who retain their original citizenship in addition to that of the Order of Malta. This schizophrenic nature of the order vis-à-vis the Holy See has created a somewhat muddy relationship with the Vatican; Pius XII tried with a notable lack of success to bring it fully under Church control, but it seems perfectly accustomed to and happy with the ambivalence of its situation.

Today, the nobly named Fra Angelico de Mojana di Cologna, a former Milanese lawyer, serves as the Maltese grand master, a position to which he was elected in 1962. Assisting him are such high-sounding lieutenants as the grand commander; the grand chancellor, who runs the day-to-day business affairs; the hospitaller; and a secretary for foreign affairs.

As with the Knights of the Holy Sepulcher, the traditional foundation of the Order of Malta was an embodiment of the medieval concept of what constituted the ideal life: service to Christ and his Church, caring for the less fortunate, honor, valor, and proficiency at arms—ideals that were inevitably very often met more in the telling than in the doing. These ancient ideals have been translated into theoretically equivalent deeds in a modern context, with the Maltese knights acting primarily as a charitable society *and*—like the Knights of the Holy Sepulcher—as strong defenders of the Church. The members' close personal ties contribute to a sort of old-boy network, said by some observers to have as its primary purpose the thwarting of international communism. But more concretely, the order has among many other notably praiseworthy deeds shipped sixty tons of dry milk to Brazil, raised ten million dollars for a Long Island center serving the handicapped, and coordinated the distribution of four and half a million dollars' worth of medicine and medical supplies to war-torn Central America.

The Order of Malta dates from 1070, when it was instituted as a hospice-infirmary, or, if you prefer, to 1113, when it was approved by Paschal II; it assumed its military-chivalric nature in 1126. It took over Malta in 1530 with backing from Emperor Charles V (its annual rent to the emperor was one Maltese falcon) and the approval of Pope Clement VII. Its 268-year dominion over the island, which Napoleon brought to a halt when he captured it in 1798, is still the basis for the order's presumption as a sovereign entity. When it didn't get it back after Waterloo (instead, Great Britain took over Malta after the 1814 Treaty of Paris), the order wandered around until 1834, when it finally settled in Rome at Pope Gregory XVI's invitation. Even the Italian state recognized the Maltese claim to sovereign status and has treated it with official goodwill; a 1935 decision by the Italian Court of Cassation (Supreme Court) upheld the order's "international personality."

The ten thousand members are organized into five grand priories and thirty-seven national associations in Europe and North and South America. (One British offshoot of the order is as a result of its interdenominational membership not under the sovereign order's authority.) Another two hundred thousand volunteers, mostly young people in their twenties, work for the order's famous ambulance corps as associate members. The U.S. membership comprises about a thousand knights, 70 percent of whom are men, about a tenth of the worldwide total. Nearly all are prominent in their fields, and some—Lee Iacocca, William F. Buckley, Jr., Alexander Haig, William Casey, Senator Jeremiah Denton, and Claire Boothe Luce among them—are internationally famous. The head of the U.S. branch is J. Peter Grace, head of President Ronald Reagan's commission for finding ways to cut the U.S. federal budget deficits.

The primary function of the order has been concentrated in caring for the sick, with special emphasis on victims of leprosy, a service in keeping with the traditions of the Knights Hospitaller of the Crusades. First aid at the Vatican itself, the sending of emergency hospital supplies and ambulances to needy nations, and other charitable and humanitarian work have gone a long way in indulging the anachronistic official stance of the order—particularly its diplomatic posturing and the emphasis on nobility. Sixteen "quarterings" of "noble" blood is required for membership, except for the category of "Knight of Magistral Grace," a device permitting nonnoble but well-deserving Catholics of some considerable station in life to join. There is also the category of "Donat"—full members but not considered knights.

A final item in this discussion of the ceremonial side of the Vatican is the recondite world of ecclesiastical heraldry, a surprisingly omnipresent but little-understood element of papal and episcopal dignity. Often acknowledged as today's foremost expert on heraldry in the Roman Catholic Church, Swiss-born Archbishop Bruno Bernard Heim is a modern Renaissance man: currently pronuncio in London capping a career in the Holy See's diplomatic service, respected adviser to popes, an accomplished heraldic artist, and enough of an authority on papal heraldry to question the brand-new Pope John Paul II on the correctness of his proposed papal arms.

Since armorial bearings—the emblems decorating arms—were military in origin and purpose, it might seem a historical oddity that clerics adopted them for their own purposes. But even though canon law forbade priests to carry arms, a taboo that carried the ultimate threat of excommunication, it became convenient for the Church's higher ranks to use such devices as their personal seal emblems. Starting in the thirteenth century, bishops had designed for themselves elaborate coats of arms, and over the next few centuries the art of ecclesiastical heraldry became bound up in the same sorts of elaborate and technically sophisticated guidelines that governed those of the profession of arms. The prelates who became popes took the art of heraldry with them into the papacy, and eventually the thousands of armorial bearings representing scores of different pontiffs that were carved in, painted on, and attached to the various architectural elements of the Vatican became unmistakable evidence of the importance of these symbols of papal identification and authority.

The armorial bearings of the pontiff are composed of several elements, as are all coats of arms; the governing rules are not fixed by canon law but are nonetheless closely observed with little deviation. The shield contains the pope's family arms, assuming his family *has* arms; if not, "family" arms will be established for the new pontiff, copying or based on the arms, if any, he used in the episcopate. The two essential symbols of papal dignity—the triple tiara and the keys—will always be part of the design: The tiara will be above the shield, the keys (one gold, the other silver) will be placed between or behind the shield, the keys held together by a cord with a single tassel on either end. The keys and tiara alone are also the symbol of the papacy during a *sede vacante* and are the major design elements of the yellow-and-white flag of the Vatican city-state (a flag that has, incidentally, been criticized for having had the arms placed on the white half, where they appear indistinct; had they been centered over both yellow and white halves, the insignia would have, according to its critics, stood out more clearly).

The specific problem that Archbishop Heim encountered with the proposed arms of the new John Paul II was the papal wish to include a large **M** on the shield, a solecism according to accepted heraldic rules. The letter stood, of course, for Mary, and in placing it there, John Paul wished to do honor to the person who commands such a large part of his personal veneration and devotion. The impasse was settled when the gold-on-blue deviation was justified as heraldically *acceptable* metal on color, not heraldically *un*acceptable color on color.

The armorial bearings of cardinals show what is supposed to be their family arms on the shield, the shield itself topped with a red hat (the kind now associated only with the cardinalature but nonetheless an element of all clerical arms). The specific mark of a cardinal's arms are the fifteen tufts (arranged in a pyramid—one at the top, five on the bottom row) on each end of the cord piercing the brim of the hat. No other devices are allowed on the arms except, if appropriate, the crosses of the Orders of Malta and of the Knights of the Holy Sepulcher.

Descent in Church rank is indicated on arms by a lesser number of the tufts; otherwise the arms are standard as far as their components are concerned. An archbishop has on each end of the cord ten tufts; a bishop, six; canons, three; and priests, one, although priests use armorial bearings only exceedingly rarely. Ecclesiastical, but never papal, arms are occasionally underlined with a motto, a pithy and sometimes euphonious two or three words expressing the professed ideals of the bearer or of his family in centuries past.

8

The Patrimony of Peter:
Finances in the Vatican

That the least praiseworthy of history's phenomena seem to be those with the greatest penchant for repeating themselves is unhappily corroborated with doleful regularity. And that of these matters the pairing of God and Mammon is one of the most prone to wickedness and corruption is an equally demonstrable observation. In the decades leading to the loss by the Roman Church of the greater part of its northern European communicants, the financial scandals—particularly those involving the sale of heavenly favors to help keep the Holy See's secular concerns afloat—were high on the list of the factors that permitted the success of Luther and the Protestant schism. They were by no means the only causes of the coming breach, but in their absence the Reformation might very likely have taken a course that would have permitted at least a degree of Roman dominion over the schismatic sects. A remembrance of those dolorous events by those entrusted with the Vatican's modern finances might well have averted the Holy See's most serious contemporary difficulties.

Since the reign of Pope Paul VI, the Church has been convulsed in a financial scandal that, if not likely to result in a second Reformation, nonetheless threatens to damage seriously the moral authority the Church has carefully built up under its post-Risorgimento popes. For the high-ranking Church figures involved, perhaps the greatest transgression has only been the exercise of poor—scandalously poor—judgment, but for the outside lay players in the still-unfolding drama, the case has been one of monumental hubris and an astonishing disregard for the good name of the Vatican's financial administration as well as the investments of thousands of small-savers.

The role of the Holy See as a world-class financial entity isn't particularly surprising in light of the Church's international mission; the Vatican's status as "one of the wealthiest institutions on earth" has long been a universally accepted axiom. But objective truth reveals a situation quite different from the popular conception. For the first three decades of this century, the government of the Roman Catholic Church came at times near bankruptcy. In 1919 the Holy See was rescued from this unenviable position by a stopgap loan from an American Catholic fraternal order, the Knights of Columbus; ten years later, the same precariousness in the state of its finances was the prime incentive in Pius XI's decision to sign the Lateran Accords with the Italian state.

With the final loss of its temporal kingdom (disappearing along with it, of course, was its major base of taxation) in 1870, the Holy See found itself at a point where expenses began substantially to exceed income, its financial worries a perpetual anxiety tormenting Peter's successors. A stubborn pride manifested in a refusal to give in to what he considered to be "usurpers" kept Pius IX from cashing the redemptory payment checks proffered annually and regularly (to the amount of $1.5 million) by the new Italian state, and the next three popes considered themselves equally bound to follow his precedent. When the Vatican was finally rescued from imminent financial disaster with the solution afforded by Mussolini in the Lateran Accords, the Holy See's modern fiscal history began. Before getting into the story, though, we'll briefly look at both the nature and the specifics of the Vatican's expenses and how an institution possessing a massive chunk of the world's movable art treasures could ever be said to be on the verge of bankruptcy.

At the outset, it should be understood that the Holy See does not itself finance all of the nearly countless worldwide activities of the Roman Catholic Church. The diocesan divisions and religious orders are expected to provide for their own expenses through the traditional means available to them—collections, earnings on investments, wills and bequests, and so on. As the central government of the Church, the Holy See's primary financial obligations are first in the area of operating the Vatican as the chief administrative center of Roman Catholicism, and second in funding the Church's still far-reaching missionary activities, not the least of which is the increasingly comprehensive *and* expensive worldwide travels of its chief evangelist, John Paul II. In the 1980s, the annual costs of keeping the Vatican afloat—including the salaries of its employees (the pope, incidentally, receives no salary, for the reason that all Vatican funds are theoretically his to do with as he wishes), maintenance, utilities, travel, and all the other normal expenses incurred in the running of any immense organization—averaged approximately $20 million less than what was taken in as revenue. The 1984 deficit was reported by the Vatican to run to more than $29 million (58.4 billion lire), with even more red ink expected in 1985.

The second issue involves the perceived wealth of the Church, including the treasures and properties of the Vatican as well as the assets of its thousands of dioceses, parishes, and religious orders around the world. As for the Vatican's fabulous and virtually priceless art treasures, the collection in fact costs more—considerably more—to maintain than it earns from paid admissions to the city-state's museums, according to the museums' administration. The historic and nonincome-producing real property within the Vatican—the churches, palaces, and museums—have a status outside of any normal definition of assets or wealth; they obviously can't be put on the market. Whatever income the Church's dioceses and parishes earn goes to support their own needs and activities, with little direct financial assistance being channeled by them to Rome. Since Vatican II, the visible splendor that has long been a central facet of the Church—the ceremonial array of its priests and especially of its prelates, the built-for-the-ages sumptuousness of new religious edifices, the rococo ostentation of papal ceremonial—have been substantially toned down to levels more in harmony with an era in which moderation in religious trappings is seen as a virtue. The many thousands of ecclesiastical buildings—convents, religious schools, headquarters of orders, and so forth—are not considered by the Church to be anything like at the free disposal of the Holy See but are "owned" by the bodies that occupy them. Although a 1976 decision of the Tribunal of the Apostolic Segnatura—the Holy See's supreme court—upheld the principle that all Church property anywhere in the world can be disposed of only with papal consent, this is not the same thing as saying that the proceeds of such disposition would automatically accrue to the Holy See.

Ironically, the beginning of the international financial scandal that as of this writing continues to send shocks through the Vatican can be said to have its origins in the event that gave the Church new economic life, the complex treaty known as the Lateran Accords. Besides legally defining the status of the Holy See and the Vatican vis-à-vis the Italian state—it was an acknowledgment on the papacy's part of the de facto situation of the Vatican as it had stood since the final loss of its secular territory in 1870—the accords most importantly produced the critical financial settlement that ended the papacy's years of relative penury.

On the rainy and historic afternoon of February 11, 1929, as thousands of church bells rang out in happy celebration all over Rome, the Vatican cardinal secretary of state received the Italian prime ministerial party in the Lateran Palace near the room in which Charlemagne had met Pope Leo III more than a millennium earlier. The leader of the Italian delegation to the signing was, of course, Benito Mussolini, Duce, prime minister, and Italy's head of state in all but name, and the treaty was a resounding diplomatic victory for him and his Fascist "corporate state." Ending the social impasse with the Church was one very valuable result for the Fascist government, but demonstrating to the world the stature and "benign reasonableness" of his regime and at the same time managing to become the idol of Catholic Italy was frosting on his cake. The three documents jointly signed by Italy's prime minister and the Holy See's secretary of state that day ended the Vatican's legal stalemate with Italy by the simple expedient of turning it into an independent state, one purposely kept as small as possible by the reigning pope, Pius IX. The secretary of state, Pietro Cardinal Gasparri, echoed Pius's wishes pithily: "We don't want to be bothered with streetcar strikes." The new state wouldn't have to concern itself with strikes, but with independence came the usual tokens of sovereignty, one of which would soon be the same economic vulnerabilities as the world's secular states.

Of the three elements of the accords—the Lateran Pact, the Concordat, and the Financial Convention—it was the third that rescued the Holy See from impending poverty. Every bit as important to the Vatican as to the Fascist government, the treaty not only gave the Holy See a state with which to garb itself in the clothing of a sovereign political entity, but also the payment from Italy became the basis for the papal kingdom's capital reserves. The terms of the Financial Convention obligated the Italian treasury to recompense the Holy See for the loss of its lands and properties in the amount of 750 million lire in cash (then worth about $39.2 million in preinflation currency) and 5 percent consolidated Italian state bonds with a face value of 1 billion lire (about $52.3 million in 1929). In a face-saving gesture on the Vatican's part, its officials went on record—in the form of a preamble to the convention—as being of the opinion that the sum was "far below" the true value of the properties seized. But as an added sweetener in the deal, the Italian government agreed to pay a salary to each parish priest in the country, a fact never overly publicized in Italy but that has remained in effect ever since.*

With this enormous windfall entirely at his disposal to do with as he thought best, Pius XI first went on record as promising he would hand it over intact to his successor, and then he went on a minor spending spree in the Vatican—among other projects, the Governatorato building was erected with a small part of the settlement, the Library and museums were reorganized, and several new curial office buildings and apartments for high-ranking prelates were constructed. Most significantly, Pius established a new administrative office called the Special Administration of the Holy See, with the authority to manage and invest the funds to the Church's maximum advantage.

The new Special Administration was also charged with administering Peter's Pence, a collection taken up by Catholic churches around the world, often on the Sunday nearest June 29, Peter's feast day, to be presented formally to the pope by bishops on their every-five-year *ad limina* visits to the Vatican. First collected in England in the eighth century, the custom spread to the Continent before being discontinued during the Reformation and was reconstituted in Paris

*A provision of the new treaty with Italy stipulates that as of January 1, 1990, salaries will be paid entirely by the church and funded by tax-deductible contributions from Church members.

in 1859 by Count Montalambert to provide funds for a Vatican rapidly becoming impoverished by the loss of its lands in the Risorgimento flood tide; the count's project eventually spread all over Europe, the Americas, and the Church's mission territories. After the final debacle in 1870 due to the overwhelming physical superiority of the insurgents, the pope was pictured to the world's Catholic faithful as a near-starving political prisoner sleeping on a straw bed in some airless Vatican garret. This tale, considerably embellishing on the pontiff's actual state, achieved the desired results and induced ever greater Peter's Pence collections from nearly every diocese in the world, especially from America's wealthy faithful, all of which was collected into the Vatican coffers and formed the Holy See's main source of revenue during its years in the wilderness. The fund is still said to vary in the amount of its proceeds in direct proportion to the popularity of the incumbent pope—high, for example, under the internationally beloved John XXIII, falling off in the years after the less-lovable Paul VI became pontiff.

After 1929, with the windfall from the Financial Convention, the funds that continued to come in from the Peter's Pence, and the uncashed checks that the Italian government had been depositing in the Vatican's account every year since 1870, the Holy See's status as a indisputably solvent financial entity to be taken with due seriousness by the international banking community was assured. During these first fat decades, the comfortably filled Vatican treasury had the singular good fortune to be managed by a man of exceptional talent. Bernardino Nogara, an engineer and director of the Banca Commerciale Italiana (and a brother of the director of the Vatican museums), through his exceptionally adroit investment skills increased the funds in the Special Administration by a considerable margin. A heavy percentage of the financial portfolio that Nogara built for the Church consisted of shares in Italian banks and utilities; gold bullion was another of the financier's favorite investments. Because of the sovereign and independent status of the Vatican, Nogara was in an enviable position of being able to avoid entirely nettlesome Italian banking and investment restrictions, allowing him to engage in just about any kind of investment activities he judged desirable, with his only responsible overseer being the pope himself. Fortunately for the Holy See, Nogara's talent and personal integrity were unimpeachable.

At the end of World War II, with the Italian economy in shambles, the Church shifted a large amount of its still-intact funds into shares on the New York Stock Exchange, a move taken on the advice of New York City's archbishop, Cardinal Francis Spellman, who together with Nogara is accounted one of the shrewdest financial experts in the Church's modern history. Nogara himself left the scene in the mid-1950s, retiring in 1954, and dying in 1958, but his place at the Special Administration was nearly filled and astonishing talents matched by a Swiss banker, Henri de Maillardoz, who happily continued Nogara's cautious but capable fiscal policies in an advisory capacity.

Assuming much of the Special Administration's responsibility and at least theoretically overseeing the Vatican's financial structure today is a 1967 Pauline creation called the Prefecture of the Economic Affairs of the Holy See, headed by a five-cardinal board of directors. The prefecture was intended to serve as the Holy See's supreme fiscal planning arm, a sort of combined Treasury Department and Budget Office for the Church. Its prefect (now Cardinal Giuseppe Caprio) reports to the pope, but his department is said to be seriously compromised by the fact that a critical financial arm of the Holy See, the pivotal Vatican Bank, is outside its control.

A year following his 1967 general curial reorganization, Paul VI made yet another major realignment in the structure of the Vatican's growing financial bureaucracy. Pius XI's Special Administration of the Holy See was combined with the even older Administration of the Properties of the Holy See into a new department called the Administration of the Patrimony of the Apostolic See, usually shortened to APSA in its Italian acronymic form. APSA is divided into "Ordinary" and "Extraordinary" sections (the names have the slightly romantic tone typical of many of the Vatican's prosaic agencies; the first is merely the section that handles duties that had come under the old Properties Administration, mostly real estate; the second covers those of the former Special Administration, mostly investments). Today the powerful department is still under the formal control of the five-cardinal board headed since John Paul's spring 1984 reorganizational blitz by Cardinal Agnelo Rossi, replacing the ubiquitous Cardinal Casaroli, himself given even greater responsibilities over the Curia as a whole.

It is believed that the beginning investment portfolio APSA inherited from its predecessor organizations at the time it was set up was worth as much as $500 million, although the Vatican's secretive nature concerning its financial affairs made the figure only an educated guess by interested financial analysts; the few hints from Curia officials concerning APSA's worth indicated—perhaps predictably—a considerably lower total. In any event, through Paul's—and APSA's—early years, the conservative investment doctrines laid down by Nogara and Maillardoz continued to be followed, and the Church enjoyed a period at the peak of its modern temporal power, financially secure and still undiluted by the weakening liberal reforms instituted in the wake of Vatican II.

The third element of the Vatican tripartite financial structure, after APSA and Peter's Pence, is the Istituto per le Opere di Religione, or Institute for Religious Works (IOR)—the reverently but nonetheless misleadingly named Vatican Bank. Established by Pius XII's personal declaration in 1942 to take over the Administration of Religious Works, which had been set up by Leo XIII in 1887 for administering the Church's funds destined for religious purposes, its modified mission was to take custody and care of the Vatican's cash as well as that of many religious orders whose funds were routed through the Vatican. At the time that Pius reordered the organization, the Vatican was faced with the mortal danger of a Fascist riptide lapping around its walls, and the bank, which was ostensibly set up merely to channel funds designated for "works of religion and Christian piety" had the real purpose of establishing both a conduit and an escape route for the Vatican's capital on a continent in which in 1942 it appeared frighteningly possible that the wrong side was within a nonce of winning. At war's end the Vatican came through physically unscathed, and the Istituto emerged as a power within a power.

The Vatican Bank is, in most respects, a "real" bank, but not exactly in the same way that Chase Manhattan or Bank of America are genuinely public, open-to-anyone banks. Although tourists can't just pop in for a look-see, it is possible to visit it under the right circumstances. An appointment with its top officer, for example, will give the visitor a chance to peruse quickly its old-fashioned and vaguely cloistered-looking banking floor—papal busts, crucifixes, etc.—before being ushered into the director's surprisingly *luxe* offices.

The bank's chief operating officer is Archbishop Paul Casimir Marcinkus, an American priest, born in 1922 and raised in Cicero,

Illinois. The man squarely at the center of the Holy See's financial
storm, he is familiarly called "Chink" by his fellow curial clerics (although not likely to his face) and sometimes referred to as the
"pope's gorilla" in reference to his six-four height and well-known
papal bodyguarding duties. In 1970 he saved the pope from a knife-
wielding madman in the Philippines, an act of courage that was said
to have understandably tightened an already close bond that was
forming between the two. Marcinkus acted as an effective advance
man for Paul VI's several mid-1960s journeys, a role he fulfilled so
agreeably in the pope's opinion that Marcinkus was somewhat in-
congruously appointed in 1968 to head the newly vacant position of
administrator of the IOR. The next year he was promoted to the
bank's presidency and two years later to chairman.

Marcinkus's authority gives him some unusual perquisites: not
only a very large office—a rarity in the Vatican—but one that is also
luxurious, modern, and unabashedly American as regards its fur-
nishings and ambience, one into which the hearty archbishop welcomed me with great courtesy on my visit. The outer office, the territory of his beautifully polite Italian secretary whose English is just
as good as is her boss's Italian, looks like that of any international
executive, a fact that's also remarkable only because of its uniqueness
in the Vatican.

The prelate presides over a banking establishment that is relatively small—it has about seven thousand depositors and about $3
billion in deposits, with its own assets about $150 million—but
whose prestige, connections, and influence put it far closer to the
aforementioned Chase Manhattan or Bank of America than to anything in downstate Illinois. Located on two levels of the Nicholas V
Tower in the Apostolic Palace, with its entrance a few hundred feet
inside St. Anne Gate, the bank's major functions are to serve as a
clearing service for Vatican officials, both secular and clerical, and to
give investment advise to the Holy See. However, for its limited
roster of privileged clients, who are mostly diplomats accredited to
the papal state, Vatican citizens, and/or top bureaucrats, as well as a
very few Italians with Vatican connections, the bank performs the
normal depository functions, all—because of the Vatican's sovereign
status—totally outside the currency and exchange control limitations that are such a bothersome feature of banking as practiced a
few yards away in economically troubled Italy. An odd requirement

for being allowed to open an account but one happily acceded to by the wealthy Italians anxious to make their money safe from the twin threats of communism and terrorism is that clients must promise that 10 percent of their accounts will be made over to the Church, either upon closure of the account or death of the depositor.

The bank is under the theoretical jurisdiction of a commission composed of five cardinals headed by the cardinal secretary of state, but it is more directly controlled by the Vatican state government, also headed by the secretary of state, Cardinal Casaroli. The pope's personal interest in the bank is such, however, that the most important elements of Marcinkus's direction are said to come directly from John Paul himself. But because the bank's director is a key financial policymaker in the inner papal circle, he has been the central figure in the explosive investment and banking scandal that has been unfolding in Italy since the mid-1970s, and it is here that the Vatican's financial story thickens.

The source of the Vatican's immediate troubles was Pope Paul VI's accurate perception that, starting in the early 1970s, Italy was quite simply in deep trouble. Since World War II, the Vatican and the Christian Democrats, Italy's bulwark against the godless left, had enjoyed a close symbiotic relationship, with the former the latter's most ardent and most important supporter. The world social revolution that came in the wake of (or, if you prefer, largely as a result of) the United States's involvement in Vietnam brought the same turmoil to Italy that it brought to the better part of the rest of the West. Socialists and, worse, Communists in powerful Italian political positions forced the Vatican to give up the tax-exempt status that had protected Vatican Italian investments, investments that suddenly began to look dangerously unsafe to the pope. Hoping that another Nogara-like financial genius might be able to help the Holy See out of this perceived danger and transfer its investments to safer climes, it settled on Michele Sindona, a good Milanese Catholic banker, an international financier, and a man who it was believed would be the perfect choice.

When Sindona went to work for the Vatican in 1969, it first looked as though he just might *be* the answer to Paul's prayers—a "reincarnation of Nogara," as writer Mike Mallowe of *Philadelphia Magazine* phrased it. Sindona's twenty-year climb up the slippery ropes of the chaotic Italian economy had given him the experience and the entrée to make his deals at the highest levels of the nation's financial world. The only problem was that the deals he began making in the name and interests of the Vatican were, as often as not, speculatively sleight-of-hand ones; he was building a financial empire that was actually little more than a house of cards, ready to crash if just one key piece should come loose. The piece that brought the house down was the collapse of Franklin National Bank, a New York–based financial institution that Sindona had taken over as a showcase American base for his operations but financed in a maneuver underwritten with funds illegally skimmed off his European operations. Franklin's 1974 collapse—the largest to that date in U.S. history—and attendant loss of around $40 million led the U.S. Securities and Exchange Commission to institute fraud proceedings against the Italian investor. This disaster started a dominolike collapse in 11 countries of Sindona's other 125 interrelated corporations, all companies existing entirely on worthless paper. The Società Generale Immobiliare, an Italian contracting and real-estate giant in which the Vatican had held shares for many years and whose interests had been taken over as a Sindona company, was seized by the Italian central bank as collateral.

The ensuing debacle naturally finished Sindona as a trusted Vatican financial adviser as well as ending his part in the management of its funds. The financier was eventually tried by both the Italian (*in absentia*) and U.S. governments on a variety of bank law violations and fraud. After having evaded American justice for a few months, Sindona finally began a twenty-five-year sentence in a New York federal penitentiary in 1980. The Vatican's investment losses in the collapse came to an estimated $240 million.

Unfortunately, the Vatican's problems didn't end here. Before his downfall, Sindona had introduced Archbishop Marcinkus to a protégé, Roberto Calvi, president of Milan's small but aristocratic and respected Banco Ambrosiano. When Calvi stepped in after Sindona's departure, he would turn mere disaster into the Holy See's greatest modern scandal, something approaching the scale of a Watergate at the Vatican.

Since World War II, Calvi's bank, named after Milan's fourth-century bishop and patron, St. Ambrose, had enjoyed Vatican patronage as a shareholder through stock purchased by the then-young IOR. But even by 1981, when the scandal first hit the fan, the total

Vatican interest in the bank came to a mere 1.59 percent of its capital, although investigative writer Penny Lernoux, author of *In Banks We Trust,* suggests that the Vatican may have actually had enough additional money invested in the bank to have been its major, albeit unacknowledged, stockholder.

The darkest facet of Banco Ambrosiano was its alleged close connections, through its president, to the murderous Italian political ultraright and the shadowy P-2, the shortened name of the Propaganda Due, a right-wing Masonic lodge in Milan. Founded in the late nineteenth century as a lodge for Masons in especially important or "delicate" positions, P-2 is totally unrelated to the American Masonic organization. P-2's membership of 962, many of whom are leaders of the Italian establishment, was headed by its *maestro venerabile,* Licio Gelli, an Italian financier and neo-Fascist. Among the most damning charges against P-2 is its purported involvement in the 1979 bombing of the central railway station in Bologna, a brutally calculated act of terrorism resulting in the random death of eighty-five people and the maiming of two hundred more. In her investigation, Lernoux asserts the unlikelihood, however, of Marcinkus's being aware of Banco Ambrosiano's P-2 connections, regardless of the fact that Calvi and the archbishop were working together closely to fill the hole that Sindona had left.

In the Church's view, its investments in Banco Ambrosiano were based on sound financial reasoning. The bank apparently had a good track record and a reasonably untarnished reputation, although its charter oddly and distastefully required that depositors be Christians, which barred the Milanese Jewish community from using the bank's services. But for reasons that appear to have their motive based on simple greed, Calvi had begun looting the bank of its reserves in 1975 and had the money directed to several fraudulent cover corporations in Central America, particularly in Panama, with the president brazenly using his Vatican connections to provide the up-front money needed to establish the bogus companies. The ultimate purpose, beyond simple greed, for all this chicanery is unclear, but some speculate that part of the money eventually wound up in Argentina to help finance its Falklands war against Britain, a war favored by some aristocratic Italian families who had emigrated from Italy to Argentina and who still maintained ties with right-wing groups in Italy. In any case, the Ambrosiano money was being transferred (i.e., laundered) through the IOR, earning the Vatican Bank large commissions and leading to the not unnatural impression—one vigorously fostered by Calvi—that the Vatican was a full partner in his business dealings. So strongly was he entrenched that he had now assumed the mantle, coined by the Italian press and once held by Sindona, of "God's banker."

The most tangible evidence that the Vatican and its bank were directly and knowingly involved in Calvi's activities is several "letters of patronage"—a form of banking endorsement sometimes called a "letter of comfort"—issued by the Vatican Bank and given to Calvi in 1981. The letters were used to assure lenders that the Vatican formally endorsed the transfer of substantial funds into the Panamanian companies, and that could be interpreted, according to writer Paul Hofmann in his book *O Vatican!*, as a "Vatican guarantee of the obscure borrowers' creditworthiness" and that were "apparently used to overcome the quite understandable reluctance of some officials in Calvi-controlled institutions and their creditors to lend large sums to companies about which they knew very little." Lernoux flatly states they were given for the very specific purpose of appeasing Banco Ambrosiano Andino, the bank's Peruvian subsidiary, which was demanding written proof from Calvi that the Vatican had controlling interest in the Panamanian companies and "was fully aware of their borrowing activities." Cardinal Casaroli would later be forced to point out publicly, rather lamely, that "the letters of patronage [were] not instruments of guarantee."

The next major event in this sad saga was the June 1982 discovery of Roberto Calvi's weighted body hanging from the under works of London's Blackfriars Bridge. How it got there hasn't yet been decided with certainty, but there is considerable circumstantial evidence that it was the result not of suicide, as the British authorities first determined, but of murder. Since 1978, the Italian banking officials had been quietly on to Calvi, suspecting that he—possibly in connection with the Vatican Bank, certainly in connection with his own Banco Ambrosiano—was stealing tens of millions of dollars. Some sources suggest the P-2 is connected with the murder because the elimination of Calvi would also eliminate the one personal link between it and the banker and possible proof of its complicity.

With the discovery of Calvi's body, the second shoe dropped on the IOR and the Vatican. Not only did the Holy See now appear to be involved, at least indirectly, in mayhem if not murder, but also the letters of patronage issued by the IOR strongly suggested the Vatican had a legal obligation to make restitution to the investors in Calvi's skein of businesses. After it declared Banco Ambrosiano a complete loss, the Italian government stated that the Vatican's liability to the investors and depositors would be at least $1.3 billion because the IOR and Banco Ambrosiano were "de facto partners." Not surprisingly, the Vatican's response was to deny responsibility for any failings on the part of those with whom it dealt financially, but it was notably the first time that a bank had failed to honor debts covered by such letters. A "surprise" document that turned up in the Vatican's possession, signed by Calvi and dated several months before his death, "cleared" the IOR of financial responsibilities and appeared to substantiate its official position of no responsibility. By this time, however, very little weight was being placed on anything that involved Calvi's word or honor.

Philadelphia's Cardinal John Krol, appointed by the pope to a fifteen-member council of cardinals charged with putting the Vatican finances back in order, suggested that the scandal had really been engineered by the Italian Communists to discredit both the Vatican and the pope, two enormous thorns in Moscow's side. A cardinal's secretary reflected this view when he told me that many clerics at the Vatican believe the real motivation to "get" Marcinkus came from Italy's far leftist opposition, a wedge of the political spectrum anxious to do anything it can to besmirch the Holy See and the Church. But Florence's Giovanni Cardinal Benelli, once considered "papabile" and a man who according to Paul Hofmann had never especially liked Marcinkus, admitted the likelihood of fault on the IOR's part when he publicly chalked up any possible error of the bank only to "incapacity and lack of experience," a sidelong but gloved slap at the IOR president.

When the scandal broke in all its fullness in 1982, Marcinkus and two of his IOR associates, after being notified by Italian officials that they were being investigated for possible bank fraud, remained in the Vatican, where they were safe from any Italian summons servers. Marcinkus explained his own move from the Villa Stritch in Rome to a Vatican apartment on the basis that he would be nearer his work, but it was noticed that he was absent from his usual position as John Paul's bodyguard on the papal trip to Spain in November

1982. The Italian authorities later made it known to the Vatican that if it assumed responsibility for at least part of the financial losses of Banco Ambrosiano, charges would not be filed against any IOR officers, a signal that permitted Marcinkus the peace of mind to be able to leave his "confinement."

As of this writing (Spring of 1985), the Vatican banking scandal still has not been completely resolved. Marcinkus has not received the red hat Vatican-watchers had long assumed he would, and in a papal statement it has been made clear that his role in the administration of the Vatican state has been subordinated to Cardinal Casaroli's overall supervision, with the permanent presidency of the state given to Sebastiano Cardinal Baggio. The archbishop was again notified, in March 1984, that his bank was being investigated for yet another irregularity, involving a $30 million loan to Italmobiliare S.p.A., the holding company of Italian financier Carlo Pesenti, but the charges were dismissed by a Milan magistrate in June 1985 for lack of incriminating evidence. Another Vatican employee, Luigi Mennini, who as managing director and the bank's highest-ranking lay executive had already spent forty days in jail for being an accessory in Sindona's fraudulent bankruptcy, was in July 1984 sentenced by an Italian court to seven years' imprisonment for "aggravated fraudulent bankruptcy" in the 1974 collapse of Banca Privata Italiana; Mennini was at the time of his sentencing avoiding Italian authorities by not leaving the protective confines of the Vatican.

The two biggest questions left unanswered in the affair are (1) whether the IOR's "lack of experience" and naïveté had lapped over into the far more ominous realm of collusion in these events, and (2) what if any financial responsibility the Vatican will see fit to take for the billion dollars in losses suffered by Banco Ambrosiano's investors and despositors in the wake of the bank's collapse. The first—and the one with the more far-reaching significance—is not likely to be discussed by any Vatican officials. As for the second, the Holy See has decided to repay to the Milanese bank's creditors nearly a quarter on the dollar—$240.9 million of the $1.3 billion of debt. The settlement money, which the Vatican considers to be recognition of "moral involvement" in the debacle, most likely was raised through the sale of its stocks and bonds, according to a report in the *Wall Street Journal*. The amount is estimated to represent nearly half the

Vatican's liquid assets. In an agreement signed in Geneva in the spring of 1984, the payment will be arbitrated by Italian courts if further disputes arise; it would be, if such happens, the first time the Vatican will have agreed to allow arbitration over its affairs by Italian law. For obvious reasons the Holy See wants the settlement, which was signed for the Holy See by Marcinkus personally, to be considered a gesture of goodwill and certainly not a legal admission of any guilt or wrongdoing in a situation in which it maintains it has been the victim, not the perpetrator. Part of the impetus for the Vatican's acquiescence to the deal came from the creditor banks' agreement, as part of the settlement, to waive threatened legal action against the Holy See. Another significant impetus to settling the matter in a manner that can be seen as generous toward Italian interests was the Vatican's desire not to jeopardize the delicate negotiations that had been carefully worked out with the Italian state over the new concordat between them, efforts the Holy See does not want to see wasted.

The fundamental impact on the Church of its financial troubles boils down most irreducibly to a loss of trust. The financial damage will be healed someday, but the spiritual wound is likely to be far graver and of considerably longer duration before becoming consigned to history. The papacy may under certain circumstances be considered infallible, but it is not invulnerable, certainly not to the kind of moral damage financial scandals leave in their wake.

In terms of international financial impact, the Sindona-Calvi-Ambrosiano affair probably can be characterized as fairly small. Even the dollar amounts involved in the Vatican itself, a financial unit whose investment assets and budget are dwarfed by those of some large dioceses within the Church, are not on a scale where recovery is questioned. Some observers have even seen positive results coming from the affair, namely the opening of at least a portion of the Holy See's financial affairs to public scrutiny, the kind of scrutiny that would make irresponsible adventurism infinitely more difficult in the future. The Vatican has a right to its confidentiality, but where the integrity of the Church's central government can be harmed so flagrantly and over such a long period, such secret activities do little to serve its interests.

9

How Saints Are Made:
The Process of Canonization

Here is the Church's treasure.

St. Lawrence

On the face of it, it wouldn't seem that Christopher Columbus, Princess Grace of Monaco, Pope John XXIII, and Palestinian nun Maria Baouardy have a thread connecting their lives. But they are indeed bound by a common link, in that these four widely disparate figures could someday share the supreme Roman Catholic accolade of sainthood if each completes the long, costly, and arduous road to canonization on which he or she is now at various stages. The mystery of sainthood and the canonic process, with all its spiritual dimensions of divine intercession, relics, and miracles, probably is the Church's greatest enigma outside the mystery of the mass itself. It is also unquestionably one of its most controversial and problematic elements for both its own members and for non-Catholics alike. Aware of the difficulties posed by the whole issue of sainthood in modern times, the Holy See has bureaucratized the process in a largely successful attempt to purge canonization of the voodoolike aspects that threatened to discredit not only this antique state of sanctity but also the religion of which it has long played, and continues to play, a central role.

Before looking at the process leading to canonization—the papal declaration of sainthood—we should try to explain just what a saint is. Not to obfuscate, but there is, unfortunately, more than one way to define the attribute of sainthood, with semantics causing the problem. In the broadest sense, the Church teaches that *every* person who enters Heaven is automatically a saint, which is to say that the attainment of the kingdom of God itself constitutes sainthood. But to understand canonization, sainthood has to be regarded as a special state restricted to those who have lived extraordinarily virtuous or holy lives in "imitation of Christ." The central and very crucial point to this latter, narrower definition is that no one becomes a saint *after* death—persons who achieved sainthood in life are merely formally being *recognized* for that merit after they die, sometimes many centuries after they die, with the recognition coming in the form of canonization. The effects of canonization are that the declared saint is forthwith officially worthy of honor and imitation by the faithful, may be prayed to for intercession with God, and requires the veneration—called *dulia* (the adoration of God through the saints)—of the entire Church. Some saints are declared the particular patrons or "protectors" of certain categories of people, or endeavors; St. Francis of Assisi is, for example, the newly appointed patron of ecology. Saints come in both universal and local varieties and in a number of subcategories—martyrs, confessors, doctors, virgins, bishops—and the rules leading to canonization vary for each of these classifications. Since the twelfth century the Holy See has been the fount of sainthood, the pope the sole proclaimer of this highest state of perfection.

In Christianity's first thousand years, declaration of sainthood was a more casual thing than what it became in the second millennium. During the Church's earliest days, the accolade was accorded automatically not only to those who had personally known the living Jesus and had been his disciples and died for it, but also to martyrs who suffered ghastly executions rather than abjure their religion and to the popes who were worked to death in the imperial mines of Mediterranean islands. The gravesites of these saints were venerated, and his or her anniversary was solemnly remembered and regarded as a holy day. In the matter of sainthood, the Church has been remarkably nonsexist, although it has tended to place an inordinately high value on females forswearing their sexuality.

Not every saint was treated equally by the entire body of the Church. Had such been the case, the ever-growing numbers would soon have turned the young religion into a sort of Occidental Hinduism. Groups centered around the graves of particular saints would keep his or her memory, while other groups would give special prominence to different saints; some have attributed the growth of the practice to a primitive urge to ancestor-worship. By the tenth century it is estimated that there were over twenty-five thousand saints, most of them local in their sphere of veneration, but the more popular ones, those recognized by the whole Church, were the superstars of their day, and miraculous favors were said to have been granted through the divine intercession of one or another saint. Eventually nonmartyrs came to be accorded the tribute of sainthood—Martin of Tours, who died at the end of the fourth century, was an early example. As residential bishops took on the role of local authority in the spreading Church, their approval was required before public honors could be paid to new saints.

As with most activities involving competing passions and ambitions, corruption insinuated itself into the flowering cults of sainthood, and in an attempt to control the growing abuses, the Church sought to bring the whole matter under the jurisdiction of the Holy See. The "official" canonization process thus began in 993, when John XV declared Bishop Ulrich of Augsburg the first papal-appointed saint, and with it slowly came the regularization of the procedures leading to sainthood. The result was that it became the sole preserve of the Holy See when in 1171 Alexander III declared papal proclamation of sainthood the only legitimate form of canonization. At the end of the sixteenth century, Sixtus V delegated the canonization procedural authority to the Congregation of Rites, and in 1634 Urban VIII laid down a rigid procedure for canonization and put an end to the growth of cults, ruling that the establishment of a cult around a person's memory would, in fact, work against a particular canonization. The roster of saints was pared down to a workable number (the Eastern Church was upset at having some of *its* most popular saints downgraded by Rome), and a sort of semiofficial list of saints was established. Between then and today, something less than three hundred new saints have been canonized, most of that number having made it in the past half century. In 1911, Pius X, himself the last papal saint, fixed an "order of dignity" for those canonized, with virgins and holy women predictably at the end of it; in 1969, Paul VI amended the order, resulting in the downgrading of certain saints—most notably St. Christopher (of dashboard fame) to local rather than universal status because he was declared to be merely "legendary."

An integral part of the issue of sainthood was the cult of relics, items associated with the person or lives of the saints. Beginning in the earliest Christian years, the pious would soak small cloths in the blood of the martyrs or touch them to the coffin of the deceased, and these *brandea,* as the cloths were called, then became objects of physical veneration in place of the mere memory of the sainted martyr. Parts of the bodily remains of martyrs, especially the easily preservable bones, attained relic status, and even items that had only been touched by the saint had a kind of second-class relic value. The disinterred bodies of saints were cut up and distributed to the faithful, some tiny bits being deposited in reliquaries and episcopal rings. The demand for these relics soon outgrew the supply, and, not unnaturally, there was a fair amount of hanky-panky in the commerce of supposedly "genuine" relics. Anything associated with Jesus himself, of course, became the most valuable relics of all, and tales of fragments of the True Cross and the Holy Grail and the Robe became the focuses of endless legends.

Today the canonic process is one of the most complex, lengthy, and costly investigative procedures in the world, let alone in the Church. The many elements leading to final recognition of a candidate's saintliness are rarely completed in one pontificate, and sometimes the first step on this road can precede the last by many centuries. Petitions for sainthood come from any source to the Sacred Congregation for the Causes of Saints, tranferred in 1969 from the Congregation for Rites, itself recently divided into two bodies, the Congregation for Sacraments and the Congregation for Divine Worship. Those that survive a first reading are comparatively few in number. There are now over a thousand dossiers in the pipeline according to Vatican officials, with some—that of Mary, Queen of Scots, for example—having been there for a very, very long time.

When the congregation officials believe a proposed candidate has the potential stuff for eventual canonization, the case file is turned over for investigation to the bishop of the diocese in which the individual died. The official put in charge of the proposed's case is called the postulator, but because the postulator remains in Rome, a local vice-postulator in the diocese is given the responsibility by the

bishop to carry out the investigational spadework. A diocesan tribunal is then formed to hear the evidence for and against the candidate,
and witnesses who knew the person or are familiar with his or her
work or life are questioned. Finally, a record of the proceedings is
sent to Rome under the seal of the country's Vatican diplomatic
representative.

This initial part of the procedure is called the informative process,
and if all goes in the individual's favor, the congregation will ask the
pope to issue a declaration of heroicity of virtues, an official statement that the person *appears* to have been virtuous to the point of
saintliness by what has been uncovered so far. Getting this far allows
the candidate to be referred to as venerable, which is nice and represents a tremendous hurdle already, but not yet enough to permit
public worship.

Now the cause, as the process of getting someone canonized is
referred to, can enter what is known as the apostolic phase, which
means it will be examined minutely and meticulously by the Sacred
Congregation itself. When a cause is accepted at this point, there is
a strong presumption that Rome considers it a likely eventual
winner, but in the decree that introduces it to the Holy See, the
pope signs *Placet Carolus*—"Karol Accepts"—rather than his usual
pontifical name; this little hedge allows him to maintain a certain
official distance should the cause later founder. Again, it should be
remembered that what's gone on so far can have covered a substantial time period in a painstaking effort to make sure no evidence has
been left unexamined.

The process now becomes a good deal *more* complicated, intense,
and expensive. A defense attorney and a prosecutor are chosen by the
congregation to thrash out the case, both naturally having titles evocative of the timelessness of the Vatican: the defense attorney is the
postulator of the cause; the prosecutor is the promoter of the faith
but is far more familiarly known as the devil's advocate. The
witnesses who testified in the first phase are called to Rome, assuming, of course, they're still living, to give their testimony again, and
are often recalled several times. The stacks of documents pertinent
to the candidate's life are read and reread. The promoter of the faith
does everything he can to explain away any outstanding virtuousness
on the candidate's part as just plain good manners, to make the venerable out as someone not necessarily undeserving, but undeserving

of the supreme accolade of sainthood; above all else, the Church does not wish to make a mistake in this critically important area calling into effect the intangibles of faith. In return, the postulator of the cause does everything *he* can to show the promoter's arguments to be nit-picking. This confrontation does not, incidentally, take place in person in a courtroom; questionnaires are sent back and forth between the two.

This is also the point where the most controversial aspect of canonization enters the picture. To reach the next stage toward sainthood, the declaration of beatification, two miracles wrought by the candidate or by a relic of the candidate must be proved—not just asserted miracles or unusual happenings, but *proven, unexplainable* miracles. The twentieth century is not an age in which the Church can with any sanguinity assume educated people will believe in miracles, happenings that by all observable laws of nature shouldn't have happened, and it is accordingly thought by many that without this requirement Roman Catholics would probably take the whole matter of sainthood more seriously, as simply an anachronistic but nonetheless admirable token of honor the Church gives to those who led extraordinarily virtuous lives. But the question of miracles takes canonization beyond the realm of recognition of "saintliness." The Church's reasoning behind the requirement of miracles is that the state of saintliness is a fact that can be made known only by God, and the miracles are God's way of divulging that he has, in effect, "overruled" the laws of nature to indicate the candidate's eligibility.

Proving that the candidate is responsible for miracles is, not unexpectedly, the thing that trips up a lot of the causes. Today miracles are, almost without exception, happenings in the realm of medical cures. In olden days, they sometimes involved real *Sturm und Drang*—the seas opening, columns of fire, and the like. Nowadays, the inexplicable remissions of seemingly hopeless cancers as a result of touching a relic, or recovering from "mortal" wounds after having a picture of the candidate shown to the victim are the evidence the canonic court is likely to be confronted with. The reputed miracles are subjected to intense and skeptical scrutiny, making sure that the most learned medical experts aren't able to justify their miraculous nature by any natural, scientific explanation.

In the recent process that led to the canonization of a nineteenth-century Philadelphia bishop, John Neumann, America's first male saint, the miracles that were accepted as such by the congregation involved a six-year-old boy being cured of the nearly always fatal Ewing's sarcoma after several visits to the Neumann shrine; a nineteen-year-old auto-accident victim suffering from a crushed skull who had a piece of Neumann's cassock applied to the wound by his mother; and a girl, eleven years old, who in 1923 had her peritonitis, in those days a hopelessly fatal condition, cured when the bishop's picture was touched to her swollen abdomen. The Vatican acknowledged these occurrences as true miracles and in 1977 rewarded the ninety-one-year-long struggle by the bishop's Philadelphian adherents by declaring Neumann a saint.

Assuming the candidate successfully gets past the first two required miracles, he will have reached the second plateau on his long journey and be accorded the status of newly beatified with a grand (but not papal-led) ceremony and mass in St. Peter's. Beatification bestows the status of "blessed" on the candidate and permits veneration on a truncated scale, veneration that could theoretically be revoked at any time if untoward evidence later turns up to indicate the candidate was less deserving than was previously believed.

To proceed to the ultimate step of canonization, all that has to be done is to prove two more miracles, but miracles that must have been wrought *after* the two that were used to get beatification. There can sometimes be papal exemptions from this requirement for the additional miracles, such as for saint-candidates who died with the status of martyrs, which was the recent case with Maximilian Kolbe (discussed later in this chapter), but the majority of causes will not go on to fulfillment without them. All of this may seem a bit like gilding the lily, but the extreme caution that accompanies canonization has a very sound justification: When a blessed is declared a saint, it is done formally and irrevocably by the pope, and that act is thus considered to come under the protection of papal infallibility. In other words, the pope *cannot* have made a mistake. Under such circumstances, the Sacred Congregation for the Causes of Saints is under enormous pressure to have done its homework with absolute, watertight thoroughness.

The initiation of the new saint into the Church's pantheon takes place in one of the most spectacular of all papal ceremonies. The pope will climax the solemn rite with the declaration and final judgment that "we decree and define that the blessed such-and-such is a saint, and we enter his (or her) name in the role of saints, ordering that his (or her) memory be religiously venerated every year by the Church throughout the world." This formula constitutes official recognition by the Church that the new saint has in fact and without doubt won a place in heaven and is there permanently residing; the newly canonized is thereafter referred to by the title Saint (*Sanctus*) before his or her name, is officially enrolled in the Canon of Saints, and is assigned a special feast day.

The achievement of canonization would appear to be filled with inconsistencies. For example, very few popes since the early ones, for whom the accolade was almost automatic, have been canonized; the only pope since the thirteenth century to have been declared a saint was Pius X, named to the Canon of Saints in 1954. Yet far, far humbler and lesser-known souls have been canonized right and left. The explanation sounds like a genuine Catch-22: The simpler and less consequential life a person has led has the effect of making it much easier to examine for circumstances that would disbar one from sainthood. How much trouble could twelve-year-old St. Maria Goretti, a rape victim, have gotten into before her death? But for a religious leader of major consequence, someone like a pope who has led a life full of heavy responsibilities, there is a great deal more to investigate, and the possibilities of unsaintly behavior consequently are that much greater.

Then there is the matter of "heroic intensity," another requirement for canonization. This says that to be considered for beatification and canonization, one has had to pursue virtues in a manner extraordinary in both motive and perseverance. It, or rather the absence of it, is said to be one of the factors that stands in the way of sainthood for John XXIII, a man who is an undoubted example of virtuousness but one who seems to have been that way quite naturally and without having had to struggle for it—without, in other words, having had the required "heroic intensity." One wonders if this same problem mightn't someday come up with Calcutta's Mother Theresa, who will surely be considered for sainthood soon after her death, because she is a woman whose goodness seems to be as innate and natural as life itself.

Although the procedures leading to sainthood are strict and strictly enforced, recent history suggests that the Congregation for the Causes of Saints will quicken the process when a reigning pope

insists on it being quickened. Being himself theoretically the guar-
antor that the sainthood was truly earned, the pope can formally
waive and even ignore some of the rules. For example, St.
Barbarigo's canonization was pushed through in a year by John
XXIII in a special procedure known as an "equivalent canonization," where a person has been considered saintly or has had a cult
for so many centuries that the canonization itself merely confirms
what had been "assumed" for so long. A more recent and still controversial example was John Paul II's October 1982 canonization of
Maximilian Kolbe, a Franciscan priest who willingly chose to die in
place of a condemned man. Ordained in 1911 in Lwów in his native
Poland and changing his given name from Raymond to Maximilian,
he developed a deep attachment to the Virgin Mary, the same kind
of attachment that John Paul today shares. Out of his special devotion Kolbe founded the Knights of the Immaculate Movement,
committed to carrying out good works in Mary's name. He later began another religious community, dedicated to spreading the gospel, called the City of the Immaculate, with its own daily newspaper
and monthly magazine. Soon after the Nazi invasion in 1939, Kolbe
was arrested, but he was released a few months later. When he went
back to his religious activities and turned the City of the Immaculate into a refugee center a little over a year later, the Nazis
rearrested him, this time sending him to Auschwitz, where Kolbe
and other inmate priests continued their pastoral work.

In July 1941, ten inmates were ordered to be executed in reprisal
for the escape of a prisoner, and it was one of these men—Franciszek
Gajowniczek, the father of a family—whose place Kolbe volunteered
to take. At first put into a starvation barracks, the priest was finally
and probably mercifully executed on August 14 with an injection of
carbolic acid. Thirty years later he was beatified by Pope Paul VI,
and on October 10, 1982, in the presence of eighty-one-year-old
Gajowniczek, was canonized by Pope John Paul II and given the title of martyr.

That John Paul would wish to do special honor not only to a fellow Pole and priest who had suffered so grievously at the hands of
their country's tormenters but also to one who had witnessed and
morally triumphed over that country's desecration by the Germans
is well within the limits of understanding. That the pope wished
Kolbe's life to be an example to his fellow priests as a personal

sacrifice imitating that of Christ is also both admirable and seemingly well within the best interests of the Church. But the controversy within the Church came over the seeming haste of the canonic process, haste that is highly unusual in this most delicate and deliberate of actions. Here, so it was felt by some within the Curia, was an example of papal wishes taking precedence over long and justifiably carefully established practice.

Kolbe was one of four canonizations by John Paul in 1982, the first performed in his then four-year pontificate. Paul VI had canonized twenty-two plus two groups of martyrs—twenty-two Ugandans and forty Englishmen and Welshmen—in his fifteen years as pope. First named was Crispin of Viterbo, a seventeenth-century Franciscan lay brother, at a ceremony in which the pope proudly declared that it was "the first time in my service in the See of Peter that I have had the joyous destiny to carry out a canonization." Beatified by Pius VII in 1806, Crispin attained saintliness through his service to the poor in his native Italy. Marguerite Bourgeoys founded a small community for Indians in seventeeth-century French Canada; the French-born missionary had been declared blessed by Pius XII in 1950. The last of John Paul's first four saints was Jeanne Delanoue, another seventeenth-century Frenchwoman who established a sanctuary for the poor in her native France; she was beatified three years earlier than Marguerite Bourgeoys.

Despite the Kolbe case, it still is apparent that the recent great and/or saintly are not rushed into sainthood. A petition for canonization for Princess Grace of Monaco, for example, stands little chance of seeing a successful conclusion in the lifetime of most who knew her. The Vatican says that there is no evidence of a large number of the faithful regarding her as saintly, explaining that fame of sanctity is a necessary ingredient for canonization. (An odd fact here is that only about fifty-four of the more than twenty-six hundred existing saints were married; whether this would have a bearing on Princess Grace's process is problematical.) If John XXIII's canonization sees the light of the fading twentieth century, it still will have been acted upon in a manner that could almost be described as hasty. Great emphasis is being placed by the Church on Third World candidates in respect of the millions of non-European Catholics who have relatively few saints of their own countries or regions to venerate. Palestinian nun Maria Baouardy, born of Greek Melkite Arab parents near Nazareth in 1846 and who founded an order of Carmelite nuns in Bethlehem, was beatified by John Paul II in November 1983. Six months later, the Pope visited Seoul, South Korea, where before a crowd in Yoedo Plaza estimated at six hundred thousand people, he canonized ninety-three Korean and ten French missionary martyrs who gave their lives for their faith over a nearly forty-year period starting in 1839. It was the first canonization ceremony performed outside Rome since the Middle Ages and was the largest number of saints ever canonized on one occasion. It also had the odd effect of making Korea—a country only about a quarter Christian— the nation with the fourth-largest number of saints in the Church, following Italy, Spain, and France.

Semantics aside, the Church still considers all those who have attained paradise to share the accolade of sainthood, a Heaven filled with countless "uncanonized saints" if you will, known only to God. There is even a special holiday for them, the feast of All Saints, celebrated each year on November 1 and held as one of the Church's holy days of obligation. Perhaps their heroic intensity was on a smaller scale and their good deeds confined to the family circle, but there is small doubt that God's love for his little saints is no less than for his heroes and heroines in the pantheon of the canonized.

10

Pontifical Treasures:
Art in the Vatican

"The Church collects and watches over all that belongs to the history of man, because nothing that is human is extraneous or indifferent to her." These words were spoken by Pope John Paul II at the January 1984 opening of a Vatican art exhibition commemorating a battle in which a Polish Catholic king defeated an Ottoman army threatening Western Christianity, but they are the cornerstone of the artistic philosophy that has guided a remarkably high percentage of the popes since the earliest centuries of the papacy. Rarely if ever has a governing dynasty been so artistically unblinkered as has the line of men who have ruled the Roman Catholic Church, a blessing that has resulted in the preservation of the Vatican as the world's cardinal repository of the Christian experience.

The largest by far of all of the functions of Vatican City, as distinct from the Holy See, is that of a museum. Visitors to the papal kingdom's vast complex of galleries and chapels and libraries, a fine-arts exchequer housing not only the artistic gold of the papacy's history but also a fair share of its dross, are inevitably astonished at the seemingly endless extent of these collections. Some of the museums frankly resemble storehouses as much as assembled collections; others are fairly overwhelming in the magnificence of their presentations. But in the aggregate, what the nearly two million visitors a year who encounter this spectacle are witness to is a more concentrated assemblage of man's artistic achievements than can be seen anywhere else on earth.

Despite its more immediate priorities, especially those involved with simple survival, the early Church had nonetheless faithfully collected the writings of pre-Christian antiquity, a happenstance in large part owed to the monastic scribes who copied and preserved these precious documents. But the sculpture and painted works of art too redolent of a pagan provenance were in the early centuries held in little regard, sometimes statues that were uncovered simply being ground up for chalk. What constituted the greater part of its public display of the objects of historic and artistic value was confined to a purely sacramental context within churches rather than in anything like organized galleries.

The Vatican museums in their contemporary sense descend from modern Europe's first art gallery open to the public. In 1471, Pope Sixtus IV, from the wealthy della Robbia family, assembled a group of his own classical sculpture and put it on display in the Capitoline Palace, the ancient seat of the Roman Senate, following this initial effort four years later with the founding of the Vatican Library. Although Sixtus's several immediate predecessors had sponsored artists of world stature, the papal capital had in the decade and a half since the reign of Nicholas V lost its lead to several other cities—Florence, Siena, even minor towns—in its prominence as an art center. But with Sixtus and his prodigious architectural and artistic endeavors, the city regained its prominence, adopting the artists of more fertile regions and making their combined work one of the most lasting legacies of the Renaissance-era papacy.

The direct progenitor of the modern Vatican museums was established in 1503 by Sixtus's nephew and the very model of the Renaissance papal monarch as art connoisseur, Julius II. In the courtyard of the Belvedere Palace, today called the Octagonal Courtyard, which was built by his predecessor Innocent VIII, Julius set up a kind of sculpture garden composed of Greek and Roman statues, including a number of Roman copies of what were then thought to be genuine Greek works. The central masterpiece was the splendid Apollo, which later became familiar as the Apollo Belvedere, a treasure Julius himself had acquired while still a cardinal. First among the other masterworks Julius added to the display were the fantastic Laocoön group, discovered in the Palace of Titus in 1506, and a monumental statuary personification of the Nile with its sixteen children, a representation of the sixteen cubits that the river then rose in flood tide, climbing over the central God figure. This museum was supposedly accessible to the public, but in actuality only its educated elements were welcome. A sign—*"procul este prophani"* (roughly "The profane keep out")—warned the unwashed away from the manicured garden with its fragrant orange trees and rippling streams.

Papal collecting continued, although the acquisitions of the succeeding popes went not to new museums but to decorate the lavish suites of apartments in the Vatican palaces, includng the long wings erected to connect Innocent's Belvedere to the older Apostolic Palace. In spite of Julius's start, two and a half centuries were to pass before anything more would be done to add public galleries to serve specifically as museums. The Sistine Library was endowed with a "Christian museum" in the mid eighteenth century and a few years later with a "profane museum," but the first authentic modern gallery in the Vatican was the great Pio-Clementine Museum completed in 1784. Named for the two popes instrumental in its establishment—Clement XIV (whose idea it was to establish it as an entity entirely separate from the Vatican Library) and Pius VI—and incorporating Julius's sculpture garden, it is still the heart of the modern Vatican museums. The actual display rooms built by Clement were really an adaptation of existing structures, but Pius's additions represented completely new galleries built exclusively as exhibition space.

The papal collection experienced its greatest modern instance of pillage shortly after the establishment of the Pio-Clementine Museum, when the Treaty of Tolentino awarded spoils to the victorious French armies, spoils that included the best of the Pio-Clementine treasures; furthermore, during the French occupation of the city, much of the Vatican Library's collections of coins, gems, and medals were also "appropriated." All were coveted by Napoleon to enrich his capital, of course. Although most of the museum's riches were returned after Waterloo, most of those taken from the library have remained in Paris to this day.

With the fall of the French, displaced art treasures that had been stolen by Napoleon's armies from all over the Papal States were returned to Rome, where Pius VII decided to keep them in the Vatican. He added the Braccio Nuovo—the "New Arm"—across the enormous Belvedere Palace courtyard parallel to the earlier arm that had been constructed for the Library, especially to house the additional classical sculpture. The recaptured paintings, among which was Raphael's exalted Transfiguration, which had been the central glory of Rome's Church of St. Peter in Montorio, formed the nucleus of the Pinacoteca, or picture gallery. Other parts of the Vatican, including the Borgia Apartments, continued to receive the overflow of the Holy See's growing mass of art.

Gregory XVI, succeeding to the papal throne in 1831, eight years after Pius VII's death, was the next pivotal figure in the development of the museums. Gregory built the Gregorian-Etruscan and Gregorian-Egyptian galleries (in 1837 and 1839, respectively), expanding the museums' scope from what had been up to then a predominantly Greco-Roman character; he also founded the Lateran Profane Museum in the Lateran Palace. It was brought together with the later Christian Museum and Missionary-Ethnological Museum in the Vatican by John XXIII, who ordered a totally modern building constructed to house the combined collections; the structure was inaugurated by Paul VI in 1971. Leo XIII restored the Borgia Apartments in the Apostolic Palace and opened it as a museum to the public; Leo's successor, Pius X, transferred much of the Vatican's Byzantine and medieval Italian paintings from the library to the picture galleries. Pius XI made many of the most major visible changes in the museums confronted by today's visitors: Besides the establishment of the museums' restorations laboratories, he constructed the largest modern architectural element of the complex, the new Pinacotheca building, a gallery displaying the best of the Holy See's immense collection of painted works, and also commissioned the enormous portal in the Vatican's north wall as a more efficient public grand entrance to the galleries complex than the prior entry through St. Peter's Square.

In terms of extending the museums into new or underrepresented realms, the remarkable pontificate of Paul VI will in all likelihood be commemorated by future generations as the Pauline Era. John XXIII's combined Christian, Profane, and Missionary-Ethnological Museum, constructed parallel to the Pinacotheca, saw its collections enormously enriched by Paul, and many parts of the papal collection were rearranged into far more distinguished settings. The new Collection of Modern Religious Art was arranged for display in the Borgia Apartments and the lower level of the Sistine Chapel, and an ultramodern subterranean gallery was built under the Pinacotheca's garden to house the new History Museum. The latest changes made, under John Paul II's pontificate, include the rearrangement of the Gregorian-Etruscan Museum; alterations in the Court of the Pine, the northernmost of the Belvedere Palace's courtyards; and a long-needed remodeling of the aged sculpture gallery in the Braccio Nuovo.

By the time the iron gates open at nine o'clock, the museums' broad entrance plaza in Viale Vaticano has already overfilled with a throng of pertinacious souvenir sellers; bands of familiar-looking mendicants; a score of sleek German tour buses disgorging riders and noxious fumes in equal parts; and already a long line of tourists, pilgrims, and art lovers anxious to push through the turnstiles leading into the museums' grand entryway piercing the slope of the Vatican hill. Air-conditioned elevators are available to take the visitors from the vestibule to the garden level, where the ticket booths are located, but most walk up the handsome double spiral ramp whose bronze balustrades are decorated with symbols of the papacy, themselves not inconsiderable objects of admiration. The circular foyer at the top looks a little like a bus station waiting room, where are housed not only the ticket offices but also a foreign-exchange booth, a post office with its own small private writing room, sales counters banked with stacks with books and postcards, and an emergency first-aid station.

A ticket to the museums (five thousand lire in 1984, about three dollars) is an extraordinary bargain, especially for the visitor who remains for the entire eight hours that the museums stay open. With exemplary charity, especially to those younger Romans to whom five thousand lire represent a considerable burden, the museums are open free of charge on the last Sunday of each month. The major issue that has to be decided by each visitor is which of the four itineraries best suits his or her time, interests, and—especially—strength. Until a few years ago, anyone could wander at will over the nearly forty thousand square yards of exhibits extending almost four and a half miles, going back and forth to reexamine favored areas of interest, skipping exhibits or galleries or even entire buildings as one wished. But with an average of almost five thousand patrons a day and twenty thousand not uncommon at the height of the summer tourist season, the museum administration was forced to institute the one-way visit system in which one of four itineraries is chosen and then maintained by following colored lines set in the floors, the primary purpose of which is to prevent backtracking.

According to the brochure, the shortest tour takes only an hour and a half, giving a visitor very little more than a peek at the top highlights but including, as do all the itineraries, the most popular sight and the one serious traffic bottleneck, the Sistine Chapel. Two other itineraries, each calculated to take the average visitor about three hours, wend through a somewhat more extensive set of galleries and museums, in some places overlapping. The Grand Slam, estimated at about five hours without any significant dawdling, takes the visitor at least *by* almost everything. But really to *see* and even minimally digest all that the museums have to offer would, at an absolute minimum, require several full days of wandering along the four-and-a-half-mile track. The complex is, fortunately, so vast that even the many thousands visiting on a heavy summer day do not constitute the kind of oppressive crowding typical of major exhibits in U.S. museums, except, of course, at the perpetually jammed Sistine Chapel.

From the vestibule, the tour of the museums proper begins, with the ten rooms of the Gregorian Egyptian Museum the first set of galleries visited. (We'll assume the Grand Slam circuit in the following description.) Built primarily by nineteenth-century pontiffs, this Egyptian collection mirrors the interest that popes shared with many other great collectors in the ancient civilization of Egypt. Most of the objects were either acquired by Gregory XVI, the museum's builder, or else have since been donated, many from the khedive of Egypt to Leo XIII, in the century and a half since the museum was formally constituted. The best of its exhibits are the mummies displayed in a series of rooms designed to look like tombs in Egypt's Valley of the Kings, although the forest of ancient Nilotic statues loses some of its impact through poor display, the effect of one magnificent example of statuary being too often reduced because of its juxtaposition with a dozen or more nearly exact mates;

many of the galleries in the complex share this problem of having so many treasures that fatigue sets in.

After the Gregorian Egyptian Museum comes the Chiaramonti Museum, named for the family of its founder, Pius VII, and affected by the same sort of overkill as the Egyptian collection. The gallery itself is so unusual, however, that the display tends to engross rather than induce satiation. Laid out by renowned sculptor Antonio Canova in his capacity as the full-time director general of the Vatican Museums, the thousand closely spaced pieces of classical Roman sculpture, dominated by bust portraits of prosperous citizens of the empire, line either side of the long Bramante corridor between the Belvedere and Apostolic palaces. A partitioned portion of the corridor beyond an ornate iron gate houses the Lapidary Gallery, closed to all except scholars who are allowed to visit it by prearrangement; its collection, which is evidently thought not to present any great attraction to the casual visitor, consists of some five thousand ancient "epigraphical testimonies," or inscriptions carved in stone or marble; the Christian examples are set in one wall, the pagan inscriptions in the other.

Doubling back on the almost tunnellike Chiaramonti gallery, the Pio-Clementine Museum comes next on the one-way route. Taking in the northernmost parts of the complex around what was the original Belvedere Palace Court (now the Octagonal Court) of Innocent VIII, the Pio-Clementine is a planned eighteenth-century museum displaying its sculpted treasures in theatrically contrived but nonetheless impressive neoclassical settings. Many of the papal collection's most familiar prizes are found in these rooms and courtyards, including the three most famous treasures of all: the Apollo Belvedere, the Belvedere Torso, and the Laocoön. Both the Apollo, a Roman copy of a Greek bronze, and the Laocoön, a marvelously melodramatic group depicting a father and his two sons entwined in the coils of a pair of great writhing serpents, are set in their own niches in the open Octagonal Court. The Apollo, perhaps the signature piece of the entire Vatican collection, represented the apogee of masculine beauty, the Laocoön the depths of human desperation. But it is the Torso, a headless and armless fragment, legs missing from the knees, that is regarded by many as the most eloquent and powerful piece of carved stone in the world. Created in the first century before Christ by the Athenian Apollonius, the work more than any other seems to have life within, and its influence was so great on Michelangelo that the sculptor proudly referred to himself as "a pupil of the Torso."

After winding one's way through the last sections of the Pio-Clementine galleries, including the majestic and dramatic Round and Greek Cross rooms, the Simonetti Stairway rises to the second-floor Gregorian Etruscan Museum, a gallery filled with artifacts of the ancient central Italian civilization, most excavated during the nineteeth century when the area comprised part of the Papal States. The Etruscan galleries include the top two stories of the half-circle gallery in the Nicchione at the north end of the Belvedere, the higher affording a spectacular view of the museum courts and, beyond, the mass of the Apostolic Palace rearing above the gallery roofs.

The course continues on the second floor down the long opposing western arm of the Belvedere, divided into three main sections before finally ending at the Raphael Stanze and the Sistine Chapel. The first of the three is the Gallery of the Candelabra, originally an open loggia, today filled with classical sculpture. A third of the distance down the corridor, the marbles give way to the Gallery of Tapestries, a corridor lined since 1838 with the "New School" work, to distinguish them from the "Old School" tapestries displayed in the Pinacoteca; many are from designs made by students of Raphael. The final third of the corridor is the Gallery of Maps, the brilliant gold and blue of the forty topographical maps of the regions of Italy on the opposing walls that are one of the museums' most successful crowd-pleasers.

Leaving these relatively modern and spacious apartments, most of which were designed to serve specifically as galleries, the "system" now takes all four tours into the far older and more cramped exhibits and rooms of the Borgia Apartments in the Apostolic Palace end of the complex, including the Raphael Stanze, a series of four rooms whose historic decorations were created by the staggeringly talented contemporary of Michelangelo in the early sixtenth century. Together with the Sistine Chapel, they constitute probably the Holy See's most valuable and renowned stationary treasure. After passing through the nearby Raphael Loggia, a corridor overlooking the St. Damase Courtyard and enclosed by windows in the nineteenth century to protect the delicately painted walls from the weather, stairs lead down to the Borgia Apartments on the level below. These rooms, directly under the Stanze and Loggia, were the private apartments of the Spanish Borgia pope Alexander VI and were lushly painted for that luxury-loving pontiff by Bernardino Betti under his alias of Pinturicchio.

A labyrinthine pathway leads down to the cellar under the Sistine Chapel, where the Pauline Collection of Modern Religious Art is displayed in a series of small, stark chambers, nearly all of which are ignored by many of the visitors after half-guilty glances into their visitor-bereft spaces. Finally, an undecorated passageway, long and claustrophobic, usually crowded, and spaced every few feet with scratchy loudspeakers giving multilingual instructions on behavior, including a strictly enforced warning forbidding photography, leads into the room on whose walls and ceiling is painted one of the greatest tourist attractions and arguably the best-known artistic accomplishment on earth.

Entry for the nearly three million tourists who troop through the Sistine Chapel is not via the main ceremonial entrance from the Sala Regia, the large and splendid architectural confection Paul III had has architect Sangallo build to impress Europe's monarchs, but merely through a low and inconspicuous door at the altar end of the room. On entering, nearly every eye unconsciously ascends to the ceiling, skipping right past the merely masterful murals on the lower side walls, the latter the work of such geniuses as Botticelli, Ghirlandaio, and Perugino. It's the ceiling and the altar wall with the two quite distinct fresco paintings of Michelangelo—the Creation and the Last Judgment, the first painted at the height of the artist's young manhood, the other a quarter century later (altogether forty-two years separate the first brushstrokes on the ceiling to the last on the end wall)—that utterly awe those who are in their physical presence for the first time. In spite of the recorded warnings and the hawk-eyed guards lining the room, every few minutes a surreptitious picture-taker will break the rules; those brazen enough to use a flash get a sharp rebuke.

The crowds in the chapel are, in the main, oblivious to the small crew of art restorers plying their esoteric craft behind and above the temporary barriers hiding the clutter of their tools from public view. Sponsored by the private television company Nippon Television Network Corporation (NTV) and under the direction of the chief

Vatican art restorer Gianluigi Colalucci, the twelve-year, three-million-dollar project, scheduled for completion in 1992, has as its goal the cleaning and restoration of the two Michelangelo fresco murals in the chapel, frescoes that were called by one writer "very likely the twelve hundred most precious square meters in all of Christendom." The work is about a third completed. Both medieval painting methods employed by the masterpieces' creator and modern technology are being used to remove the five centuries of dust, dirt, and soot (the latter from the torches and tallow candles used to illuminate the chapel in the years before electric lighting was instituted at the turn of the twentieth century) in the murals' first thorough cleaning. Unfortunately the overpainted loincloths on the altar fresco cannot be lifted without irreparably damaging the original; the wisps of paint rest on a second layer of plaster, which is bonded to the bottom layer.

M. Kobayashi, head of NTV, convinced his skeptical board of directors to finance the project with the reasoned plea that "we are a public service and have obligations to our viewers, one of them being to let the [Japanese] public know of the culture of the West." The return on NTV's investment, aside from any spiritual satisfaction, is the exclusive right to film and distribute documentary television programs on the work, both during the project and for three years after the completion of each phase of the work. Even the Italians have been quietly pleased with the arrangement, realizing that this is the first time in art history that the public will be able to follow the minute-by-minute restoration of one of mankind's supreme cultural treasures.

At the main doors at the front end of the chapel, the entrance used by the Sacred College when it enters en masse to elect a new pope, tourists can stick their heads over the barriers to see, at an unfortunate angle, the Sala Regia. Sadly the Pauline Chapel with its two Michelangelo murals and the long and richly polychromatic Sala Ducale are just out of visual range and are not shown to the public.

Upon leaving the Sistine Chapel, the route again returns to the long corridors of the Belvedere, now the first-floor west wing that houses the public museum part of the Vatican Library. The two Belvedere cross wings are seen on this part of the route—the Library Arm with its spectacular golden Sistine Salon, and the New Arm, a sculpture gallery attached to the Chiaramonti Museum. At the end of the library corridor, the visit to the Belvedere and Apostolic palaces parts of the museums gives way to the new museums built since the establishment of the Vatican state.

The Pinacoteca is the museums' main picture gallery, a "conventional" museum designed along the same general lines as those in any large city in Europe or America. The difference is, of course, that very few museums can match the nearly endless stores of art that centuries of popes have collected for posterity and their own enjoyment. The supreme masterpiece of the Pinacoteca is Raphael's *Transfiguration,* but the galleries and corridors are filled with works by Melozzo da Forli, Titian, Veronese, da Vinci (his spiritual *St. Jerome* is one of the most haunting paintings ever created), Caravaggio, Cranach, and other great artists. Striking an ecumenical note is a Thomas Lawrence work, a huge portrait of England's King George IV, a papal ally in the defeat of Napoleon; the painting was a personal gift to Pius VII from the British King.

The Historical Museum, a creation of Paul VI, is an underground gallery divided into roughly equal halves, with papal transportation—nineteenth-century coaches, twentieth-century cars—at one end, uniforms and decorations of the pontifical armed forces at the other. To build this museum, the formal Pinacoteca garden was removed, the museum was built, and the garden was put back in place. The tours end at the back of the Pinacoteca, between it and the Vatican wall, with the modern museum housing the Pio-Christian collection, the Gregorian Profane Museum, and the Missionary-Ethnological Museum, all having been artfully wedged into the very limited confines.

The conditions that permitted the Medici pope Leo X to spend six hundred thousand ducats a year on the acquisition of art in an age when a family could live comfortably on an annual income of two hundred ducats have long since vanished from the Holy See. Vying with Europe's other secular princes, the popes often maintained the leading position as international sponsors of talented artists and purchasers of the finest work being created, sometimes funding their passion with income realized from the sale of indulgences, episcopates, and Roman titles of nobility. The artistic patrimony that Peter's successors accumulated today amounts to hundreds of thousands of items, of which perhaps half are on actual display in the museums, the remainder still in storage or waiting to be cataloged.

Since the age of papal acquisition of art has given way to one primarily of the preservation of its collections, the most common method by which the Vatican museums continue to be enriched is through the gifts of both generous nations and private donors, the individual museums also acquiring items through internal transfer. The Missionary-Ethnological Museum, for example, has received gifts of valuable and rare carpets from Iran and Afghanistan, and other galleries have similarly received bequests from sources all over the world.

The museums' administration is a branch of the Governorship of the Pontifical Commission for the Vatican city-state called the General Administration of the Pontifical Monuments, Museums, and Galleries and thus is subject to the state's governing board of six cardinals, led by Agostino Casaroli, the papal secretary of state; the body also has final approval authority over its annual budget. Of the millions of dollars required to administer and maintain the papal art complex annually, only a fraction is derived from admission fees, an amount just adequate to pay the salaries and wages of the 250 people needed to maintain the facilities. Included in the staff are only 10 curators and 30 conservators and restorers but 130 guards; all are under the direct command of a Roman-born archaeologist and the museums' director general, Professor Dr. Carlo Pietrangeli, a Knight of Magisterial Grace of the Order of Malta and successor to the famous Deoclecio Redig de Campos (director general from 1971 to 1979 and now director general emeritus). Pietrangeli's responsibilities include not only all the pontifical museums but also all of Rome's pilgrimage basilicas except St. Peter's.

The two major concerns for the museums, in terms of both cost and difficulties, are in the areas of security and restoration. Security considerations today have switched from outright thievery to the more perplexing and, in many ways, harder to prevent "vandalism to make a statement," usually a political statement, as for example the attack on Michelangelo's Pieta, which led to the placing of this most delicate example of the sculptor's work at a safer remove from the public. The twelve dozen or so guards provide only a thin line of security in the vast stretches of galleries, so it was necessary to encase behind glass the most famous paintings and statues, and therefore most desirable targets, a solution that to an annoying if slight degree decreases the viewer's ability to see the works as the artists intended. The precautions have been proved necessary: on one morning—one would hope not an entirely typical one—security searches of visitors' personal belongings carried past the entrance uncovered a Bowie knife, a jackknife, a kitchen knife, a pair of scissors, a saw-bladed kitchen knife, five penknives, and a loaded revolver, this last belonging to a man who styled himself a "private detective."

If our era is in fact one of expert and caring conservation, such was rarely the case in past centuries. Even granting the lack of anything resembling modern technology in the way art is preserved, past guardians of these treasures were by today's standards remarkably cavalier in the treatment of their artistic heritage. The altar candles, censers, torches, and braziers in the Sistine Chapel were allowed nearly to blacken the lower part of the Last Judgment; fragments of ancient sculpture were "fixed" by having ersatz limbs added; frescoes in the open Apostolic Palace loggias were left for centuries to the demaging effects of the elements; armies rampaging at periodic intervals through the papal treasures did immeasurable and irremediable damage; the Reformation-era Grundyism defaced masterpieces; and the delicate fibers in the splendid tapestries disintegrated through carelessness in the way they were handled.

To repair some of the damage wrought by time and folly, the Restoration Laboratories, founded by Pius XI in the 1920s, today bring to bear some of the Vatican's most impressive miracles in technology. The workshop where the sumptuous and invaluable tapestries of the Holy See's collection are restored reveals a prime example of the talents that have been assembled to work these modern miracles. Next to the offices of L'Osservatore Romano in the St. Anne district, several white-habited nuns of the French order of the Missionaries of Mercy toil at their arcane occupation in a room lit by natural sunlight pouring through the six skylights high overhead, a work of devotion and discipline, painstaking and little acknowledged. But the tapestry restorations are only a single example of the efforts being made by the Vatican's museums administration to repair and preserve the papacy's artistic patrimony for posterity. Under Dr. Pietrangeli's direction, work on paintings, statues, frescoes, and many other objects, projects ranging from the well-documented restoration of the Sistine ceiling and the reconstruction of the Apollo Belvedere to the all-but-unknown efforts being made to preserve early Christian manuscripts speak to the Holy See's commitment to hand over its heritage intact to new generations.

The "spectacular" was praised and excoriated, admired by many and called "pompous" by a few. But irrespective of the critical carping that blunted its impact, the 1983–84 Vatican exhibit in the United States was a seminal event for the Holy See and a signal honor for the 2.2 million Americans who, for the first time in history, saw a significant part of the papal art collection outside its permanent home.

The exhibit, titled "The Vatican Collections—The Papacy and Art," came about directly as a result of a request by New York's archbishop, Cardinal Terence Cooke, to Pope John Paul II on his 1979 visit to the United States, but the groundwork had been building for many years. The fact that the cardinal was president of a group called The Friends of American Art in Religion that had long collected works for the Vatican's Modern Religious Art Gallery and was lobbying for such a tour, had a strong impact on the Holy See's decision. Firmly believing that the cultural patrimony of the papal state should be allowed to travel to transmit its spiritual message to a worldwide audience, John Paul accepted the cardinal's entreaty. In Dr. Pietrangeli's words "The Church recognizes its duty to communicate the benefits of its heritage to mankind." Three eminent American museums were settled on to display the broadly based selection of pontifical treasures. The Metropolitan Museum of Art in New York, on whose board Cooke also served as a trustee, was the responsible authority of the exhibition and chose the Art Institute of Chicago and the M. H. de Young Memorial Museum of the Fine Arts Museum in San Francisco as the other two museums. Washington's National Gallery had also attempted to get the exhibit but lost out in the final planning; J. Carter Brown, the gallery's director, had even written directly to the pope proposing a small ancillary exhibition on Raphael for his museum. The final decision between New York and Washington was reported to have at least partially hinged on the former's greater Catholic population as well as the relatively small turnout in Washington during John Paul's 1979 visit to the capital.

The choice of the pieces to form the exhibit was, not unexpectedly, the object of most of the criticism directed against the show;

most of the works were specifically requested by the Metropolitan staff. Although it was obvious that the exhibit planners took quality into account, the primary consideration in selecting the items was gathering a representative sample over the enormously broad spectrum, both in terms of time and taste, of the Vatican's collection of papal acquisitions. In an address in the Nervi Audience Hall, John Paul himself characterized the purpose of the exhibit along these lines: "To relate the long and interesting relationship between the papacy and art throughout the centuries . . . they will speak of history, of the human condition in its universal challenge, and of the endeavors of the human spirit to attain the beauty to which it is attracted." Pietrangeli called the theme of the exhibition "the devotion with which the popes have collected, protected, conserved, and made available to all an incomparable patrimony of works of art and historical and cultural documents." In short, the show would, at center, represent both historic and artistic triumphs of Roman Catholicism and its papacy.

The museums' directors had as a major consideration the consequences of leaving the Vatican's galleries themselves so stripped of their most popular works as to court disgruntling the roughly two million people who would visit them during the fourteen months the items would be on display in the United States. Pietrangeli hopefully explained that "the wealth of our museums is such that the public will not be disappointed if a few works, however important, are absent from their customary home for several months," but the Vatican nonetheless required the borrowers to provide exact duplicates of the sculptured pieces to display in place of the temporarily missing authentic pieces, and little placards were put in front of each of these copies for the duration informing the museum visitors of the switch.

Most of the Vatican museums and venues contributed to the final collection of more than two hundred works of art and artifacts in the exhibition. From the Pio-Clementine complex in the Belvedere Palace came the show's star piece, the Apollo Belvedere, along with such outstanding works as the Belvedere Torso and the Laocoön group. The Pinacoteca sent the *Deposition* by Caravaggio and frescoes by Melozzo da Forli, and the Chiaramonti contributed the magnificent statue known as the Augustus of Prima Porta, one of the greatest sculpted portraits ever found of any of the Roman emperors. Some of the Vatican's most magnificent woven pieces came from the Tapestry Gallery, especially the luminous "Miraculous Draught of the Fishes" after a cartoon by Raphael, and the Basilica of St. Peter's lent a thirteenth-century bust of Boniface VIII and a floridly intricate cross and two candlesticks made for Cardinal Alessandro Farnese in the sixteenth century.

One of the primary factors that had mitigated against any substantial loan of the Vatican's treasures in the past was the obvious, critical, and uniquely dangerous risk of injury. But extreme caution coupled with modern moving techniques—along with the inevitable recognition that works of art face considerable risk even in their own home—overcame any objections on that score. The director general pointed out that the injury to the Pietà happened not on its 1960s visit to the United States but tragically in its own setting in St. Peter's, and proffered further examples: the Night Watch being damaged in its Amsterdam Museum and the Mona Lisa being stolen from the Louvre. In any event, the collection was ensured for fifty million dollars (any meaningful monetary appraisal of these irreplaceable items was, of course, impossible), and they were transported in several shipments geared to the realistic calculation that if one plane goes down, you don't lose everything

The Vatican museums published a newsletter for their patrons that included a detailed description of the procedures employed in moving the art. It may be a bit technical in its specifics, but an abbreviated recounting of the main points demonstrates the extraordinary precautions and care taken in the art's transfer from the Vatican to the United States. The first job tackled was the restoration to the greatest extent possible of each of the two hundred chosen items. Oil paintings and frescoes were cleaned and the sculpture was strengthened—the Apollo, for example, was taken apart (it can be dismantled into thirteen pieces), and stainless steel rods were inserted inside the limbs, enabling it for the first time to stand securely without the supporting iron rod that had braced it in its Vatican position and that, incidentally, made it impossible in its own home to be seen easily from all sides. All of the stages of the restoration process were furthermore meticulously documented with photographs. Over a year's period, the temperature and relative humidity of the paintings' environment in the Vatican were recorded, and three weeks prior to packing the paintings were put into environmental chambers reproducing the temperature and relative humidity of that moment, with the crates, made of new, dried, vermin-free lumber, and the packing material—wood, padding, buffering, and silica gel. The custom-made crates represented one of the show's highest individual items of cost. The environment in the chamber then was slowly changed to the median to which each painting was accustomed, and the receiving museums were notified of the readings and required to provide these exact same conditions until returning the works to the Vatican.

Finally the pieces were packed. The frameless panels (ten of the paintings were executed on wood rather than canvas) were kept stable inside the packing cases with the help of wooden rods fixed to the head of each panel. Nonrigid padding material was inserted along the sides to keep the precious contents in place, but enough room was allowed to expand if needed; painted surfaces were covered with a protective lint-free, nonadhering soft fabric, and a sheet of plastic film was finally put around the entire contents. The silica gel, a substance chosen because of its ability to maintain an even relative humidity during the travel period, filled what room remained in the cases. Each case was placed inside a second case, and, for some paintings, this was placed inside a third container. Padding material was inserted between each to further absorb shocks, vibrations, and accidental drops.

Each procedure was checked along the way by Vatican experts as well as representatives of the receiving museums, the shipping agent, and security officials, and, because the items had to traverse Italian territory to get to Rome's airport, the cases were sealed in the presence of Italian customs officials. Vatican museums couriers accompanied the complex parcels on each flight. After studies by museum officials, it was decided that the jar of a jet's touchdown would represent less danger to the art than the constant vibrations involved in an ocean journey, and regularly scheduled and thus unobtrusive flights were chosen to minimize the risk of loss to terrorism. Fifty million dollars in flight insurance, the maximum provided for international traveling exhibitions under the U.S. government's Art and Artifacts Indemnity program, was taken out on the cargo. Pan American, the official carrier, donated its services, a gift valued at half a million dollars.

On the shipment's arrival in New York, the unloading procedures involved a police-escorted caravan from the airport to the Metropolitan Museum, and the storing of the cases in a controlled environment for twelve to twenty-four hours before being opened. Vatican and Metropolitan conservators supervised the opening, a reversed-order duplicate of the packing at the start of their trip in the Vatican. This exact procedure was followed down to every painstaking detail when the work was sent from New York to Chicago, again from Chicago to San Francisco, and finally from San Francisco back to their Vatican home.

The show was incredibly complicated and incredibly expensive to mount: Philip Morris, Inc., gave a three-million-dollar grant, the largest corporate grant ever given in support of an art exhibition, and Standard Oil of California gave seven hundred thousand dollars, with a five-dollar-per-person admission cost helping to fill in the remainder. However, the endeavor was received with acclaim and gratitude by the American museum-going public in spite of the faultfinding from art critics because every piece wasn't on a level with the show-stoppers. In fact, much of the art was displayed in more congenial and dramatic settings than are possible in the Vatican itself, where the historical surroundings can't easily be altered or arranged to highlight individual items. An estimated 2,194,000 people saw the exhibit in the three museums; a very large share of these people probably would have little opportunity to see the papal treasures in their home setting. If it was John Paul II's wish that the Vatican's material treasures be shared with a wider audience and that the sharing reflect generously on his Church, then the pontifical exhibit was an unqualified success.

Postscript

At the end of this journey through the kingdom dedicated to the memory of the prince of apostles, a last word regarding its course in the years ahead is fitting. The nature of society's problems suggests there will be little or no lessening of the crush of apparently insoluble problems facing the man elected to the throne of Peter. The Vatican is beset on many fronts: pummeled by the "liberation theologists" of the Third World, revolutionaries who would make a separate church for the poor; challenged by militant feminists in North America and Western Europe, Catholics who see the hierarchy's views on human reproduction and women in the priesthood as anachronisms; disdained by the growing body of "preconciliar" conservatives, Catholics who believe the Church has lost its traditional footings; ignored by another equally impassioned body of Western European and North American liberals, their concerns persuasively expressed in the voices of eloquent theologians; and not least, perplexed by the still relatively little-understood problem of black African Catholics attempting to adapt—"inculturate"—their own pre-Christian experience and customs into the liturgy and rites of conventional Roman Catholicism.

Christians have long expected the papacy to provide guidance, but today the holder of the office has come to be looked to for moral inspiration by peoples in all corners of the world. A modern pope is universally *required* to be a voice for reason. Pope John Paul II has often expressed his hope to personally lead his Church into its third millennium. But whether the fifth of the planet's population that calls itself Roman Catholic will continue to heed the moral imperatives coming from Rome at the beginning of the twenty-first century will depend in large part on the wisdom of this pontiff, the successor to 261 men who have gone before him as the guardians of the patrimony of Peter. Although the intransigent difficulties so much a part of the late twentieth century world won't be erased with even the most Solomonaic of papal wisdom, the fact remains that the Church's influence at the beginning of its third thousand years will nonetheless be measured by the decisions being made today in Peter's kingdom.

Appendix:
A Guide to the Popes

Petri dignitas, etiam in indigno herede, non deficit.
The dignity of St. Peter is not lacking, even in an unworthy heir.

Leo I

The papacy dawned at a time coincidental with the beginning of its first—and almost last—antagonist, imperial Rome. It was in the reign of the second emperor, Caesar Tiberius, that the newly martyred founder of the Christian faith passed to his chosen successor, the apostle Simon but whom he called Peter, his supreme authority on earth. Of the lives of the earliest successors of Peter, relatively little is known with certainty. What is historically indisputable is that, speaking in the aggregate, they managed to defend and shepherd Roman Christianity through storms of deadly peril, delivering their growing flock to each successor in turn, until the Church grew into a power no force on earth could stop.

The diversity of station, character, and ability of the 262 men who have legitimately occupied Peter's throne is almost boundless. Their backgrounds have ranged from the heights of the landed nobility to the poverty of itinerant monkhood, their private lives from unarguable saintliness to bottomless venality, their discharge of the office from a level equal to history's greatest heroes to a point where only the institution's momemtum saved the Holy See from disintegration. At the time of their election, the popes have covered an age span from the eighty-six-year-old Gregory IX to the eighteen-year-old Benedict IX. In terms of academic achievement, they range from scholarly graduates of the world's great universities to utter illiterates.

223

In the main, the papacy has been a remarkably middle-class institution. Of the 262 incumbents, the great majority have emerged from the middle rungs of society. A few have been princes or upper bourgeoisie, a few peasants, but the Church hasn't been snobbish about whom it has allowed to become Jesus's vicar and master over the world's emperors. The promise of native ability, still the primary quality sought among young clergymen, has generally been the paramount qualification among the stepping-stones to the pontifical throne.

We see themes constantly repeated during the course of papal history: debilitating wrangling over the fine points of theology; nepotism that became an accepted and much-abused *droit du roi*, practiced, to the Church's detriment by many of Peter's successors; the priest-kings' focus on temporality as an integral part of their office, even to the often shameful denigration of spirituality. But, and it's a mighty but, they always brought their office forward, an *office* intact in its spiritual significance and for many centuries secure in the accepted scheme that mankind had ordered for itself.

The story of the Vatican is, in great part, the accumulated stories of the popes' lives, stories that have filled libraries. I hope that these brief profiles of the men who have sat on the throne of Peter will help the reader better understand not only the Vatican, but also how it became the popes' kingdom.

Much of what is "known" about the early popes is from *Liber Pontificalis* (*Lives of the Popes*), an early history not generally considered to be particularly rigorous documentation. This list is the roster of *official* popes as listed in *Annuario Pontificio*. Anti-popes, thirty-seven false claimants to the Holy See from the third through the fifteenth centuries, were generally elected by dissident or schismatic groups. A total of 262 legitimate popes (264 pontificates) are considered canonically elected. The last anti-pope was Felix V, who died in 1449.

Peter—42–67 (years of pontificate; until the middle of the first millennium, the dates are disputed): Although Peter is called the first "pope," it is inaccurate to think of him, or his early successors, as filling that office in the modern sense of the papacy. As Jesus's closest collaborator, Simon bar-Jona of Galilee always occupied first place among the band of Apostles who followed him on his evangelical journeys throughout what became Palestine. The change of his name from Simon to the Greek Peter, meaning *rock*, gives rise to Jesus's famous epigrammatical charge to his first Apostle that "upon this rock I shall build my Church . . . and I will give you the keys of the kingdom of heaven." According to tradition, Peter served as "bishop" for the Christians of Rome for twenty-five years. He held a position of unique authority within the fledgling community before he was martyred during the reign of Emperor Nero. Condemned to crucifixion, the legend states that Peter asked for, and was granted, the special consideration of being nailed to the cross upside down, so as not to emulate directly the manner in which Jesus died. The office of Peter, as head of Rome's Christians, was the precursor of the bishopric of Rome, and it is from this title that all popes have derived their authority. No successor has taken Peter's name on being elected pope, holding to the traditional notion that the last pope will again be named Peter.

Linus—67–76: The single, although lasting, contribution credited to Linus is the requirement that women cover their heads in church, a custom not relaxed until the reforms of the twentieth-century Second Vatican Council.

Cletus—76–91: Also known as Anacletus, though it will probably never be known what he called himself, Cletus was of Athenian origin. Like his two predecessors and many successors, he died a martyr's death, in his case during the reign of Domitian.

Clement I—91–100: Clement is the first pope designated by an ordinal number, the Roman numeral that follows a ruler's name. Early popes who bore the same name as a predecessor called themselves *junior,* or if the third of the name *secundus junior,* and so on. It was not for another six hundred years that ordinal numbers were used on official documents, and it didn't become common until the tenth century. Even today, the pope's ordinal number is omitted from the most formal papal documents. Clement is best remembered for his letter to the Corinthians chastising them for the schism within their Church that was threatening the authority of the Roman bishop. According to some accounts, Clement's martyrdom occurred when he was thrown into the sea with an anchor tied around his neck.

Evaristus—100–5: Son of a Jew and a Greek, he assigned seven deacons the special task of scrutinizing the teachings of bishops for possible errors in dogma, a function anticipating the later Holy Office.

Alexander I—105–15: Almost nothing is known of Alexander, but during his reign as head of the Church, Trajan's persecutions of Christians were in full force as Rome's preeminent public spectacle.

Sixtus I—115–25: Sixtus is remembered primarily for settling on a movable date for Easter, which hardly settled the matter. It was one of the initial and growing differences between the eastern and western halves of the Church that eventually sundered them. Sixtus also decreed that only priests should be allowed to touch the ceremonial vessels used in the mass, a step toward permanently raising the clergy as a separate and elite class.

Telesphorus—125–38: Established the set number of seven weeks for the pre-Easter fast known as Lent. Telesphorus also authorized a midnight mass on Christmas, an enduring custom since his time.

Hyginus—138–40: Although he was almost a complete mystery personally, the first charges of heresy were then cast against him. Defined as "diluted" or "perverted" teachings or thinking, heresy led to unbelievably brutal passions in coming centuries.

Pius I—140–54: Pius was this pope's actual given name and the first man to bear the name that has come down to our age. The changing of names after election to the papal throne wasn't generally prescribed until shortly before 1000, although a few earlier popes with names of pagan gods such as Mercury and Octavian changed theirs out of respect for the office. Since 1000, only two pontiffs, the Renaissance popes Adrian VI and Marcellus II, kept their baptismal names. Theoretically they were taking the names of earlier Adrians and Marcelluses. As for the first Pius, it is certain only that he was an Italian.

Anicetus—155–66: *Liber Pontificalis* says he forbade the clergy to grow long hair and that he further stimulated the controversy over the date for the Easter celebration. The matter would remain unsettled for a good while longer. Anicetus is thought responsible for building the first memorial over Peter's alleged gravesite.

Soter—166–75: Women had been gaining a larger share in liturgical Church practices, but some historians say that Soter prohibited them from touching the consecrated altar cloth, an ominous sign of things to come.

Eleutherius—175–89: Eleutherius had to contend with the Montanists, a group that believed that inspiration rather than hierarchy should guide Christians. The threat to the papacy inherent in the notion is obvious, but records show that the pope was lenient with the sect.

Victor I—189–99: Victor was African in origin and is known for a treatise he wrote on, of all things, dice-throwing. Under his pontificate, Greek ceased to be the only official language of the Church, eventually replaced by Latin. Victor saw himself as unquestioned head of the *whole* Church and dealt vigorously with dissent. Victor's rule as the bishop of Rome approached our modern definition of a pope.

Zephyrinus—199–217: Besides dealing with renewed state persecution, Zephyrinus handled charges of heresy raging around his office, including that of the troublesome Theodotus the Tanner, who rovingly proclaimed that Jesus wasn't the son of God. Like each of his predecessors to date, Zephyrinus died a martyr at the hands of civil authorities.

Calixtus I—217–22: Hippolytus, history's first declared antipope, set himself up in opposition to Calixtus, whom he considered too lenient with repentant sinners. Calixtus is thought to have built Rome's first Christian basilica in his native Trastevere district. Legend attributes his death not to official persecution but to a crowd of drunken idolaters who threw him out a window. This is but one of several fatal defenestrations in the history of European "culture."

Urban I—222–30: It isn't known why Urban is historically accorded the status of martyrdom, for times were relatively peaceful for Christians during his pontificate. Emperor Alexander Severus, a faily decent sort, even had a statue of Jesus in his home pantheon, probably an act of bet-hedging. During his pontificate, Urban's biggest problem was still the rival Hippolytus. All sources list Urban's one lasting contribution as the edict that sacramental vessels be made of silver rather than glass, a further drift away from the sect's simple origins.

Pontian—230–35: As *Liber Pontificalis* puts it, Pontian was "crowned with martyrdom"; they might have added "in spades." Still plagued by Hippolytus and burgeoning schismatic sects, Pontian had the misfortune to witness mild Alexander Severus replaced on the throne by the brute Maximinus Tracius. Pontian was eventually shipped off to the mines of Sardinia, where the sort of treatment he received was earlier described. Before he met his grisly end, he talked Hippolytus out of his heresy and welcomed him back to the fold, an admirable act of Petrine charity.

Anterus—235–36: His forty-day pontificate is pretty much a historical blank, although he is credited with ordering the recording of the martyrs' acts, a proclamation much appreciated by historians.

Fabian—236–50: Reputedly dedicated to exposing of heretics, Fabian is the subject of the pretty legend of a dove settling on his head as a mark of grace, thus leading his brethren to elect him pope. In fact, almost nothing is known of him.

Cornelius—251–53: Another antipope, this one named Novatian, surfaced to plague Cornelius. His biggest struggle was against the Novatianus schism, a rigorist ideology contemptuous of what it considered a too-easygoing pope.

Lucius I—253–54: Lucius continued Cornelius's charitable policy of forgiving repentant sinners and readmitting them to the sacrament of communion.

Stephen I—254–57: The major event recorded from Stephen's reign was the vexatious matter of baptism renewals carried out by schismatics, an act the pope vigorously condemned. A lesser matter was Stephen's edict that priests not use their sacramental robes for street wear.

Sixtus II—257–58: The first pope to have the same name as a predecessor, he was known in his day as Sixtus, Junior. During his pontificate, he tried to patch up shaky relations with the African and Asian branches of the Church. Emperor Valerianus carried out ghastly persecutions of Christians, Sixtus naturally among those caught in the wholesale massacres.

Dionysius—259–68: Valerianus's persecutions were so brutal that they paralyzed the Christians from choosing a new pope for some time after Sixtus's death. When Dionysius was finally chosen, he had a number of nasty schisms to deal with, heresies that if left unchecked might eventually fragment and destroy the young Church. The miracle is that the popes were able to handle such matters when the authorities were systematically terrorizing them for their religious activities, held as treasonous by the state.

Felix I—269–74: Felix, not unexpectedly, spent most of his time dealing with heresies. He is thought to be the first pope to die a natural death.

Eutychian—275–83: Nothing is known for certain about this pope personally, but the Aurelian persecutions proceeded at a furious pace during his time in office, followed by a long period of peace between the state and the Christians.

Caius—283–96: As in the case of his predecessor, little is known about Caius's personal life, but many reports hold that he issued the edict that bishops should first be priests, today a fundamental tenet of canon law. The peace of the latter part of the previous reign followed through that of Caius.

Marcellinus—296–304: The peaceful interlude for the Christians ends with the Diocletian bloodbaths at the turn of the fourth century, the longest and most severe of those ordered by any Roman emperor. In the middle of this persecution the beleaguered pope was accused by a heretical sect, the Donatists, of offering up sacrifices to idols. After his execution, his headless body was said to have lain in the street for twenty-six days before being buried by a priest.

Marcellus I—308–9: The four-year hiatus in choosing a new pope was due to the turmoil in the Church caused by Diocletian. *Liber Pontificalis* says Emperor Maxentius "condemned" Marcellus to work in his stable as a sign of humiliation. If that's the worst thing that happened to him, he was relatively lucky.

Eusebius—309 or 310: Eusebius fought against the heretical notion that penance was useless in the rehabilitation of Church members who had fallen into sin. This un-Christ-like behavior was basically the work of Heraclius, whose followers set him up as an antipope.

Miltiades—311–14: Another African, Miltiades was of Greek and Berber parentage and supposedly had dark brown skin. Some sources list him as the only black successor to the papal throne. His reign correlated with the epoch of Emperor Constantine, the single person after Christ most responsible for the triumph of Christianity. Constantine credited his famous military victory at Saxa Rubra to divine intercession after claiming he saw the sign of the cross in the sky the evening before the battle. He forgave the Christians their heresy, openly befriended the faith with the zeal typical of a convert (which he wasn't, yet), declared Christianity the official religion, and gave the Lateran Palace to Pope Miltiades as a gift to be used for Church headquarters. Because the bishop of Rome had his official seat, or see, at the Lateran Palace, it would forever serve as the cathedral of Rome.

Not least of Miltiades's joys was that when he died, he did so in his own bed, which from then on became the normal course of affairs. In the wake of the accrued power that accompanied Christianity's transformation from an outlaw sect also came arrogance and luxury, two factors that eventually debilitated the Church almost to the point of its destruction.

Sylvester I—314–35: Thanks to the imperial protection now extended to the sect, things got a great deal easier for the Christians. The alliance between Church and state initiated the transformation of Christianity into a universal faith. This also established, not entirely for the good, the temporal character of the hierarchy, which would conflict with its spiritual nature until well into the twentieth century. Of primary importance was the famous "Donation of Constantine," wherein the emperor purportedly bestowed the Church's primacy on the pope, an official act by the medieval papacy justifying the foundation for its claims of temporal power. Historians now believe the Donation document, which didn't turn up until 800, was a forgery never granted by the emperor, but it nonetheless played an indisputedly important part in the later history of the papacy. Sylvester's towering achievement was convening the Council of Nicea, whose aim was to put down yet another heresy but that instead brought the Church its central article of faith, the Nicene Creed. This article proclaims the divinity and "consubstantial" nature of Jesus as God the Son to God the Father. Constantine founded his new eastern capital during Sylvester's pontificate; no emperor would ever again return to Rome to take up permanent residence. However, the illusion of its role as the legitimate capital of the empire remained for another century.

Mark—336: Mark first conferred the pallium on the bishop of Ostia as a symbol of episcopal authority. These white wool bands are still worn today around the shoulders of the pope and residential archbishops and are consecrated annually by being lowered by the pontiff into Peter's tomb in the Confession of St. Peter's Basilica.

Julius I—337–52: Constantine died shortly after Julius's installment, and the empire was divided under the emperor's sons, Costanzo, Costante, and Constantine II. This factor, among many, would eventually contribute to the splitting of the Church into Roman and Byzantine halves.

Liberius—352–66: He ordered the construction of Rome's pilgrimage basilica of St. Mary Major but was forced into exile by the Emperor Costanzo in a showdown over who, pope or emperor, was really in charge of the Church. The emperor still commanded greater strength and thus prevailed. When Costanzo died, Liberius resumed his role as head of the Church in both halves of the empire.

Damasus I—366–84: A scholar and a gentle pope, he prompted Lucifer of Cagliari to quit the Church in disgust at Damasus's manner of easy forgiveness. Lucifer went off and started an new rigorist schism. St. Jerome, a friend of the pope, wrote the first Vulgate version of the Bible during this pontificate. Damasus reaffirmed that the papacy's power was derived solely from its succession from Peter.

Siricius—384–99: Siricius wrote on matters still at the heart of Roman Catholicism and still controversial: priestly celibacy, virginity and marriage, Mary's immaculate conception, and the need for priestly sanctity. The Jovinian heresy, again involving rigorism, was put down by the pope. Siricius built the Roman pilgrimage basilica of St. Paul Outside the Walls, which stood until it was destroyed in an 1823 fire (though it was later entirely rebuilt). In 395, paganism was officially declared illegal in the empire, with Christianity now the sole religion. The imposition of priestly celibacy failed at the time, but the attempt resulted in a strong social cleft between clergy and laity, the clergy being placed on a pedestal of superiority, which strengthened the authority of the Church.

Anastasius I—399–401: Like almost all the popes since Sylvester, Anastasius was chosen by the Roman assembly and ratified by the emperor (some were appointed directly by the emperors), while the Roman city clergy came to be called "cardinals" and functioned as the popes' chief helpers. Anastasius was a friend of three of the greatest men Christianity has produced, Augustine, Jerome, and Paulinus, all now termed Fathers of the Church. The last of Rome's great families were converting from paganism to Christianity.

Innocent I—401–17: Imperial Rome, weakened beyond help by the combined effects of population decrease, war, pestilence, emigration to Constantinople, and poverty, finally fell to Alaric the Visigoth. Jerome wrote, "Fallen has the city to which the world once fell." Innocent was safe in Ravenna, where he had gone to persuade the incompetent western emperor Honorius to come back to Rome to put up a fight for the city. The Rome Innocent returned to had been sacked for five days by the Visigothic flood, and it was more by his own effort than by the emperor's that order was eventually restored in the city. Innocent also had trouble with his eastern flank when the legitimate patriarch in Constantinople, (St.) John Chrysostom, was deposed by Arcadius, the emperor of the empire's eastern half.

Zosimus—417–18: Zosimus put down the Pelagian heresy, a cult whose primary deviation was denying original sin, a fundamental tenet of Christianity. It may seem, in retrospect, that the popes expended an inordinate amount of effort in suppressing what seem to be philosophical brushfires, but their undeniable success in bringing their office and Church through many horrifically violent centuries attests to the evident necessity of their actions. *Liber Pontificalis* reports that Zosimus ordered priests not to drink in public, a problem that must have been getting out of hand.

Boniface I—418–22: During Boniface's reign, the Church was bothered by an excess of state interference, and Boniface suffered another antipope. Both men appealed to the emperor in the de facto western capital at Ravenna for his still important recognition. Antipope Eulalius gathered up a gang of thugs and seized the papal residence in the Lateran Palace, but a council of bishops called by the emperor decided Boniface was the true pope. All the while, the pesky Pelagianists were still giving Boniface problems.

Celestine I—422–32: Among Celestine's acts, he sent St. Patrick to Ireland to convert that island to Christianity, and he called a third ecumenical council, in Ephesus, which condemned the Nestorian heresy. This sect maintained Mary was the mother only of the earthly Jesus, not of Jesus as God.

Sixtus III—432–40: Because of the triumph of Mary at the council of the prior reign, a new basilica of St. Mary Major in Rome was ordered to replace the old one, built by Pope Liberius. It is still the city's primary Marian shrine.

Leo I (the Great)—440–61: A new era for the papacy. Leo had the mixed fortune to be pope during the time of the fearsome Hun and its beastly leader, Attila, called the "Scourge of God." But in taking the Hun by the horns, as it were, Leo earned the title of "Great" by which he is known to history. He was a strong backer of the absolute primacy of the Roman see against all heresies and especially against the machinations of the eastern throne and see in Constantinople. The latter still considered itself, in the sense of "ruler as the appointed representative of God," the governor of the universe. Matching his loyal devotion to the Roman see, Leo just as strongly defended the Church against the depredation of the Asian invaders. By the time Attila was preparing to pounce on Rome, the imperial authorities were all but impotent, leaving matters of defense to the Church. Leo went north to meet the advancing Scourge and miraculously talked him out of his plans to take, and undoubtedly rape, the city. Nobody is quite sure how he did it, though it is said that he spoke to the Hun with such "forceful eloquence" that Attila was "persuaded" to retreat, but history happily records Leo's success. Although many more nasty invaders would course over Rome in succeeding centuries, the strongest threat to its continuance as the heir to the Roman empire was turned back. The papacy was hereafter generally recognized as the preeminent, decisive factor in European affairs, with the empire's western anchor effectually the capital of the bishop of Rome.

Hilary—461–68: Almost all that is known with certainty about Hilary is that he was a great church-builder. Arriving in the wake of a strong predecessor tends to place this pope in his shadows, but Hilary's reign was peaceful.

Simplicius—468–83: The official empire in the West finally expired during this pontificate. When Odoacer forced Romulus Augustulus to abdicate, imperial Rome ceased to exist in Italy. The European Middle Ages began, and although the eastern Roman emperors in Constantinople still claimed authority in Italy, the Church of Rome soon became the West's de facto authority of final resort and defender of its civilization.

Felix III—483–92: Having been married and widowed before entering the priesthood, Felix has the relatively rare papal distinction of being the direct ancestor of another pope, as the great-grandfather of Pope Gregory the Great. Felix assumed the ordinal "III" even though Felix II had been an antipope.

Gelasius I—491–96: More schisms and heresies to contend with—the Acacians, the Manicheans, the insufferable and seemingly indestructible Pelagians.

Anastasius II—496–98: Dante consigned Anastasius to hell in *The Divine Comedy,* but later historians cleared this pope's reputation. Even *Liber Pontificalis,* though, says he was struck dead by "divine will." All the controversy over Anastasius's character related to a misinterpretation of his supposed leniency with a schismatic archbishop.

Symmachus—498–514: On the same day Symmachus was elected, an antipope, Laurentius, was also elected by the anti-Byzantine faction, and it was this usurper who was actually installed in the Lateran. (One wonders how the laity ever kept track of all this.) Symmachus still showed a certain amount of spirit, though, by sending a sharp letter to Emperor Anastasius in Constantinople, chastising him for giving support to the Monophysite heresy, a struggle over the relationship of the divine will versus the human will in Jesus. Part of the reason for the Church's Eastern factionalism was the east's preoccupation with dialecticalism, sophistry, and symbolical interpretations of almost everything. The Roman see, on the other hand, remained strictly orthodox, tolerating few deviations from the original faith passed on by Peter.

Hormisdas—514–23: Best known for the "formula of Hormisdas," in which the primacy of the Roman see was clearly enunciated and agreed upon over the signatures of twenty-five hundred bishops. The document became a constitutional element of Roman Catholicism regarding papal authority. The famous Emperor Justinian came to the Byzantine throne in 518.

John I—523–26: Another martyred pope, John was thrown into prison by the Ostrogoth emperor/occupier in Ravenna, Theodoric. John died soon thereafter, still in prison.

Felix IV—526–30: Theodoric died, and his successor, Atalaricus, treated John's successor, Felix, somewhat more kindly. Some sources say

Felix "chose" his own successor by giving Boniface (see the next entry) the pallium off his own shoulders as he lay on his deathbed; others say the act was only a "signal of his wishes." In any case, this sort of thing was highly irregular even then, although Boniface did indeed become the next pope.

Boniface II—530–32: Felix's high-handed maneuver backfired and the Roman clergy and populace chose an antipope, Dioscorus. There probably would have been a battle to decide matters if the latter hadn't conveniently died a month later. Boniface first tried to justify his predecessor's act by declaring that he, too, would name his own successor. The unhappy mob that gathered in the streets led him to see the error of his ways, and he wisely gave up his dangerous plan. Had things gone differently, this might have started a tradition of popes choosing their own heirs.

John II—533–35: More heresies. The first pope to change his name on election—his given name, Mercury, that of a pagan god, obviously was inappropriate for a pope. Justinian still reigned in the East.

Agapetus I—535–36: In order to deal personally with the tiresome and potentially dangerous Monophysite schism in the East, Agapetus went to Constantinople. There the emperor's famous wife, the former entertainer Theodora, was giving aid and comfort to these heretics and persuaded her husband to confirm a bishop with Monophysite tendencies as patriarch of·the city. Agapetus was successful in finally getting Justinian to put down the heresy, but Agapetus died before he was able to return to Rome.

Silverius—536–37: Another papal descendant, Silverius was Hormisdas's son, the latter having been married before becoming a priest. Theodora was still trying to control the reins and did her best to get her favorite, the Monophysite-leaning patriarch, reinstated in Constantinople. Justinian sent an army to Italy to expel the Goth usurpers, and the general leading the expedition had Silverius removed from the Lateran, at Theodora's orders. The Theodoran-inspired successor, Vigilius, had Silverius sent to the island of Palmaria, where he soon died of one of that pesthole's many plagues.

Vigilius—537–55: Vigilius wasn't recognized at first as the legitimate pope, but after Silverius died, chaos might have erupted had Vigilius been shunned. Justinian brought the pope to Constantinople to encourage him to make some concessions to Monophysitism, its adherents becoming so numerous in the East that the emperor felt something significant must be done to placate them, but the pope at first refused. After a certain amount of seesawing, Vigilius was forced to submit, and the emperor magnanimously sent him back to Rome with the so-called Pragmatic Sanction, an official document that gave the papacy legal control over many temporal matters in the West. Meanwhile, Rome was brutally sacked in the wake of a war between Byzantine and Goth. Elsewhere, a monk named Benedict was establishing the framework for western monasticism.

Pelagius I—556–61: He spent most of his time rebuilding Rome and defending papal rights in the West against temporal meddling from the East, citing the Pragmatic Sanction as his authority.

John III—561–74: Justinian died, another set of Huns invaded Italy, and the pope kept the crumbling catacombs from falling apart.

Benedict I—575–79: Yet another invasion, this time by the Lombards, lasted through Benedict's pontificate. The pope asked for help from Constantinople, which wasn't forthcoming. The empire in the East had by now all but abdicated military authority in the West.

Pelagius II—579–90: Because of the immediate danger from invaders (the pope fortunately managed to work out a truce with the wild men), Pelagius was consecrated without imperial confirmation, the prerequisite up to that time. He spent his ecclesiastical energies on, among other things, promoting celibacy among the western clergy.

Gregory I (the Great)—590–604: As is the case with most dynasties, the Roman papacy occasionally produced a genuinely great leader among the many unexceptional men who have occupied Peter's throne. Gregory was one such man, leaving the Church a far stronger institution than it was when he came to its leadership. He was the first pope who was undisputed head of western Europe in all religious matters, and in political affairs he was the rival of the eastern emperor. Gregory was a staunch military defender of Italy against the still-dangerous barbarian hordes from the North, but his greatness lay more in the brilliant manner in which he administered a fractious Church. In anticipation of the Vatican's artistic greatness, Gregory fought the iconoclasts of his time, defending religious art not as something to be worshiped but "solely for instructing the minds of the ignorant." The growth of monasticism and monasteries, refuges in a terrorized Europe, added to the prestige and strength of his office and received his active support and encouragement. His name is immortalized in the Gregorian chant, and his epitaph aptly suited his contributions: God's consul.

Sabinian—604–6: Little is known of this pontificate other than that it was an extremely difficult period, with attempts to alleviate famine occupying much of the pope's time.

Boniface III—607: There was controversy over the use of the title "universal bishop" assumed by the patriarch of Constantinople, an act guaranteed to upset the bishop of Rome.

Boniface IV—608–15: The emperor formally gave Rome's Pantheon to the pope, which was thoughtful even though it really wasn't his to dispose of anymore. Boniface immediately turned it into a church named St. Mary Rotunda.

Deusdedit—615–18: (alternately known as Adeodatus I): Like that of Sabinian, the pontificate of Deusdedit was plagued by trouble, with both rebels and natural disasters. Rome was hit by a disastrous earthquake in 618, and the pope was in the front lines of those caring for the victims. The papal "bull" or proclamation, the pope's final word on any issue, supposedly started with Deusdedit: The leaden seal on his documents was taken from the Latin word for seal, *bulla*. Deusdedit was buried in St. Peter's.

Boniface V—619–25: During his pontificate, a new religion was born in Arabia that grew to be Christianity's greatest rival and the source of endless rivers of blood on both sides. Islam eventually swept over much of Europe itself and required the Church's undivided attention in repulsing it. Boniface took a special interest in the infant British Church and sent gifts to that island's royal family in an attempt to convert it to the Roman faith.

Honorius I—625–38: Honorius followed up his predecessor's efforts to convert the British Isles with personal contacts through the archbishops of Canterbury and York, but his overall pontificate was a failure in doctrinal and dogmatic areas. In 680 the fourth ecumenical council condemned him for not taking vigorous enough action against various heresies.

Severinus—640: A generally weak pope, he wasn't in office long enough to do much other than order the building of the apse for St. Peter's.

John IV—640–42: The Church aimed its proselytizing efforts at both Ireland and the pope's native Dalmatia, part of today's Yugoslavia.

Theodore I—642–49: The primary heresy that continued to take up the pope's energies was the new Monothelite dogma coming out of the East. This particular doctrine held that if Christ had no human will, he could not be a true man, perhaps nitpicking but dangerous enough to be a threat to Rome's authority. The heresy started in Severinus's reign and continued to be a thorn in the popes' sides.

Martin I—649–54: Another victim of the machinations of the emperor in Constantinople, Martin was imprisoned in the Crimea, and was the last pope to be venerated as a martyr. This situation was predicated on minutely differing interpretations of dogma and theology, which served as a convenient excuse for the very real power struggle still going on between emperor and pope.

Eugene I—654–57: Elected while Martin was rotting in the Crimean jail, he had the hypocritical temerity to condemn the emperor for his ill treatment of his predecessor. Eugene also denounced yet another theological deviation issued from the patriarch of Constantinople.

Vitalian—657–72: Emperor Constans decided to go to Rome to try to patch things up with this pope as well as to remind the Italians that he was still in charge. He never made it back to Constantinople, knifed in his bath during a rest stop in Sicily. But his successor, Constantine IV, ushered in a happier relationship with the pope.

Adeodatus II—672–76: An exceedingly kindhearted man according to all reports.

Donus—676–78: Donus ferreted out a group of Syrian monks in Rome who were brazen enough to practice their Nestorian heresy right in the pope's own backyard. Their group was broken up immediately.

Agatho—678–81: The Third Ecumenical Council of Constantinople was held, partly to give the Monothelites a chance to present their case, but really to put down the heresy once and for all. For a time, the breach between Rome and Constantinople was healed when the latter accepted the formula that "Peter had spoken through the mouth of Agatho." Agatho is still venerated as a saint by both the Roman and Greek churches.

Leo II—682–83: The primary act of his papacy was the formal confirmation of his predecessor's ecumenical council.

Benedict II—684–85: Benedict was so well thought of by the emperor that he asked him to adopt his two sons, a touching formality sealed with the mailing of locks of the boys' hair to the pope.

John V—685–86: During either John's pontificate or the one previous (sources disagree), a dispensation was received from the emperor in Constantinople that officially eliminated the need for imperial confirmation of the papal elections.

Conon—686–87: The next emperor renounced the aforementioned dispensation, putting the matter back at square one.

Sergius I—687–701: Many of these seventh-century popes served very short reigns, not only because of the insalubrious Roman climate and the appallingly primitive level of medical knowledge, but also because popes were generally elected at very advanced ages. Sergius finally broke the mold. He is remembered for baptizing the king of the West Saxons, starting those still-wild men on their path to Christianity. The two antipopes of the time were Theodore and Paschal, a pair who undoubtedly gave Sergius sleepless nights.

John VI—701–5: Two events during John's pontificate heralded the advancing temporal power of the office that would in many ways overshadow its spiritual nature: The pope saved the emperor's representative in Italy, the exarch, from the wrath of a Roman crowd disgusted with remnants of Byzantine domination in Italy; and the pope then, with the help of the duke of Benevento's army, stopped the latest Lombard invasion.

John VII—705–7: Although things went a little better with the Lombards during this pontificate, their king even restoring some of the papal estates he had stolen, relations with Constantinople were poor. Emperor Justinian II, whose nose was sliced off in battle and was thus known as the "Slit-nosed one," kept after John to approve one of his pet heresies.

Sisinnius—708: A twenty-day pontificate.

Constantine—708–15: Calculating that honey might gain him more than vinegar, Justinian II invited Constantine to be his honored guest in Constantinople with the intention of getting him to approve what John VII had not. Constantine evidently made soothing sounds, and the emperor was satisfied. But Justinian soon died, and his successor, Philippicus, was, of all things, a confirmed Monothelite. Furthermore, he intended to make this blasphemy the true religion of the empire. But the crisis passed, as Philippicus soon died and was replaced by an orthodox successor, at last condemning Monothelitism to the dustbin of ecclesiastical history.

Gregory II—715–31: When the emperor starting meddling in what the pope considered strictly Church matters, Gregory excommunicated him. This angered the emperor exceedingly, who sent an assassin to Rome to do Gregory in, but it and several repeat attempts failed. The important point is that a bigger wedge was driven between the two leaders of the empire, hastening the day when Rome would completely break with Byzantium.

Gregory III—731–41: Troubles on both the imperial and Lombard fronts. Gregory appealed to the Frankish king for help with the latter, but Charles was busy battling the Arabs at Poitiers and couldn't spare the troops. The pope was kept busy at home excommunicating iconoclasts.

Zachary—741–52: Through the force of his amiable personality, Zachary got the Lombard king to back off and initiated a twenty-year truce with the invaders from the North. The pope supported the Frankish de facto ruler Pepin in his determination to dethrone the lethargic Merovingians and become legal king; Zachary's opinion that "he who does the work of a king should *be* king" was all the encouragement Pepin needed to proceed with a coup.

Stephen II—752: The shortest pontificate in history—four days. Because he died before his consecration, *Liber Pontificalis* and *Annuario Pontificio* omit him; most other lists include him, however.

Stephen III—752–57: He ruled under the title "Stephen II" because at the time his predecessor wasn't considered to have been truly pope; history has revised the situation. The Lombards were threatening Ravenna, the seat of the exarch, and the pope sent to Pepin for help, solemnly naming him and his two sons, Charles and Carloman, "kings" as an inducement. Pepin at last came to the pope's aid. When the emperor assumed that the Frankish king would restore his exarch in Ravenna, Pepin responded that he had come only to help the pope, not the emperor. This was the end of any kind of Byzantine control in Italy and the birth of the Papal States, comprised of large tracts of Lombard lands in central Italy given to the papacy in the famous Donation of Pepin. Stephen was its first pope-king.

Paul I—757–67: Paul had the unique distinction of being the brother of his immediate predecessor, Stephen III. He continued his sibling's policy of political alliance with Pepin and had to contend with seemingly never-ending Lombard problems. Paul was noted for nocturnal visits to prisons to comfort prisoners.

Stephen IV—768–72: Two antipopes, one backed by Constantinople, the other by the Lombards; the former had his eyes torn out for his impertinence when Stephen got hold of him. It's interesting to note that this incredibly cruel pope is venerated in parts of Sicily as a saint, but the Vatican doesn't officially consider him as such.

Adrian I—772–95: The Seventh Ecumenical Council, held in Nicea, defined the Church's stand on iconoclasm and the worship of images, stating honor must be shown to such images because their purpose is to conjure up the goodliness of the saints they represent. The council also brought about a temporary unity between the Eastern Church and Rome. To help him throw out the Lombards, Adrian called on Pepin's son Charles (Charlemagne), whose assistance was soon forthcoming. Charles also confirmed his father's "donation."

Leo III—795–816: Many small local insurrections on his lands' flanks caused the pope to lash out repeatedly at these troublemakers. Rome's jealous first families tried to assassinate Leo with a then-popular form of mutilation: first blinding the victim and then cutting his tongue out. Leo barely escaped with his life. During his pontificate came another watershed year, commencing with the coronation of Charlemagne as emperor in Rome on Christmas Day 800. The pope surprised the emperor by quickly producing a crown and royal robe of state. In doing so, he revived the Augustan age, acclaiming Charlemagne "Charles Augustus" in the new Holy Roman Empire, and, more to the point, a European Christian empire in which kings would rule but popes would rule kings. It was to last exactly one thousand and six years. Voltaire made the famous comment that it was "neither holy, nor Roman, nor an empire," but it was, of course, all three—at least in the beginning. By this act, the pope demonstrated that all power, political and otherwise, comes from God *only through the pope,* the significance of which would in time grow immensely. At the time, however, this act somewhat irked the new emperor, who already considered his own authority perfectly sufficient. The East, rapidly becoming an Islamic sea, was, for the time being, written off.

Stephen V—816–17: Now that the Roman clergy had formally expunged eastern interference in the election of the pope, they made sure that the new emperor in the West wasn't going to get the opportunity to involve himself in the process. Stephen made the journey to Rheims, then an arduous undertaking, to crown Louis the Pious as Emperor Charlemagne's successor. However, without Charlemagne's personal protection, much of the strength the Church had gained quickly dissipated.

Paschal I—817–24: The pope devoted a large share of his energies to evangelization, sending missionaries to his special concern, the Danes. Known as a kind man, he used the treasury of St. Peter's to ransom Christians captured by Saracens on their raiding parties.

Eugene II—824–27: The western emperor—the new Holy Roman one—was officially recognized as military protector of the Holy See. In 826 a council in Rome solemnly forbade simony, the practice of buying and selling of pardons and sacred objects; had this injunction been faithfully observed in the centuries to come, the Reformation might never have happened.

Valentine—827: An upper-class Roman, he died forty days after his pontificate started.

Gregory IV—827–44: Just as earlier popes encountered jurisdictional and dynastic problems with the eastern emperors, so popes from this time on continued to have the same sort of difficulties with the new western emperors. In Gregory's case, they involved the sons of Ludwig the Pious, Charles the Bold and Ludwig the German, among whom the empire was divided into three kingdoms. Europe was at the threshold of an especially agonizing period of the dark Middle Ages, with Norsemen making life hellish for coastal and riverine area dwellers, Saracens running amok elsewhere, and intractable internecine squabbles among the successors of Charlemagne. Gregory reaffirmed his primacy over the emperor. November 1 was established as All Saints' Day.

Sergius II—844–47: Giovanni, an antipope, set himself up in Rome. Sergius exiled the scoundrel. The Saracens attacked Rome, but its walls held and the city itself was spared. St. Peter's was not spared, however, located as it was outside the city's protective walls and therefore prey to looting attacks upon much of its gold and silver. The papacy was at one of its lowest points of degradation in history.

Leo IV—847–55: The new pope, determined to avoid the kind of disaster that befell his predecessor, constructed walls around St. Peter's and the Vatican, creating the famous Leonine City. This gave the area its first real protection against marauding invaders, a plague from which the feuding descendants of Charlemagne were no longer able to protect Italy. It also saved the medieval papacy more than once from its two even greater enemies, the emperor and Rome itself. At the same time the walls were being built, restoration work was in progress on the basilica to restore it to its presack state. Leo crowned two monarchs, Emperor Louis and King Alfred of West Saxony. As the Carolingian power ebbed, that of the local Roman nobles grew, and they began to covet an increasing role in the power and possessions of the papal throne.

Benedict III—855–58: The famous "Pope Joan" is said to have sat on Peter's throne between the reigns of Leo IV and Benedict III. Actually, there's no historical evidence to confirm such a pontificate, probably the product of overheated medieval gossip. To illustrate the sort of nonsense connected with this legend, it is said that her sex was discovered only during a papal procession in which she gave birth to a child, causing her death shorty thereafter. For some centuries after this tale first arose, new popes underwent a sort of sex test, being installed at their coronation ceremonies on a throne with an open seat, which a deacon would look under and, seeing evidence of masculinity, shout, *Habet!* whereupon the assembly would joyfully respond, *Deo gratias!*

Nicholas I (the Great)—858–67: The last of only three popes on whom history has accorded the title of "Great," Leo I and Gregory I being the other two. The Byzantine emperor formally declared the separation of the Roman and Greek churches, an act, known as the Schism of Photias, that led to his excommunication by the pope. This, however, didn't alter the fact that the churches were indeed growing dogmatically and irreconcilably distinct; the break took another two centuries to become final. Nicholas was an extremely active pope regarding the civil affairs of the Papal States and the empire, and during his pontificate effectively asserted the primacy of the papacy.

Adrian II—867–72: The pope called a council in Constantinople to protest the eastern schism, and for a while things were patched up. He had less success in his attempt to end the squabbling among the Carolingian kings.

John VIII—872–82: Plagued on all sides by barbarians, Norsemen, Saracens, local troublemakers, schisms, and Byzantine radicals, John didn't have an easy pontificate. Even the western empire was crumbling, with ineffective emperors unable to fill Charlemagne's role example. By some accounts, John was assassinated, but the story remains more legend than fact.

Marinus I—882–84: Marinus was the first bishop ever transferred from his own see to become bishop of Rome and pope.

Adrian III—884–85: The Roman nobility was sinking to new depths of depravity, a sad state of affairs for the capital of the papacy. Despite the pope's decree that future emperors must be Italian nobles, the moribund throne passed from the Carolingians to the Germans a few years later.

Stephen VI—885–91: The authority of the Holy Roman emperor in the West had declined enormously with the breakup of the empire into a number of small, independent states. The actual title was still much coveted, though, and the Pope conferred it on the duke of Spoleto to assuage this bothersome noble, an act that later caused the papacy endless problems. Rome still railed at Constantinople's heresies.

Formosus—891–96: Formosus governed in a competent manner, but in taking away the imperial title from the Spoletans he damaged the memory of his legacy. He crowned German king Arnulf emperor, the most likely of Charlemagne's heirs, but when Arnulf was disabled with paralysis, the Spoletan ex-empress-mother swore to have her revenge someday on the pope who took the title away from her son.

Boniface VI—896: Twenty days on the throne. The Magyars, too, were now on the rampage, adding to Europe's miseries.

Stephen VII—896–97: An unhappy pontificate. Stephen was put on the throne with the backing of the Spoleto faction and immediately proceeded to put the propped-up and decaying corpse of Formosus on trial. He asked it why it had "usurped the apostolic seat," waited for an answer, and when none was forthcoming, convicted it, at the same time declaring invalid all of Formosus's ordinations. These macabre events inflamed the easily inflammable Romans, who captured Stephen in a riot and strangled him.

Romanus—897: Very little is known about Romanus, but it is believed he had the strength of character to denounce the despicable actions taken by his immediate predecessor.

Theodore II—897: Like that of Boniface VI, another twenty-day reign. A lamentable time for popes.

John IX—898–900: John ushered in one of the papacy's most trying, dangerous, and miserable centuries, but he himself was a capable pope. Had he lived longer, he might have been able to spare the Church some of the unhappiness it faced in the coming tenth century. The confused state of the imperial throne left the matter of papal elections completely under the sway of the exquisitely corrupt Italian nobles.

Benedict IV—900–3: The major action during this pontificate was an unrelieved jockeying for power *and* the magic imperial title by the princely Italian nobles, who apparently had little else to occupy their time or their thoughts.

Leo V—903: Nothing happened that was out of the ordinary for papal life as it was lived in the tenth century. Leo is believed to have died in prison, a victim of the constant intrigues then plaguing the pontifical throne.

Sergius III—904–11: Sergius despised Formosus, who had appointed him bishop to a backwater just to keep him from becoming pope; as a consequence, he stirred the muddy waters of the corpse trial, recondemning

Formosus's memory and praising Stephen VII for having conducted the trial. This was the first pope whose election was controlled by the unsavory but politically savvy house of the Roman noble Theophylact, whose wife and daughter Marozia (Sergius's child-mistress) were instrumental in this role throughout the next two thirds of the century. Much tenth-century gossip was attached to Sergius, making him one of the more interesting of that era's popes.

Anastasius III—911–13: As with Leo V, little is known of Anastasius. He was, so it is recorded, honored with a state visit to Rome by the Welsh king Howel the Good.

Landus—913–14: Another Theophylactic choice, the high papal official who appropriated so much power that the popes themselves became almost powerless for a few decades. Not only was Theophylact a considerable mover and shaker, but also his wife, Theodora, and daughters Theodora and, especially, Marozia were equally unable to resist the heady Roman brew of papal power politics. Marozia was a particular problem, a scheming hustler motivated in part by her insatiable nymphomania.

John X—914–28: Although most of the Theophylactic popes were unfit for office, the papacy was fortunate to gain one capable incumbent in the person of John X. An uncharacteristically venal act on his part was naming a five-year-old as bishop of Rheims, designed to assuage a petty but militarily powerful local noble. But John was too independent for the by-now all-grown-up and powerful Marozia, and she had the unfortunate man imprisoned, where depending on one's source, he may or may not have been smothered with a pillow. In any case, he died soon after his incarceration.

Leo VI—928–29: Marozia was now running events in Rome, completely overshadowing the emasculated pope.

Stephen VIII—929–31: An uneventful pontificate. Marozia ruled Rome, having appropriated for herself the titles of senator and patrician.

John XI—931–36: The high-water mark of the House of Theophylact, John was the *son* of Marozia and completely under her somewhat inefficient but extremely cunning sway. When Marozia remarried a French noble who swaggered into Rome as if he owned it, John's disillusioned brother Alberic staged a coup, imprisoned their mother, locked the pope in the Vatican, and took over the temporal affairs of the papacy.

Leo VII—936–39: Alberic held all control, but Leo tended to his strictly spiritual concerns in a capable manner. Indicative of the age and an augury of worse things to come, he allowed the bishop of Mainz to drive out of the city any Jews who wouldn't accept an enforced conversion to Christianity.

Stephen IX—939–42: Still under Alberic's domination, the pope nonetheless had spiritual powers at his command. When a group of French nobles tried to oust the legitimate and capable Louis IV from the French throne, Stephen warned the miscreants that he would excommunicate them if they didn't desist, a threat that accomplished its purpose.

Marinus II—942–46: Completely under the domination of Alberic.

Agapetus II—946–55: The beginning of the German domination of northern Italy. Holy Roman emperor Otto I invaded Italy when the lack of any strong Italian nobles in the area left an irresistible power vacuum. Agapetus is remembered for making a number of changes in the organization of the Church's dioceses.

John XII—955–63: The next-to-last of the line of Theophylactites in the person of Alberic's son, Marozia's grandson. Elected by the Roman nobility at the age of twenty at his father's insistence, he was called Octavian before he changed his name when he became pope, the first pope since John II to do so. John XII was a true debauchee (referred to by some sources as an "incestuous satanist"), partly as a result of his pampered upbringing. John was allegedly fatally stricken (possibly apoplexy) in the midst of an adulterous act; he lingered eight days before expiring.

Benedict V—964: The imperial pope, Antipope Leo VIII, was repudiated by the Romans in favor of Benedict, an act that caused Emperor Otto to lay siege to Rome. Famine forced the Romans to surrender, and Benedict was deposed in favor of Leo. Benedict was exiled to Hamburg, where he is said to have passed a happy life.

Leo VIII—963–65: Leo's name in the list of popes is somewhat anomalous, omitted in some sources, but included in others, and most significantly in the authoritative *Annuario Pontificio*. He was a layman at the time of his election, not uncommon during these years of the papacy. Always unpopular with the Roman citizenry, Leo possessed the all-powerful imperial backing. When the Germans took Rome, he ordered Benedict's deposition, which the now deacon calmly agreed to.

John XIII—965–72: John was hated by the Romans, who favored Benedict, because he was a friend to the emperor. Ironically, John was a member of the House of Theophylact but had little in common with his kinfolk. John is adjudged a kind man and a good pope, although under the emperor's sway.

Benedict VI—972–74: Considered a pope under imperial control, he was thus plotted against and strangled by dissident Roman nobles.

Benedict VII—974–83: He fought against the ever-present practice of simony and passed new laws to suppress it.

John XIV—983–84: An antipope, Boniface VII, had John locked up in the Castel Sant'Angelo, where he died. Boniface then lost the all-important favor of the mob and met a bloody end himself, having his corpse skinned and hauled through the streets of Rome by the same rabble who did him in.

John XV—985–96: Crazy local politics and power plays continued in Rome, beggaring anyone's ability to follow or comprehend it all. An interesting event in John's reign, the halfway point between Peter and the present, was the first recorded canonization in Church history when Ulricus was declared a saint.

Gregory V—996–99: The first pope of German nationality, he was the grandnephew of Emperor Otto I. It wasn't hard for dissidents and locals to rouse the Roman mobs against a German pope, who captured and threw him into prison. The papacy still remained unsafe.

Sylvester II—999–1003: The pope who ushered in the second millennium, when much of Christendom was anxiously awaiting a cataclysmic Judgment Day. Many people even gave away their worldly goods to the Church, which were gleefully accepted as a sign of their repentance. Sylvester sent the famous Crown of St. Stephen to the Hungarians. Some sources say Sylvester was murdered, others that he merely fled when the Roman nobles turned against him.

John XVII—1003: If one follows closely, one notices that John XVI is missing from this catalog of popes. The reason is that he was an antipope, and *this* John skipped the number. As for John XVII, all we know of his reign is that it was short, and it seems he may have died by being poisoned.

John XVIII—1003–9: The last medieval king of Italy fell to the emperor, and the pope put an end to one of many obscure eastern schisms.

Sergius IV—1009–12: Like his predecessor John XIV, Sergius was also named Peter but changed it out of respect to the first pope. The Saracens ravaged Jerusalem's Church of the Holy Sepulcher, an act that incited the first glimmerings of the idea of a crusade to the Holy Land. It was intended as a mission to teach the heathens a lesson and reclaim sovereignty for Christ *and* the West.

Benedict VIII—1012–24: Benedict apparently had good intentions to raise the Church from the depths to which it had fallen, but at the end of his pontificate its character was little changed.

John XIX—1024–32: The brother of the preceding pope, the second time this occurred, John took over the papacy through some strong-arm methods normal at the time. He considered accepting a peace overture from the Byzantine patriarch but was sadly talked out of it by the Cluniac monks around the throne. During this period, the Cluny monks, the Jesuits of the day, formed an extremely powerful organization, one no pope was willing to alienate.

Benedict IX—1032–44: One of history's most enduring games is settling on who was the worst pope; Benedict gets a lot of first-place votes. A depraved lecher infinitely more concerned with carnal pleasures than with the business of running the papacy, he was liked by nobody and was set upon by practically every faction. It is a wonder that he survived for the relatively long period of twelve years. Like Nero, he achieved the extraordinary: Both managed to shock their contemporaries.

Sylvester III—1045: He was deposed after a one-month reign, when Benedict IX reoccupied the throne for a few days.

Gregory VI—1045–46: Gregory paid his predecessor to leave, a wise action for the reputation of the papal throne but one that tainted him for having purchased the papacy. Emperor Henry wanted to remove this non-German, and, calling him a simonist for his payment to Benedict, forced Gregory to abdicate.

Clement II—1046–47: Suidger, bishop of Bamberg, became Clement II. The choice of a pope had been placed entirely in the hands of the German emperor Henry III. The following story is indicative of the debased level to which papal excommunication (then defined as and fervently believed in as an eternity in the fires of hell after a life outside the pale of society) had fallen. While the pope and emperor were on a progress through the South, the townspeople of Benevento refused to open their gate for the imperial/papal party, an understandable reluctance considering the ferocity of the times. Henry simply ordered the pope to excommunicate the whole town. Religious government by excommunication, anathema, and interdict was a sad fact of life in the medieval world.

Damasus II—1048: When Clement died, Benedict IX quickly reoccupied the papal throne before the emperor's choice, Bishop Poppo of Brixen in Bavaria (Damasus II), could occupy it himself. (Benedict IX is counted thrice in the *Annuario Pontificio* list of popes.) Henry was furious and ordered the local worthies to get rid of Benedict. They obeyed the emperor, but poor Damasus wasn't accustomed to the sultry Roman heat and expired before all the trouble his protector had gone to could pay off.

Leo IX—1049–54: Canonized by the Church, Leo was both a good pope and a good man in a mean age. Not only did he promulgate badly needed reforms, but he actually fought to carry them out as they were intended. The lasting tragedy of his pontificate was the final and irrevocable split between the Roman and Greek churches, when in a fit of pique over a long litany of dogmatic differences, the patriarch in Constantinople excommunicated the pope in Rome!

Victor II—1055–57: The weary though not-yet-defeated Benedict made one more attempt to get his old throne back, but was routed by the Romans. Victor continued the reform policies of Leo, demonstrating that even during the worst days of the papacy good men still could be found to occupy Peter's throne.

Stephen X—1057–58: Stephen benefited from the fortunate circumstances of having the truly extraordinary Cardinal Hildebrand, the future Gregory VII, as an adviser.

Nicholas II—1059–61: Nicholas promulgated extremely important papal election decrees, one of which restricted the vote to the cardinal bishops and excluded the rest of the clergy and the laity from the process. This innovation didn't last, but it resurfaced a couple of centuries later. He also specified that the pope should, if possible, be a Roman bishop, and that the election should be held in Rome. It almost goes without saying that the emperor didn't like to see his interests jeopardized in this manner, and he even went so far as to declare the pope officially deposed.

Alexander II—1061–73: Another zealous would-be reformer who deposed simoniacal bishops, he paved the way for the great and lasting reforms of his famous successor.

Gregory VII—1073–85: Father of the medieval papacy and the pope who first claimed to be the universal ruler not only of men's souls but of their bodies as well, Hildebrand was a Benedictine monk born near Siena sometime around 1015. Because he had served a succession of reforming popes, the clamor for his election was strong on Alexander's death, and he was elevated to the papal throne by "popular" acclamation on the day of his predecessor's funeral. He decreed and confirmed the absolute power of the pope to depose emperors, adding for good measure that no one could ever depose a pope. He also declared that the pope alone can demand to have his feet "kissed by princes." His greatest fame arose from his struggle with the powerful and proud Emperor Henry IV, in which the pope fought for the absolute denial of lay authority in ecclesiastical appointments, something that struck at the heart of the feudal system. Henry eventually attacked Rome, forcing the pope to take refuge in the musty old Castel Sant' Angelo. Henry put an antipope, Clement III, on the papal throne as his toady. But the process started by Gregory of breaking up the old feudal system greatly changed Europe, the position of the papacy within it, and the relationship of the clergy to the laity. From now on, the papacy was regarded throughout Christendom as a moral power with which every evil-doer, whether king or peasant, had to reckon. But with Gregory's strengths came an undesirable legacy: Europe was split into two opposing forces—the lay and the clerical—and the pope's "independence" for his Church very often equated to tyrannical clericalism.

Victor III—1086–87: He attempted to follow the policies of Gregory but died before he could accomplish much.

Urban II—1088–99: Urban witnessed the first of the crusades, a project inspired by Gregory VII to wrest Jerusalem from the Seljuk Turk invaders. He died too soon to hear the city was successfully overtaken by the Christian army.

Paschal II—1099–1118: Paschal had to endure three antipopes. Henry V, the new emperor, came to Rome demanding that Paschal crown him and cease his attempts to overthrow the feudal system, a world order the emperor very much liked. The pope refused, and Henry kidnapped him for his insolence. The emperor then demanded that the captive Paschal officially sanction lay investiture. Paschal, envisioning the empire's gain the Church's loss, but threatened with having his throat slit if he refused, gave in. This was taken as a dreadful act of cowardice by Rome's anti-empire party, but they weren't facing Henry's blade.

Gelasius II—1118–19: Gelasius's entire pontificate was a year-long cat-and-mouse game, the upheaval centering on who was *really* in charge. It was an exceedingly unseemly year, with rampant brutal activity.

Calixtus II—1119–24: The Diet of Worms was held by Henry to settle formally the lay investiture question, a course he was forced to take because of increasing public disgust with the debilitating struggle between emperor and pope. The Treaty of Worms essentially confirmed the independence of papal authority, while somewhat placating Henry. This didn't spell the complete end of lay interference in these matters, but it was thought at the time to be a great Church victory. Calixtus also decreed that marriages contracted by priests were not only sinful, which they had been considered for centuries, but were now null and void.

Honorius II—1124–30: When strong Calixtus was replaced by weak Honorius, it was business as usual in Rome—intrigue, machinations, and jockeying for position.

Innocent II—1130–43: Innocent's major accomplishment was his Lateran Council of 1139, which by its decrees confirmed Gregory's reforms.

Celestine II—1143–44: War raged over Europe, with the pope in the middle of the power struggles that kept the battlegrounds soaked with blood.

Lucius II—1144–45: Trouble at home with the Romans, who were so angry at the pope's peace overtures to the emperor that they set up a short-lived rump republic in the papal capital.

Eugene III—1145–53: Another pope hexed by the eternal "Roman problem"—internecine warfare among the city's factions. Order was almost impossible to maintain in Rome. Pope and republic came to an agreement that in essence restored most papal authority.

Anastasius IV—1153–54: Anastasius was old and infirm when he began his short pontificate, and little of importance was achieved during his term of office.

Adrian IV—1154–59: Born Nicholas Breakspear, Adrian is famous as the only English pope in history. He put down the factious Romans by the then-horrendous expedient of suspending all religious functions except baptism and the last rites until the warring rebels agreed to a truce.

Frederick Barbarossa of Hohenstaufen, the German emperor, battled the pope for temporal supremacy and invaded Italy. In the end, the Romans again turned against Adrian, forced him to flee Rome, and shortly thereafter he died.

Alexander III—1159–81: A very successful pope, he continued his predecessor's struggle with Frederick Barbarossa. When he died, Adrian was on the verge of excommunicating Red Beard; Alexander finally carried this out. In doing so, he met the challenge of four successive antipopes the emperor set up to oppose the Roman pontiff. In league with the Milanese, the pope finally defeated the excommunicated emperor and forced him to accept the Truce of Venice. Frederick was then given absolution, and came to like Alexander. In the Third Lateran Council, the pope promulgated the requirement that two thirds of the cardinals' votes were required to elect a new pontiff. Alexander stands out from the ranks of his predecessors for taking special pains to protect Jews from their legions of tormentors.

Lucius III—1181–85: More trouble from the Romans. Lucius and Frederick agreed on the need for another crusade. In his single-minded quest for aggrandizement, Frederick married his daughter to the Norman ruler in Sicily, seemingly a smart move at the time. However, it effectually set the stage for the bloody thirteenth-century war between the imperial Hohenstaufens and the papacy, ruining the former and causing grave injury to the latter.

Urban III—1185–87: More struggles in Italy with the restrengthened Frederick. The Saracens overran the Christian kingdom of Jerusalem, news that some sources say induced the pope's fatal grieving.

Gregory VIII—1187: To recapture Jerusalem, the primary goal of his time, Gregory knew he had to promote peace within the empire, a laudable task he initiated in his short pontificate.

Clement III—1187–91: Clement began the Third Crusade, which included Philip II of France, Richard Plantagenet (Lion Heart) of England, and Emperor Frederick Barbarossa, who died en route. The Saracen Saladin forced the surviving two to make peace. Clement freed the Scottish Church from the authority of the English archbishop of York.

Celestine III—1191–98: This aged but capable diplomat was consecrated as pope the day after he was ordained a priest, so anxious were the cardinals to have his talents dedicated to the papacy. Celestine excommunicated the Austrian duke Leopold for imprisoning Richard Lion Heart on his return from the Third Crusade.

Innocent III—1198–1216: If Gregory VII was the Julius Caesar of the medieval papal empire, Innocent III was its Augustus. Elected at age thirty-seven, he was younger than any pope elected since. Innocent, a reformer, carried out his papacy as much an emperor as a pope and is remembered as one of the greatest and certainly the most powerful of the medieval pontiffs, a "dispenser of kingdoms." A strong asserter of papal power over the Christian princes, he also reached out for conciliation with the schismatic Eastern Church. In the Fourth Lateran Council, called by Innocent, the rule was established, still valid today, that Catholics must receive communion at Eastertime. Innocent encouraged both Dominic and Francis of Assisi to start their orders; the Dominicans and Franciscans have remained two of the Church's strongest arms. The savage Albigensian crusade against heresy in Languedoc destroyed that area's political independence as well as much of its culture. Even more shameful was the crusade Innocent sent out to win back the Holy Sepulcher, one that was diverted instead to concentrate on the capture and sack of Constantinople. This deed was said to be more responsible than any other single factor for breaking the last tenuous ties between the two halves of Constantine's old empire.

Honorius III—1216–27: His biggest problem was the treacherous emperor, Frederick II, whose Italian power politics were a mortal threat to the papacy. Honorius placated Frederick, but by doing so merely passed on the danger to his successors. Relations were, for a short while, good enough with Byzantium that Honorius crowned the Eastern emperor Peter Courtenay in 1217. Except for vast amounts of energy wasted on aborted crusade attempts, Honorius's papacy was successful enough, with papal diplomats scurrying all over Europe on their missions of political peacemaking. Even the all-but-unpleasable Romans thought the pope was a fairly decent fellow.

Gregory IX—1227–41: Two important religious events took place during this pontificate: the canonization of Francis of Assisi and Dominic; and the establishment of the Inquisition, an institution that later brought infamy to the Church.

Celestine IV—1241: Pope for seventeen days, although he was never crowned.

Innocent IV—1243–54: It took the cardinals seventeen months to choose a new pope. In a war-filled reign, Innocent's ongoing bloody struggle with the imperial House of Hohenstaufen devastated Italy and weakened the papacy, causing it to lose allies and deplete its treasure. Frederick's furor with the papacy foreshadowed a laical, anticlerical theory of the state in Europe.

Alexander IV—1254–61: Another pontificate characterized by civil difficulties, warfare among factions, and meting out excommunications to punish recalcitrant princes.

Urban IV—1261–64: A good man, Urban tried to mitigate the harshness of the Inquisition and allow the repentant absolution, but he was stymied by the continuing fight with the Hohenstaufens. Urban instituted the feast of Corpus Christi.

Clement IV—1265–68: The most important event of his reign was the final defeat of the Hohenstaufens by a papal ally, the end of one of the most important families in European history. It was not long, however, before there were new nemeses for the popes to worry about.

Gregory X—1271–76: After what is probably the longest *sede vacante,* or interregnum, in papal history, Tebaldo Visconti was elected as Gregory X. Rudolph of Hapsburg was elected Holy Roman emperor, ending the interregnum that also existed with the imperial crown. A brief reunion was established with Byzantium by this capable pope, one that might have proven permanent if it had been more carefully nurtured by his successors.

Innocent V—1276: The start of new jealousies between Germany and France, disputes that the pope tried to mediate in his short reign.

Adrian V—1276: A reign of a few days, one of the shortest in history.

John XXI—1276–77: A physician, he was the only Portuguese pope. John worked to keep up the reunion with the Greek Church. He was killed when his observatory roof crashed in upon him.

Nicholas III—1277–80: A comparatively capable pope who is looked upon by history, largely as a result of accusations by Dante in his *Inferno,* as the originator of serious papal nepotism.

Martin IV—1281–85: Despite Nicholas II's reforms, by now ignored, papal elections had degenerated into an almost unrelieved mess, paralyzed by lengthy deadlocks among factions supporting one or another of the candidates. Martin embroiled the papacy in a disastrous twenty-year-long war over Sicily; at one point, he excommunicated the whole island en masse.

Honorius IV—1285–87: The Carmelite order of nuns was founded during his papacy. Fighting continued in Sicily.

Nicholas IV—1288–92: Feuding betwen the two noble Roman families of Orsinis and Colonnas was temporarily settled through Nicholas's intervention. In 1291, Acre, the last Christian outpost in the Holy Land, fell to the sultan of Eygpt.

Celestine V—1294: History's oddest pope. In one of their usual unbreakable deadlocks, the cardinals got the strange notion to name as pope the venerated but otherworldly hermit Peter Murrone, which in our day might be like choosing a Timothy Leary for the post. In an act that must have taken the mostly Italian cardinals aback, Celestine soon named twelve new cardinals, seven of them French. But it didn't take long for him to realize he was massively ill-suited for the papacy, and he chose to abdicate. (Dante contemptuously called it *il gran rifuto,* the great refusal, placing him in the worst circle of hell in his *Inferno.*) Celestine's own decision embodied the force of law, since there was no higher authority on earth to approve it.

Boniface VIII—1294–1303: Boniface issued the famous bull *Unam Sanctam,* which stated, "there are two swords, one spiritual and one temporal, the first being of the Church and the second for the Church," a good appraisal of medieval papal notions regarding the use of warfare in the defense of its own interests. In 1300, Boniface proclaimed the first jubilee, which brought almost two million pilgrims to Rome. A furious and bloody fight ensued between the pope and the Roman noble family of Colonna, who allied with the French. The latter's attempt to murder the pope scarred this papacy. The end of Boniface's reign is considered the end of the feudal age in Europe and the beginning of the era of the nation-state.

Benedict XI—1303–4: Benedict's appeasement policies were an attempt to make peace with the French and the Colonnas but weren't entirely successful.

Clement V—1305–14: With Clement began the "Avignon papacy," lasting for more than seventy years. Rome, which proved too fractious to remain the center of Christianity, fell into anarchy, decay, and despair. Invited by an accommodating French king to set up the court at peaceful Avignon, in Provence, which was not then French territory but belonged to the Angevin princes of Naples, the popes naturally came under the control of the velvet-covered fist of the French monarchy. Clement never once visited the Roman see during his papacy, and he named a veritable horde of French cardinals, who soon came to control the papacy. Of the 114 cardinals named in Avignon between 1309 and the papacy's return to Rome in 1377, 113 were French.

John XXII—1316–34: A fine administrator, he led a relatively quiet papacy in the tranquillity of Avignon, in stark contrast to the appalling conditions in Rome. During these years without the protection of the papal administration, Rome turned into a sink of degradation.

Benedict XII—1334–42: After considering a return to Rome, the new pope signaled that he was settling in for a long stay by building a lavish new papal palace in Avignon.

Clement VI—1342–52: Clement actually bought the whole town of Avignon for eighty thousand gold florins from the owner, Joanna, queen of Naples and countess of Provence. In Rome, Cola de Rienzi set up an aborted republic in the absence of papal control. The Black Death, Europe's worst disaster in history, struck Avignon with a fury, carrying off a greater percentage of Europe's population than World War II. However, the pope spent lavishly and generously to comfort the victims. Recalling the early pagan persecutions of the Christians, the Jews were blamed and killed in large numbers, but Clement did what he could to protect them.

Innocent VI—1352–62: The plague returned for a curtain call in Avignon, carrying off seventeen thousand more people, including nine cardinals. Charles IV's famous Golden Bull ended the four-hundred-year struggle between papacy and empire and made the empire a solely German entity from this time forth. Innocent began to pave the way for the papacy's return to Rome.

Urban V—1362–70: Urban returned the papal court to Rome in 1367. He reconciled with the Eastern emperor on the steps of St. Peter's but was unable to persuade Europe's princes of the urgency of an alliance to save Constantinople from the coming Islamic onslaught. Because this French pope felt he could accomplish more in Avignon, not to mention its greater comforts, he returned there in 1370, much against the wishes of ordinary Romans.

Gregory XI—1370–78: As we saw earlier, St. Catherine of Siena is given historical credit for persuading Gregory to return the papacy permanently to Rome. This was a remarkable thing for the French-born pope to carry out and one for which he thought of himself as a "martyr to the necessities of the Church." The Rome he returned to was, alas, as bloody and battlesome as ever, and he resolved to return to Avignon, and would have had death not intervened.

Urban VI—1378–89: Finally another Italian, and the last pope who wasn't a cardinal before coming to the papal throne. The French cardinals were furious at this reemergence of the Roman-Italian papacy and elected their own pope, Antipope Clement VIII, seated at Avignon. This initiated the Great Schism, which lasted for forty years and helped precipitate the inevitable Reformation.

Boniface IX—1389–1404: The effect of the Schism was not antireligion but confusion, for the people didn't know which papal court was the "right" one. The two popes wantonly excommunicated each other and tragically ignored the far greater dangers to Christendom that their folly was sowing. To finance his extravagant *curia,* or court, Boniface became a simonist on a massive scale, brokering spiritual favors.

Innocent VII—1404–6: His chief concern was to end the Schism, but he failed.

Gregory XII—1406–15: Popes and antipopes proliferated, with their supportive retinue of cardinals. If modern readers struggle to keep everything in order, the uneducated peasants of the time, the vast majority of the population, were hopelessly unable to understand what was going on, although their illumination was not considered of much importance anyway. A council was called in Constance by one of the antipopes, John XXIII, and there the Schism eventually was ended. One of its conditions, however, was that Gregory abdicate, which he fulfilled by retiring to live out his life as a cardinal.

Martin V—1417–31: Martin was elected by the council at Constance and recognized by virtually all the disputants, an act that brought relief to Christendom. Although one might think the people were fed up with the papacy after these decades of venality, the institution was still thought of as the bulwark against a far darker anarchy that the papacy buffeted. Not equal to the task of healing the papacy after the damaging Schism, Martin did not carry out needed reforms, although his pontificate did see the first blush of the Renaissance when he initiated a program to restore the city's ruined churches.

Eugene IV—1431–47: A council at Basel decided that it, not the popes, was the supreme authority in the Church and tried to make a kind of parlimentary regime of the papacy in a long, bitter dispute with Eugene; it even elected its own antipopes. Eugene, who governed the Church chiefly from Florence, died before besting the mutinous councilors, but the papacy survived the onslaught. The last of the Byzantine rulers asked for reunion with Rome, knowing his empire was doomed by the Ottomans. Fra Angelico was painting in the Vatican.

Nicholas V—1447–55: The first and best of the Renaissance popes and one of the greatest Christian humanists of his time. The Schism ended along with the councillor danger to the authority of the papacy. While the West stood and watched, Mohammed II swept over Constantinople in 1453, and the twelve-hundred-year-old eastern empire of Constantine and Justinian was eradicated. The humanist Nicholas was a great supporter of the arts, and the Renaissance flourished at the papal court. When the plague reappeared in Rome, Nicholas was one of the first to recognize that it was carried by humans. Until it passed, he shut himself up in a castle outside Rome and forbade everyone, even cardinals, from coming closer to it than seven miles, on pain of excommunication. With the help of the Florentine architect Alberti, Nicholas drew up the first plans for the reconstruction of both the Vatican and St. Peter's, plans that were realized by later artists in a form remarkably similar to those of this pope and his architect. In 1452, Frederick III became the last Holy Roman emperor crowned at Rome. Perhaps the greatest contribution of Nicholas, a great admirer of classical Greek literature, was the founding of the Vatican Library, endowed partly from his own remarkable collection of beautifully bound books.

Calixtus III—1455–58: The first of the noble Catalan-Spanish Borgias on the papal throne, Calixtus held strong feelings on the subject of crusades and sold the papal jewels to send an army to defeat the Turks. He was famous for his nepotism, naming two nephews cardinal, one of whom dragged the papacy into the gutter when he later came to throne himself as Alexander VI. Calixtus and his successors in the Renaissance period emulated Nicholas's patronage of the arts but ignored many of the important spiritual and administrative duties they were expected to fulfill by their election to the office.

Pius II—1458–64: Known as Aeneas at his own wish, in memory of the hero of Virgil's *Aeneid,* he was pontiff at a time that bordered on two eras—the end of the Age of Faith, and the beginning of the sharply anticlerical Renaissance, a time when man started living a life not solely in preparation for the hereafter but in enjoyment of the life at hand. Pius's great mission in the papacy was to unite the Christian princes in a crusade against the Turks when Sultan Mohammad II insolently ignored a papal demand that he convert to Christianity. The pope even started his own crusade when he couldn't convince the national rulers of its urgency, knowing it would fail without the western allies, support. He died while preparing to set forth on his journey to the East. Pius canonized Catherine of Siena, the woman who was instrumental in persuading Gregory XI to return the papacy to Rome. Pius had his hometown, Corsignano, renamed Pienza after himself and turned it into a small jewel of early Renaissance architecture.

Paul II—1464–71: Remembered as an antihumanist, he believed that he was only checking the humanist extremes that were giving the Curia a reputation as undisciplined hedonists. Like his predecessor, he also tried unsuccessfully to awaken Europe to the danger from the East. Paul reduced the interval between Holy Years from fifty to twenty-five, and started building the Palazzo Venezia, the papal residence for the next hundred years.

Sixtus IV—1471–84: Extravagant almost to the point of bankruptcy, he built the chapel named for himself in the lee of St. Peter's. Two crusades were carried out during his pontificate. Sixtus tried to check the excesses of the Spanish Inquisition, but his great failing was nepotism. He placed grossly immoral, generally lecherous, and inevitably incompetent relatives in high Church positions, bringing dishonor to his memory and decadence to the papacy. The popes were becoming little more than secular Italian princes, utterly absorbed by temporal interests. Estates, freely handed out to papal nephews, sometimes led to the Holy See's involvement in wars to protect these landholdings.

Innocent VIII—1484–92: Another pope of unquestioned corruption and little historical merit. His unworthy pontificate was characterized by office-selling to raise funds, flagrant nepotism, and his own dubious personal morals. His illegitimate sons, including one world-class lecher, lived in the Vatican. Europe was disgusted with the degenerating papacy, and Martin Luther was just over the horizon. Innocent's major contribution to the Vatican itself was a summer villa, called the Belvedere, today part of the museum complex.

Alexander VI—1492–1503: Another Borgia, Alexander was a debauchee whose spiritual concerns were almost entirely overshadowed by matters of flesh, gold, and aggrandizement. As the father of the famous

Lucrezia and Cesare, he made his son a cardinal at age eighteen, despite the fact that he wasn't a priest. In time, Cesare became the de facto ruler of the Papal States. The central tragedy of Alexander's reign was that his policies were openly dominated by the interests of his bastards before those of his flock. While some historians account Alexander the worst pope who ever reigned, much of the contemporary criticism against him was slander, probably including the more highly colored stories of orgies in the papal Borgia apartments. One of his undoubted accomplishments was the revitalization of the moribund University of Rome. Alexander was famous for drawing the line of demarcation in the New World between Spanish and Portuguese spheres of influence.

Pius III—1503: Pope for less than a month. Although he was made a cardinal at the age of twenty, he didn't become an ordained priest until he was elected pope.

Julius II—1503–13: Grandson of a Ligurian fisherman and a nephew of Sixtus IV, Julius II is one of history's towering popes-as-monarch, an eminent prince of the Renaissance and a pontiff who believed Christianity was best defended by force of arms. He placed himself literally at the head of Christ's army, when as the former Cardinal della Rovere, he had earlier commanded Innocent VIII's formidable legions. Julius retook through his brilliant and brutal generalship, those portions of the Papal States lost in earlier pontificates; their borders would remain essentially the same for nearly four centuries. As one of the greatest and most discriminating patrons of the arts ever known to the Church, he turned much of Rome into a city of beauty, initiating the reconstruction of St. Peter's, with Bramante and Michelangelo his two chief artistic geniuses-in-residence. In the final account, however, Julius's triumphs were not in the spiritual realm, which was the kingdom his office, at least in theory, was dedicated to upholding. He subjected Italy to a bloodbath, but, as Barbara Tuchman noted in *The March of Folly,* the military gains he won at such frightful cost in men and treasure made little difference in averting the disasters that befell Roman Catholicism within a decade of his death.

Leo X—1513–21: Giovanni de' Medici was the son of the Florentine Lorenzo the Magnificent and became a cardinal at age thirteen. Martin Luther began preaching what amounted to religious revolution during Leo's pontificate, a threat the pope seriously underestimated. During this time of extreme but largely unrecognized, or perhaps unacknowledged, danger to the Church, it was unfortunately led by a luxury-loving Medici when it needed a strong-willed Hildebrand. Leo peddled cardinalates, created new offices sold to the highest bidders, and took the proceeds of the sales of indulgences to pay for his lavish excesses, a practice started by Julius II, refined by Leo, and the primary spark that set off Luther's criticisms. Leo was famous for being Raphael's patron and for the comment singularly appropriate to his pontificate, "Let us enjoy the papacy since God has given it to Us." The Renaissance papacy died with this pope.

Adrian VI—1522–23: Adrian was the last of the forty-six non-Italian popes until John Paul II was elected in 1978. In the second millennium only Adrian and Marcellus II retained their baptismal names for their pontificates. Adrian turned Italy into a battlefield again when he sided with the empire, England, and several Italian states against France, which was attempting to win power in Sicily. With protesting Lutherans on one flank and Turks on the other, the reform-minded Adrian had little chance of extricating the papacy from the mire into which it had sunk. The Catholic Counter-Reformation was taking shape under this pious Dutchman, and had he lived longer, his stern attempts to root out the wickedness in the Holy See might have averted some of the excesses of the Protestant schism. Romans celebrated Adrian's death by hailing the papal physician as their liberator.

Clement VII—1523–34: Another Medici priest-king, one of the handsomest popes, and an appallingly industrious nepotist. Now the alliance tables were turned, and the German emperor, Charles V, was Rome's enemy. In 1527 the imperial army invaded the papal capital, and the ensuing sack left it a city of eight thousand butchered corpses, the Roman Renaissance dying in the gore. The pope, bedeviled on all sides, was left an underfed prisoner in his "refuge" of Castel Sant'Angelo, watching the drunken German and Spanish mercenaries below his windows riding by, dressed in priceless vestments, singing obscene songs that mocked the prisoner in the fortress. Another disaster for the papacy had more lasting effects: Henry VIII of England wanted a divorce because his queen hadn't produced a son and heir. Unfortunately for Clement, Queen Catherine was the aunt of the emperor, thus sadly tying the papal hands. The pope refused the divorce, and Henry, in effect, took the English Church out of the Roman Church's control. Had Clement pursued a single-minded and vigorous policy of reform, he might have taken much of the wind out of the Protestants' sails before they had a chance to consolidate their schism; when he didn't, the opportunity was lost forever.

Paul III—1534–49: The true founder of the Catholic Reform, more often called the Counter-Reformation, Paul started the process of replacing the Renaissance playboy cardinal-princes with real spiritual leaders and cleaning up the badly degenerated papal Curia. The Society of Jesus (the Jesuits) was approved in his reign, and the Index of Forbidden Books came into existence. Paul convoked and opened the reform-minded and very lengthy Council of Trent. The pope made his favorite bastard, Pierluigi, duke of Parma and Piacenza.

Julius III—1550–55: The English schism was briefly healed under the Catholic Queen Mary but was reopened when her sister Elizabeth succeeded as Protestant monarch. Julius continued with his predecessor's reforms. His personal tastes were typical of those of potentates of his time. He raised his favorite, a fifteen-year-old boy named Innocenzo, to the cardinalate and then commanded his brother to adopt the lad. Innocenzo was eventually given a harmless sinecure in the Secretariat of State.

Marcellus II—1555: Pope for less than a month, Marcellus is perhaps better remembered by history as one of the Vatican Library's great directors.

Paul IV—1555–59: A furious enemy of heresy and debased morals, Paul reinstituted the work of the Roman Inquisition, understandably causing widespread hatred of him among pleasure-loving Romans. He saw himself, of course, not as an intemperate extremist but as a reformer of the last of Renaissance libertinism.

Pius IV—1559–65: The watershed Council of Trent, which drew up a platform of practical reform, ended so successfully for the Church that it was the last council to be held for three hundred years. Pius was well served by his nephew and secretary of state, Charles Borromeo, whom he made a cardinal and whom the Church later canonized. Pius curbed the Inquisition but did not stop the reforms of the Church.

Pius V—1566–72: He excommunicated England's Queen Elizabeth, and at the same time freed British Catholics from obedience to her. Christendom, at Pius's goading, finally united against the Turkish threat, and the Ottoman fleet was beaten at the decisive Battle of Lepanto. The pope, a former grand inquisitor, was a hell-and-brimstone pontiff, attacking heresy and immorality with a vengeance, efforts for which he was canonized. Pius was famous for giving thirty statues from the Vatican's collection of pagan sculpture, gratis, to the municipality of Rome in a misguided effort to restore "decorum" to the papal court.

Gregory XIII—1572–85: On religious and political issues, Gregory followed his predecessor's harsh policies. He donated a new building for the Jesuits' Roman College, memorializing him under its renamed title of Gregorian University, today still run by the Society of Jesus. Gregory's name is also associated with the calendar reforms he instituted to correct the cumulative errors in the Julian calendar.

Sixtus V—1585–90: The resolute Sixtus did much to cure the crippling banditry plaguing the Papal States, with pursuit and punishment of the reprobates carried out vigorously. "While I live, every criminal must die!" the infuriated pontiff vowed. The dome of St. Peter's was finished, the Quirinal Palace was built, and Spain's armada was defeated by the English. Sixtus is probably most noted for his curial reorganization, particularly the transformations of the old dicasteries into fifteen "congregations," and for the requirement that bishops make *ad limina* ("to the threshold," meaning routine) visits to Rome, as they still do today every five years. This enabled the Holy See to keep closer tabs on the episcopate. Elizabeth of England paid him a famous compliment when urged to choose a husband: "I know of but one man who is worthy of my hand, and that man is Sixtus V."

Urban VII—1590: Pope for thirteen days.

Gregory XIV—1590–91: The office of the cardinal secretary of state was gaining power. There was Spanish interference in papal elections, with Philip II trying to make the pope a sort of Spanish court chaplain.

Innocent IX—1591: A two-month papacy.

Clement VIII—1592–1605: Clement obtained a measure of freedom from Spanish control and interference, and solved many of the problems the Church was having in France. On converting to Catholicism and taking the French throne, the formerly Protestant Henry of Navarre made his famous remark, "Paris is worth a mass."

Leo XI—1605: He caught a cold at his coronation and died twenty-seven days later.

Paul V—1605–21: Paul was another hard-line pope, putting evildoers to the ax with abandon. A furious feud between Venice and the papacy almost turned into a general European war before Henry IV of France mediated the fracas. Another nepotist, Paul made his family, the Borghese, powerful and rich. The devastating Thirty Years' War started in 1618. St. Peter's façade was completed.

Gregory XV—1621–53: Founder of Propaganda Fide (Congregation for the Propagation of the Faith), the Vatican's secretariat in charge of worldwide missionary activities. He established rules that are still in effect governing papal elections, the most important being the secret vote. The Thirty Years' War, one of the ghastliest butcheries the Continent has ever known, was turning Europe into a charnel house.

Urban VIII—1623–44: A member of the famous Florentine Barberini family, Urban formalized the processes of beatification and canonization, bought Castel Gandolfo for the papacy, and gave cardinals the style of "eminence." The pope's friend Galileo was convicted of heresy for his scientific and rational theories questioning eternal verities, injuring papal prestige. To Urban's credit, he later gave Galileo a pension and even administered the last sacraments to the scientist. The pope wisely employed Gianlorenzo Bernini, creating between himself and the young artistic prodigy the relationship only once seen before at the Vatican, that between Julius II and Michelangelo. History also remembers Urban as the last pope to practice nepotism on a grand scale. He saw St. Peter's to its final architectural completion, and he consecrated the basilica in a ceremony in November 1626 that lasted two days. Europe was still engaged in the Thirty Years' War during Urban's reign, three decades of political maneuvering in which Catholics slaughtered Protestants, Protestants slaughtered Catholics, all the while further weakening both the papacy and the Papal States.

Innocent X—1644–55: The Thirty Years' War at last ended with the Peace of Westphalia, vindicating religious tolerance and opening a new secular era, in effect, a Catholic loss to Protestantism. Innocent condemned the heretical and burgeoning Jansenist movement.

Alexander VII—1655–67: St. Peter's colonnade was built. The biggest burr under Alexander's saddle was the arrogant and imperialistic young Louis XIV of France. In 1655 Alexander welcomed history's most glamorous convert, Christina of Sweden, to Rome. The pope briefly considered moving his entire court and Church administration to the Quirinal Hill to be near his favorite residence, the Quirinal Palace, rapidly becoming the center of papal life in the city.

Clement IX—1667–69: He adopted a relatively benevolent attitude toward Jews, something rare in his day. Many writers have commented on the fact that Clement himself heard confessions in St. Peter's, then an unusual act of personal piety for a pope.

Clement X—1670–76: Eighty years old at the time of his election, he concentrated on spiritual matters, letting his nephew run the Holy See.

Innocent XI—1676–89: An anti-nepotist, he quashed the practice of popes appointing their nephews as chief advisers. The victories against the Turks at Vienna and Budapest, which finally turned back the Moslem threat from central Europe, were due in great part to papal financing and encouragement. The independent Louis XIV had refused to help in this enterprise, and for that reason among many others the pope excommunicated him. England saw a brief Catholic monarchy under James II until he was booted out of the country in the Glorious Revolution.

Alexander VIII—1689–91: The last nepotist pope, although on a somewhat diminished scale, Alexander showered favors on his family, mainly in the form of court appointments. Little of lasting importance was accomplished during his short reign.

Innocent XII—1691–1700: Innocent made peace with Louis XIV on his own terms, dealing royal absolutism a serious blow. His reform bill against nepotism, specifically decreeing that popes no longer had the right to give money or estates to family members except for "the kind of assistance normally given to any of the poor," made the debilitating practice all but impossible for his successors. This decree gave new prestige to the papacy, even among Protestants.

Clement XI—1700–21: The long-lived, troublesome Jansenist heresy in France, an austere, anti-Jesuit predestinationist sect created a near-schism, giving this pope as much grief as it had his last several predecessors. The Austrian-French war over the Spanish succession, in which the papacy tried to remain neutral, was another rich source of problems for Clement.

Innocent XIII—1721–24: He was well intentioned, inconsistent, peace-loving, and ridden with kidney stones. Not much was accomplished in his three-year pontificate.

Benedict XIII—1724–30: Benedict engendered a great deal of ill will through the appointment of the self-aggrandizing Cardinal Coscia as one of his chief advisers and administrator of the Papal States. He lifted Innocent X's long-standing automatic excommunication of anyone caught using tobacco in St. Peter's.

Clement XII—1730–40: Blind during his papacy, he ruled almost the entire ten years from his bed. He had the good sense to dismiss Cardinal Coscia. Clement condemned the practice of Freemasonry, then a redoubt of the anti-Christian tendencies of the Age of Enlightenment. As was the trend during the reign of most of the other eighteenth-century popes, the monarchs-*cum*-despots of Europe paid increasingly little attention to papal wishes.

Benedict XIV—1740–58: Generally considered one of the best popes and greatest conciliators of the century, his passing was genuinely mourned by most of Europe at his death. His scholarly demeanor and conciliatory brand of diplomacy were sorely needed on a continent that was engaged in the War of the Austrian Succession when Benedict came to the throne and in the Seven Years' War when he left it. During this time, the theoretically neutral Papal States were used as a kind of military training ground by the belligerents.

Clement XIII—1758–69: The matter of the Jesuits, accused of being agents of the papacy and troublemakers in the states ruled by the Bourbons, was beginning to vex the papacy and demand a "solution." The Bourbon monarchs plotted against the order not only because of its intense loyalty to the pope but also because they sorely hungered after the considerable Jesuit properties. Clement had the moral courage to defend the order. Rome was in its usual state of disorder; during Clement's pontificate, there were four thousand murders in the city.

Clement XIV—1769–74: Clement relented and suppressed the Jesuits, partly because even Maria Theresa of Austria joined the cry against them, motivated by a desire not to jeopardize the impending marriage of her daughter, Marie Antoinette, to the French dauphin. A famous portrait shows Clement announcing the "dissolution, extinction, and quite abolition" of the order to a pleased Spanish (i.e., Bourbon) ambassador. Clement said it was necessary for the "tranquillity of the barque of Peter." (Pius VII later restored the society, in 1814.)

Pius VI—1775–99: The first of two popes bitterly humiliated by the new scourge of the Continent, Napoleon, who solemnly declared the papal institution an "obsolete machine." The viciously anticlerical French Revolution was a tremendous blow to the papacy, a virtual loss of the Church's "first daughter," and an event that effectively reshaped the existing European political and social order. The anticlericalism was understandable, however, in light of Church excesses under the *ancien régime*. Italy was invaded by Napoleon, Rome was sacked, a Roman republic was declared in 1798, and Pius was kidnapped and then imprisoned in the French fortress of Valance, the humiliating state in which he died.

Pius VII—1800–23: Pius VII was the last pope physically abused. The culprit was, of course, Napoleon. Pius is seen in the famous David portrait of Napoleon's coronation, watching helplessly while the upstart emperor crowned himself. The pope also watched helplessly as Napoleon and his armies picked off the Papal States one by one. When he was at last excommunicated, the furious Napoleon ordered Pius's arrest and carted him off to France as a political prisoner. Like his predecessor, he was also incarcerated, in his case for four years. The Papal States were finally restored in 1815 by the Congress of Vienna. After all he underwent, Pius finished his long reign relatively peacefully.

Leo XII—1823–29: Leo transferred his residence from the Quirinal Palace to the Vatican. Although he was a pious and pastoral pope, Leo's pontificate was unsuccessful. A reactionary, he tried to reverse the liberalization that was changing Europe; he even withdrew the few tentative steps Pius VII took toward allowing lay involvement in the governance of the Papal States. Leo's reaction, although understandable in light of his two predecessors' treatment at the hands of "liberalism," was deeply resented.

Pius VIII—1829–30: Had the comparatively liberal Pius served a longer pontificate, he might have been able to avert the coming total disintegration of the Papal States.

Gregory XVI—1831–46: Gregory greatly strengthened the papal army, but the final fall of the papacy as a temporal kingdom began under his archreactionary regime. He was opposed to any reforms, either within or without his own territories. Rebels abandoned any hope of peaceful negotiations toward a secular state and took up arms against the papacy.

Pius IX—1846–78: The famous Pio Nono was the last of the papal kings and the longest-reigning pontiff in history. Pius started his papacy on a path toward liberalism, but the bloody revolutionary events of 1848 disabused him of most of his liberal tendencies. Driven out of Rome by a mob, he was forced to flee into exile in Gaeta, in the kingdom of Naples. He was restored to his office in Rome with the help of several thousands of Napoleon III's French soldiers, the French thereafter becoming his protector against the Italian revolutionaries. In the 1860s, the patriots Cavour and Garibaldi captured most of the Papal States for their new kingdom of Italy, and by 1870, the process was completed when Rome itself was taken and the temporal rule of the papacy ended. This began a period often referred to by the Vatican's partisans as "The Great Injustice." Pius retired to the Vatican, where he remained a self-declared "prisoner" for the rest of his reign. Pius's two greatest ecclesiastical contributions were the dogma that Mary was created "immaculately," without original sin, and, out of the First Vatican Council, the dogma that the pope is infallible when speaking *ex cathedra*—officially and solemnly, "from the throne"—on matters of morals and faith.

Leo XIII—1878–1903: As with every pope from Pio Nono until Pius XI, Leo's election was, in effect, a sentence of incarceration to the Vatican. Since the pontiffs in this period would not recognize the authority of the Italian state, they did not leave their self-imposed confines at the Apostolic Palace and the Vatican grounds. Except in his relations with Italy, Leo's policies were generously conciliatory, and he started the papacy on its purely religious path to worldwide moral influence that it continues to travel to this day. Leo's most memorable bequest was his encyclical *Rerum Novarum,* which first condemned the evil social practices that kept workingmen in misery and subjugation; he was known as the "socialist pontiff" for advocating the rights of workers.

Pius X—1903–14: Pius reformed the Roman Curia, the government of the Church. He stressed the need for children to receive communion and for adults to receive it more frequently. He died on the eve of World War I and was canonized by Pius XII as the great "pope of the Eucharist," the last of at least eighty popes to be venerated as saints.

Benedict XV—1914–22: The new Code of Canon Law, largely prepared during his predecessor's reign, was promulgated. Benedict's reign was marred by World War I and his belief that as father to all Catholics, he should remain strictly neutral, a policy for which he was condemned by both sides in the conflict as being in favor of the other. But the frail pope did his best to alleviate the suffering of prisoners of war on both sides by establishing communications with their families as well as organizing diplomatic missions both during and after the war to mitigate its disastrous effects. Ironically, he came close to bankrupting the Holy See by giving away its funds, and even his own personal resources, to care for refugees and war orphans.

Pius XI—1922–39: Pope of the Lateran Treaty, which ended the stand-off between Italy and the Vatican. This made the latter an independent political entity and tidied up its muddy and uncertain state of affairs while also ending the status of popes as prisoners in the Vatican. Pius condemned communism in an encyclical and said in no uncertain terms that anti-Semitism was un-Christian.

Pius XII—1939–58: While elected at a dangerous time for Europe, Pius was a strong statesman in light of his long diplomatic experience. The single greatest issue of Pius's reign and still one of history's most bitterly argued controversies is whether he might have done more, if only by speaking out with greater force, to help the Jews and other groups who suffered under the Nazi regime. The question is far from being resolved, regardless of polemicists on one side who think Pius's "guilt" is transparent, and those on the other who argue that had he done so both Jews and Catholics in Nazi-controlled states would have been put in even greater jeopardy. The modern era of monolithically conservative Catholicism ended with Pius XII.

John XXIII—1958–63: Beloved and already considered by millions a saintly figure. John's reign, however, is coming under increasing historical controversy because of the liberalizing effects on the placid Pacellian Church brought in the wake of the watershed Second Vatican Council he called in 1962. His passing was eloquently, truthfully reported as "a death in the family of mankind."

Paul VI—1963–78: The council that John convened, Paul finished. For the same reasons that controversy now surrounds the former, so the enormous changes wrought in the Church under Paul's reign are being subjected to increasingly severe criticism as to their long-term desirability or perceived inevitability. Many of Paul's efforts were involved with heresies and schisms, matters he confronted with vigor. Paul was the first pope to travel extensively, beginning his ten globe-hopping jet voyages with a December 1963 ecumenical trip to Jerusalem, embracing the Greek Orthodox patriarch after a nine-hundred-year break between Rome and Byzantium. The most lasting and damaging controversy from the Pauline years involved his encyclical *Humanae Vitae* ("On Human Life"), in which he condemned, against the advice of the commission of cardinals he set up to advise him on the subject, the use of artificial contraceptives in birth control, stating, "Every conjugal act must be open to the transmission of life."

John Paul I—August 26–September 28, 1978: Considered a pastoral candidate, John Paul was expected to concentrate on the Church's religious matters and to take relatively little interest in international political affairs.

He died after a one-month reign, leaving the papal throne to the greatest diplomat-pope of the modern era.

John Paul II—1978– Gloriously Reigning (see chapter 3): The most traveled pontiff in history, the first non-Italian pope in four and a half centuries, and one of the most charismatic leaders ever to occupy Peter's throne. The former cardinal-archbishop of Cracow has since the outset of his papacy tried to steer the church rightward from the liturgical and social changes that came in the wake of the Second Vatican Council, while at the same time compassionately addressing the problems of poverty-stricken Catholics in the Third World.

Bibliography

ADLER, BILL, and SAYRE ROSS. *The Pope John Album.* New York: Hawthorn Books, 1966.

AMBROSINI, LUISA, with MARY WILLIS. *The Secret Archives of the Vatican.* Boston: Little, Brown, 1969.

ANCIAUX, PAUL. *The Episcopate in the Church.* Staten Island, N.Y.: Alba House, 1965.

ANDRIEUX, MAURICE. *Daily Life in Papal Rome in the Eighteenth Century.* New York: Macmillan, 1969.

APOSTOLIC VATICAN LIBRARY. *Library Guests of the Vatican During the Second World War.* Vatican City, 1945.

ARADI, ZSOLT. *The Popes—History of How They Are Chosen, Elected and Crowned.* New York: Farrar, Straus & Cudahy, 1955.

ATTWATER, DONALD. *Penguin Dictionary of Saints.* Baltimore: Penguin, 1965.

———, ed. *A Catholic Dictionary.* New York: Macmillan, 1962.

Baedeker's Central Italy. Leipzig: Karl Baedeker, 1909 et al.

BARRETT, WILLIAM E. *Shepherd of Mankind—A Biography of Pope Paul VI.* Garden City, N.Y.: Doubleday, 1964.

BEGNI, ERNESTO, ed. *The Vatican—Its History—Its Treasures.* New York: Letters & Arts, 1914.

BENEDICTINE MONKS OF ST. AUGUSTINE ABBEY OF RAMSGATE, comp. *The Book of Saints.* New York: Macmillan, 1947.

BENNETT, MELBA B. *Key to the Apostolic Vatican Library.* Palm Springs: Welwood Murray Memorial Library, 1967.

BENY, ROLOFF, and PETER GUNN. *The Churches of Rome.* New York: Simon & Schuster, 1981.

BENZIGER BROTHERS. *Catalogue of Church Vestments.* New York: Benziger Brothers, 1873.

BERGERE, THEA and RICHARD. *The Story of St. Peter's.* New York: Dodd, Mead, 1966.

BERTARELLI, L. V. *Roma e Dintorni.* Milan: Guida d'Italia della Consociazione Turistica Italiana, 1938.

BOLTON, PRESS GLORNEY. *Roman Century 1870–1970.* New York: Viking Press, 1970.

BONOMEO, JACQUES. "The Tabernacle of the World's Memory Is Resealed," *Figaro,* March 3–9, 1984.

BOORSCH, SUZANNE. *The Building of the Vatican.* New York: Metropolitan Museum of Art, 1980.

BRODERICK, ROBERT C. *The Catholic Encyclopedia.* Nashville: Thomas Nelson, 1976.

BRUSHER, JOSEPH S. *Popes Through the Ages.* Princeton: D. Van Nostrand, 1959–64.

BULL, GEORGE. *Inside the Vatican.* New York: St. Martin's Press, 1982.

BURTON, MARGARET. *Famous Libraries of the World.* London: Grafton, 1937.

CALVESI, MAURIZIO. *Treasures of the Vatican.* Cleveland: World Publishing, 1962.

CARDINALE, HYGINUS E. *Orders of Knighthood, Awards and the Holy See.* Gerrards Cross (London): Van Duren, 1983.

CARNAHAN, ANN. *The Vatican.* London: Odhams Press, 1950.

CHAFFAJON, ARNAUD. *La Merveilleuse Histoire des Couronnes du Monde.* Paris: Fernand Nathan, 1980.

CHAMBERLIN, ERIC R. *The Bad Popes.* New York: Dial Press, 1969.

CHEETHAM, NICHOLAS. *Keeper of the Keys.* New York: Charles Scribner's Sons, 1982.

COLIMODIO d'ALLORO, LUCIANO, and NINO NAPOLITANO. *The Popes—Album of Icons.* Naples: Aldo Fiory, 1964.

COLLINS, MSGR. HAROLD E., *The Church Edifice and Its Appointments.* Philadelphia: Dolphin Press, 1940.

CORNWELL, RUPERT C. *God's Banker.* New York: Dodd, Mead, 1984.

DALLAS, PHILIP. "The Papal Gardens—Castel Gandolfo in the Alban Hills," *Architectural Digest,* January 1977.

DAL MASO, LEONARDO B. *Rome of the Popes.* Rome: Bonechi Edizioni, 1975.

DAUGHTERS OF ST. PAUL. *Pope John Paul II: He Came to Us as a Father.* Boston: St. Paul Editions, 1979.

DELL ARCO, MAURIZIO F., ed. *The Vatican and Its Treasures.* London: Bodley Head, 1982.

DI FONZO, LUIGI. *St. Peter's Banker.* New York: Franklin Watts, 1983.

DOUILLET, JACQUES. *What Is a Saint?* New York: Hawthorn Books, 1958.

DRAGADZI, PETER. "Good Knights of Malta," *Town & Country,* April 1984.

ESCOBAR, MARIO, and ANDREA LAZZARINI. *Vaticano e Chiesa Cattolica.* Genoa: Stringa, 1954.

FENICHELL, STEPHEN S., and PHILLIP ANDREWS. *The Vatican and Holy Year.* Garden City, N.Y.: Halcyon House, 1950.

FITZGERALD, GEORGE, C. S. P. *Handbook of the Mass.* New York: Paulist Press, 1982.

FOY, FELICIANO A., ed. *Catholic Almanac.* Huntington, Ind.: Our Sunday Visitor, 1984.

GAHLINGER, ANTON, K. S. G. *I Served the Pope.* Pittsburgh: St. Joseph's Protectory, 1953.

——————— *Papal Heraldry.* Cambridge, Mass.: W. Heffer & Sons, 1930.

GALBREATH, DONALD LINDSAY. *Papal Heraldry.* London: Heraldry Today, 1972.

GANTER, BERNARD J., J. C. L. *Clerical Attire: A Historical Synopsis and a Commentary.* Washington, D. C.: Catholic University of America Press, 1955.

GERLACH, MARTIN. *Kronen-Atlas.* Vienna: Verlag M. Gerlach, 1878.

GESSI, LEONE. *The Vatican City.* Rome: Grafia SAI, 1930.

GIORDANO, MARIO. *La Cité du Vatican.* Paris: Librairies de France, 1934.

GOLLIN, JAMES. *Worldly Goods.* New York: Random House, 1971.

GONTARD, FRIEDRICH. *The Chair of Peter.* New York: Holt, Rinehart & Winston, 1964.

GRAHAM, ROBERT A., S.J. *Vatican Diplomacy—A Study of Church and State on the International Plane.* Princeton, N.J.: Princeton University Press, 1959.

GRANFIELD, PATRICK. *The Papacy in Transition.* Garden City, N.Y.: Doubleday, 1980.

GREELEY, ANDREW M. *The Making of the Pope 1978.* Kansas City, Kans.: Andrews & McMeel, 1979.

GRICHTING, PAUL. *Die Schweizer in Rom.* Brig, Switz.: Rotten-Verlag, 1975.

GRISSELL, HARTWELL DE LA GARDE. *Sede Vacante*. Oxford: James Parker, 1903.

HALE, J. R., ed. *A Concise Encyclopedia of the Italian Renaissance*. New York: Oxford University Press, 1981.

HALL, KATHRYN E. *The Papal Tiara*. Published by author, 1952.

HAMMER, RICHARD. *The Vatican Connection*. New York: Holt, Rinehart & Winston, 1982.

HARDON, JOHN A. *Modern Catholic Dictionary*. Garden City, N.Y.: Doubleday, 1980.

HASSAN, BERNARD. *American Catholic Catalog*. San Francisco: Harper & Row, 1980.

HATCH, ALDEN. *Pope Paul VI*. New York: Random House, 1966.

HEBBLETHWAITE, PETER. *The Papal Year*. London: Geoffrey Chapman, 1981.

HEENAN, DR. JOHN. *The Vatican State (March of Times* series). London: Pilot Press, 1943.

HEIM, BRUNO B. *Armorial*. Gerrards Cross (London): Van Duren, 1981.

HELYOT, P. *Costumes de la Cour de Rome*. Paris: Ancienne Maison Silvestre, 1862.

HESTON, EDWARD L., C. S. C. *The Holy See at Work*. Milwaukee: Bruce Publishing, 1950.

HIBBERT, CHRISTOPHER. *The Popes (Treasures of the World* series). Chicago: Stonehenge Press, 1982.

HITCHCOCK, JAMES. *Pope John Paul II and American Catholicism*. New York: National Committee for Catholic Laymen, 1980.

HOEFLER, RICHARD C. *Designed for Worship*. Columbia, S.C.: State Printing Company, 1963.

HOFMANN, PAUL. *O Vatican!* New York: Congdon & Weed, 1984.

HOLISHER, DESIDER. *The Eternal City*. New York: Frederick Ungar, 1943.

HOLLIS, CHRISTOPHER, ed. *The Papacy*. New York: Macmillan, 1964.

HYNES, REV. HARRY G. *The Privileges of Cardinals*. Washington, D.C.: Catholic University of America Press, 1945.

IRVINE, LEIGH H. *Irvine's Dictionary of Titles*. San Francisco: Crown, 1912.

JAVERS, RON. "The Making of a Saint," *Philadelphia,* May 1977.

JENKINS, GRAHAM. *The Making of Church Vestments*. Westminster, Md.: Newman Press, 1957.

JUNG-INGLESSIS, E. M. *St. Peter's*. Florence: Scala, 1980.

KAROLAK, TADEUSZ. *John Paul II—The Pope from Poland*. Warsaw: Interpress Publishers, 1979.

KEMP, ERIC W. *Canonization and Authority in the Western Church.* London: Oxford University Press, 1948.

KINNEY, EDWARD M., ed. *The Vatican.* New York: L. H. Horne, 1964.

KITAO, TIMOTHY K. *Circle and Oval in the Square of St. Peter's.* New York: New York University Press, 1974.

KITTLER, GLENN D. *The Papal Princes.* New York: Dial Press, 1960.

KORN, FRANK. *From Peter to John Paul II.* Canfield, O.: Alba House, 1980.

KRAUTHEIMER, RICHARD. *Three Christian Capitals.* Berkeley: University of California Press, 1983.

KUEHNER, HANS. *Encyclopedia of the Papacy.* New York: Philosophical Library, 1958.

LAFFONT, ROBERT. *A History of Rome and the Romans from Romulus to John XXIII.* New York: Crown, 1960.

LEES-MILNE, JAMES. *St. Peter's.* London: Hamish Hamilton, 1967.

LERNOUX, PENNY. *In Banks We Trust.* Garden City, N.Y.: Anchor Press, 1984.

LESAGE, ROBERT. *Vestments and Church Furniture.* New York: Hawthorn Books, 1960.

LETAROUILLY, PAUL M. *The Vatican and the Basilica of St. Peter.* London: Alec Tiranti, 1963.

LEVY, ALAN. *Treasures of the Vatican Collections.* New York: New American Library, 1983.

LIBRERIA EDITRICE VATICANA. *Annuario Pontificio.* Vatican City: Libreria Editrice Vaticana, various years.

LOBELLO, NINO. *The Vatican's Wealth.* London: David Bruce & Watson, 1968.

LYDON, REV. PATRICK J. *Ready Answers in Canon Law.* New York: Benziqer Brothers, 1934.

MCCLOUD, REV. HENRY J. *Clerical Dress and Insignia of the Roman Catholic Church.* Milwaukee: Bruce, 1948.

MACEOIN, GARY, and the COMMITTEE FOR THE RESPONSIBLE ELECTION OF THE POPE. *The Inner Elite—Dossiers of Papal Candidates.* Kansas City, Kans.: Sheed, Andrews & McMeel, 1978.

MALINSKI, MIECZYSILAW. *Pope John Paul II.* Garden City, N.Y.: Doubleday, 1982.

MALLOWE, MIKE. "The Kingdom and the Money," *Philadelphia,* March 1983.

MARTIN, MALACHI. *The Decline and Fall of the Roman Church.* New York: G. P. Putnam's Sons, 1981.

MAYER, FRED, photo. *The Vatican*. New York: Vendome Press, 1979.

MELLOR, CAPT. F. R. *The Papal Forces*. London: Burns, Oates & Washbourne, 1933.

MENEN, AUBREY. *Speaking the Language Like a Native*. New York: McGraw-Hill, 1962.

METROPOLITAN MUSEUM OF ART. *The Vatican—Spirit and Art of Christian Rome*. New York: Harry N. Abrams, 1982.

MICHELIN. *Rome*. Paris: Pneu Michelin, 1978.

MORGAN, THOMAS B. *Speaking of Cardinals*. New York: G. P. Putnam's Sons, 1946.

MURPHY, FRANCIS X., C. S. R. *John Paul II—A Son from Poland*. South Hackensack, N.J.: Shepherd Press, 1978.

———. *The Papacy Today*. New York: Macmillan, 1981.

———. *This Church These Times*. Chicago: Association Press, 1980.

NAINFA, REV. JOHN A. *Costumes of Prelates of the Catholic Church*. Baltimore: John Murray, 1909.

NAVAL, MARGARET. *Rome Off the Record*. Vienna: Wilhelm Frick Verlag, 1960.

NEUVECELLE, JEAN. *The Vatican—Its Organization, Customs and Way of Life*. New York: Criterion, 1955.

NEVILLE, ROBERT. *The World of the Vatican*. New York: Harper & Row, 1962.

NICHOLS, PETER. *The Pope's Divisions*. New York: Penguin Books, 1981.

NOEL, GERARD. *Anatomy of the Catholic Church*. Garden City, N.Y.: Doubleday, 1980.

NORRIS, HERBERT. *Church Vestments—Their Origins & Development*. London: J. M. Dent, 1949.

OLIVERI, MARIO. *The Representatives—The Real Function and Nature of Papal Legates*. Gerrards Cross: (London) Van Duren, 1980.

PALLENBERG, CORRADO. *Inside the Vatican*. New York: Hawthorn Books, 1960.

———. *Vatican Finances*. London: Peter Owen, 1971.

PANCIROLI, ROMEO. *L'Appartamento Pontificio delle Udienza*. Rome: Editalia, 1971.

PATTON, PHIL. "The Master's Work," *Geo*, October 1981.

PEPPER, CURTIS G. *The Pope's Back Yard*. New York: Farrar, Straus & Giroux, 1966.

PINE, L. G. *The Story of Titles*. Newton Abbot, Devon: David & Charles, 1969.

PIRIE, VALERIE. *The Triple Crown*. Gaithersburg, Md.: Consortium Books, 1976.

POCKNEE, CYRIL E. *Liturgical Vesture*. Westminster, Md.: Canterbury Press, 1961.

POTTER, MARY KNIGHT. *The Art of the Vatican*. Boston: L. C. Page, 1902.

PYCROFT, FRANK. *Catholic Facts and Figures*. London: Sheed & Ward, 1977.

RAHNER, KARL, S. J. *Bishops: Their Status and Function*. Baltimore: Challenge Books, 1963.

REDIG DE CAMPOS, DEOCLECIO. *Art Treasures of the Vatican*. Englewood Cliffs, N.J.: Prentice-Hall, 1974.

————. *I Palazzi Vaticani*. Bologna: Cappelli Editore, 1967.

REED, OLWEN. *An Illustrated History of Saints and Symbols*. Buckinghamshire, Eng.: Spurbooks, 1978.

SCHREIBER, REV. PAUL F. *Canonical Precedence*. Washington, D.C.: Catholic University of America Press, 1961.

SHARKEY, DON. *White Smoke over the Vatican*. Milwaukee: Bruce, 1944.

SPINA, TONY. *The Making of the Pope*. New York: A. S. Barnes, 1962.

STERLING, CLAIRE. *The Time of the Assassins*. New York: Holt, Rinehart & Winston, 1983.

SULLIVAN, RT. REV. JOHN F. *The Externals of the Catholic Church*. New York: P. J. Kenedy & Sons, 1959.

SZOSTAK, JOHN M., and FRANCES SPATZ LEIGHTON. *In the Footsteps of John Paul II*. Englewood Cliffs, N. J.: Prentice-Hall, 1980.

THOMAS, GORDON, and MAX MORGAN-WITTS. *Pontiff*. Garden City, N.Y.: Doubleday, 1983.

TISSERANT, MSGR. EUGENE, and THEODORE WESLEY KOCH. *The Vatican Library*. Jersey City, N.J.: Snead, 1929.

TRASATTI, SERGIO, and ARTURO MARI. *Journey in Suffering*. Bergamo: Editrice Velar, 1981.

TUCHMAN, BARBARA W. *The March of Folly*. New York: Alfred A. Knopf, 1984.

TYACK, GEORGE S. *Historic Dress of the Clergy*. London: William Andrews, 1897.

URTUSUN, JOSEPH. *What Is a Bishop?* New York: Hawthorn Books, 1962.

VAILLANCOURT, JEAN-GUY. *Papal Power*. Berkeley: University of California Press, 1980.

VAN DER VELDT, JAMES A., O. F. M. *The City Set on a Hill.* New York: Dodd, Mead, 1944.

———. *Exploring the Vatican.* London: Hollis & Carter, 1947.

VAN LIERDE, P. C., and A. GIRAUD. *What Is a Cardinal?* New York: Hawthorn Books, 1964.

VASI, MARIANO. *A New Picture of Rome.* London: Samuel Lee, 1819.

Vatican City—A Special Edition for the Museums and Papal Galleries. Trento: Industria Grafica, 1973.

Vatican Radio 1931–1971. Rome: Società Grafica Romana, 1971.

VON MATT, LEONARD. *Die Paepstliche Schweizergarde.* Zurich: NZN-Verlag, 1948.

WALL, BERNARD. *The Vatican Story.* New York: Harper & Brothers, 1956.

WALSH, JAMES J. *Our American Cardinals.* Freeport, N.Y.: Books for Libraries Press, 1969.

WALSCH, JOHN EVANGELIST. *The Bones of St. Peter.* Garden City, N.Y.: Doubleday, 1982.

WERNER, ALFRED. "The Vatican," *Horizon,* January 1962.

WHALE, JOHN, ed. *The Man Who Leads the Church.* San Francisco: Harper & Row, 1980.

WILLIAMS, CAROLINE. *Saints—Their Cults and Origins.* New York: St. Martin's Press, 1980.

WOLLEH, LOTHAR. *The Council—The Second Vatican Council.* New York: Viking Press, 1965.

WOODWARD, KENNETH L. "The Corridors of the Vatican," *Geo,* March 1982.

YALLOP, DAVID A. *In God's Name.* New York: Bantam Books, 1984.

YOUNG, NORWOOD. *The Story of Rome.* London: J. M. Dent, 1901.

INDEX

Note: Popes not mentioned in the text have not been included in the index. All popes are listed, in chronological order, in the Appendix.

273

Julius II, Pope, 12, 23–24, 27, 34–35, 134, 204, 255
Justice, Palace of, 16
Justice and Peace Commission, Pontifical, 108, 112
Justinian, Emperor, 19–20

Kabongo, Emery, 60
Knighthood, pontifical, 168–73
Knights of Hospitaller of the Crusades, 173
Knights of Columbus, 129, 177
Knights of St. Lazarus, 170
Knights of the Golden Collar, 169
Knights of the Holy Sepulcher, 170
Knights of the Immaculate Movement, 200
Knights Templar, 170
Kobayashi, M., 212
Kolbe, Maximilian, 198, 200–201
Krol, John, 189
Küng, Hans, 106

Laocoön group, the (sculpture), 204–5, 209, 217
Laity, Council for the, 111–12
Lapidary Gallery, 209
Largo di Porta Cavalleggeri, 7
Largo Sant'Uffizio, 105–6
Last Judgment (Michelangelo), 23, 87, 211–12
Lateran Accords, 14, 65, 169, 177, 179–80
concordat, 101–2
Laterni family, 20, 32
Lateran Pact, 180
Lateran Palace, 22, 24, 140, 206, 228, 231
Lateran Profane Museum, 206
L'Attivita della Santa Sede, 120
Laurenti, Camillo Cardinal, 87
Lawrence, Thomas, 213
Lefebvre, Marcel, 107
Legates, 103–4
"Legatin, right of," 100–101
Leger, Paul, 77
Lent, 162, 225
Lentini, Tommaso, 139
Leo I, Pope, 90, 231
Leo III, Pope, 33, 238
Leo IV, Pope, 21, 26, 239
Leo X, Pope, 151, 213, 255–56
Leo XIII, Pope, 27, 85, 117, 123, 128–29, 183, 169, 170, 206, 208, 262
Leone IV, Via, 6
Leonina, Piazza della Città, 80
Leonine City, 21, 239
Leonine wall, 21, 22, 26, 27
Lernoux, Penny, 187, 188
"Liberation theology," 69, 106, 107
Library, Court of the, 24
Liechtenstein, pilgrims from, 143–45
Lombards, the, 21
Lopez, Trujillo, Alfonso Cardinal, 77
L'Osservatore della Dominica, 118
L'Osservatore Romano, 9, 97, 113, 114, 117–19
Luce, Clare Boothe, 173
Luther, Martin, 127, 176

Maderno, Carlo, 34, 38–39, 40, 44, 65
Maestro di Camera, Office of the, 113
Magee, John, 113, 141, 142
Majordomo, Office of the, 113
Mallon, Vincent, 100
Mallowe, Mike, 185
Maniple, 162–63
Maps, Gallery of, 210
Marcinkus, Paul Casimir, 183–90
Marconi, Guglielmo, 115
Mario, Monte, 9
Marshal Courtyard, 11
Martin, Jacques, 61, 113, 142
Martin, Malachi, 82
Martin V, Pope, 75, 252
Martin of Tours, 194
Martinez-Somalo, Eduardo, 96
Mary, Queen of Scots, 195
Mass, celebration of
choir dress, 162–68
funerals, 155
inaugurals, 153, 154
and John Paul II, 61
Novendiale masses, 53
papal, 149–51
at public consistitories, 78
Master of Pontifical ceremonies, 141
Matrons of the Holy Sepulcher, 170
Maxentius, Emperor, 18–19
Mayer, Augustine, 108
Medici family, 27
Melchiades, Pope, 20, 228–29
Menen, Aubrey, 14, 30
Mennini, Luigi, 190
Metropolitan, 92
Metropolitan Museum of Art (New York), 216, 219–20
Meltzer, Charles, 127
M. H. de Young Memorial Museum (San Francisco), 216, 220
Michelangelo Buonarotti, 11, 23, 34, 46, 138, 210, 211–12
design for St. Peter's, 36–37, 46–47
Last Judgement, 23, 87, 211–12
Milizia Urbana, 135
Milvian Bridge, 17, 18–19
Minutanti, 98
"Miraculous Draught of the Fishes" (tapestry), 218
Missionaries of Mercy, 215
Missionary activities, 110, 178
Missionary-Ethnological Museum, 27, 206, 214
Miter, 152, 164–65; papal, 166–67
Modern Religious Art, Collection of, 207, 211, 216
Momo, Guiseppe, 14, 15
Mondale, Walter, 153
Monsignor, 93, 158–59
Montalambert, Count, 181
Mooney, Cardinal, 85
Motion Pictures, Pontifical Commission for, 131
Mozart, Wolfgang, 169
Mozzetta, 164, 166

277

278

279